"Thoroughly analyzes the context within which journalism's version of "John Henry" was played out with nary a witness. Harrington's character is revealed humanly with neither romanticism nor cynicism."
  —Dr. Richard K. Olsen, Chair, Communication Studies, University of North Carolina Wilmington

"A fascinating and comprehensively documented discussion of North Carolina newspapers handwritten by a maverick, Civil War-era journalist. Smith perceptively analyzes the underappreciated value of print journalism without a printing press."
  —Dr. Douglas S. Campbell, Lock Haven University of Pennsylvania, author of *The Supreme Court and the Mass Media* and *Free Press v. Fair Trial*

"Highly readable and reveals a portion of American journalism that needs to come to light. Harrington's vision for a free press and his work to that end show the spirit of a vibrant medium with the power to shape America's future."
  —Dr. Dennis E. Hensley, Director, Professional Writing Division, Taylor University

"A rare peek at an original "indie" journalist who lived a century and a half before Matt Drudge stumbled on his first insider scoop."
  —Dr. J. Matthew Melton, Dean, College of Arts and Sciences, Lee University

"A valuable piece of family and local history. I am richer for having read it."
  —Sion H. Harrington III, Harrington descendant and Military Collection Archivist, Special Collections Branch, North Carolina Division of Historical Resources

March 2011

A FREE PRESS
in *Freehand*

Michael Roy Smith

A FREE PRESS

in  Freehand

*The Spirit of American Blogging in the Handwritten News-
papers of John McLean Harrington 1858-1869*

Michael Ray Smith Ph.D.

foreword by
Roy Alden Atwood, Ph.D.

preface by
Quentin J. Schultze, Ph.D.

e

edenridge press
GRAND RAPIDS, MICHIGAN

Published by
Edenridge Press
Grand Rapids, Michigan USA
service@edenridgepress.com

Quantity discount pricing is available.
service@edenridgepress.com

Book design by Matthew Plescher
Photographs by Michael Ray Smith and Geneva Harrington Cameron

HIS036050 HISTORY / United States / Civil War Period (1850-1877)

ISBN-13: 9780982706329 (pbk.)
ISBN-10: 0982706324 (pbk.)

ISBN-13: 9780982706312 (cloth)
ISBN-10: 0982706316 (cloth)

Library of Congress Control Number: 2011920923
Library of Congress subject headings:
Journalism—United States—History.
Penmanship, American—History.
Graphology.
North Carolina—Politics and government—1858-1869.
Harrington, J.M. (John McLean), 1838-1887.
Press—United States—History.

For Os and Ceedie, my favorite Southerners

Acknowlegements

I am indebted to the North Carolinian Society for two Archie K. Davis Fellowships to study John McLean Harrington. I thank Dr. Ronnie W. Faulkner of Winthrop University for his great insight into this historic period and for his many suggestions. In addition, I thank historian James Martin for his ideas. I am grateful to the North Carolinian Society and the work of many colleagues around the nation, including researcher Sion Harrington, military archivist in the Special Collections Branch, North Carolina Division of Historical Resources, Department of Cultural Resources. I also thank Beth Hayden of the State Library of North Carolina. I also want to express appreciation to the Southern Historical Collection, Manuscripts Department, Wilson Library, at the University of North Carolina at Chapel Hill. In addition, I gratefully acknowledge Sara McCarthy Acosta for her editorial suggestions, Campbell University for its generous support of this project, and Drs. M. Dwaine Greene and Mark Hammond. I am grateful to Barbara MacLean for her assistance with the Lois Byrd Local History Collection of Harnett County Public Library System. I also thank librarians from Campbell University for their help: Marie Berry, Jennifer Carpenter, Ron Epps, Derek Hogan, Borree Kwok, and Siuki Wong. I also acknowledge scholar Debra Reddin van Tuyll for her summaries of the best books on the Civil War press. I am grateful to Zachary Elder of the Rare Book, Manuscript, and Special Collections Library at Duke University. In addition, I wish to thank to Deborah Joe Blue of Campbell University's Photographics, and Tara Matney and Cheryl Cruickshank, formerly of the Department of Mass Communication.

Many scholars across the nation offered welcomed suggestions. They include but are not limited to: Dr. Jim Martin of the University of North Alabama; Drs. Ford Risley and John S. Nichols of Pennsylvania State University; Drs. Adam English, J. Dean Farmer, Edward A. Johnson, Barry Jones, Mark Merry, Edward Fubara, David Whiteman, Carl Broadhurst, and Benjamin Hawkins, all of Campbell University; Dr. David Sloan of the University of Alabama; Dr. Sheridan Barker of Carson-Newman College; Professor John Lawing and Dr. Dennis Bounds of Regent University; Dr. Dennis E. Hensley of Taylor University; Dr. Michael Longinow and Dr. J. Douglas Tarpley, both of Biola University; and many others such as writers Cecil Murphey and

Jim Watkins, the Rev. Dennis Fulk, editors Manny Garcia, George Archibald, and James W. Curtis, academics Brian Cannon, Michael Graves, and Scott Marshall, and supporters Ronald W. Smith and Stanley R. Smith. I am also grateful to Melissa Lilley for her editing and friendship, and Dr. Louise Taylor for her suggestions. I am indebted to editors Amy Tol and Marsha Daigle-Williamson, and Matthew Plescher and Quentin J. Schultze of Edenridge Press for their work.

Universities across the nation are involving students in educational endeavors that benefit the community through meaningful service. This project took a similar tack. Students at Campbell University studied handwritten newspapers of the Civil War era along with the press of that period in a communication class called Research Methods. Over several semesters, students examined microfilm, visited libraries, conducted in-depth interviews, visited historic sites, and worked to appreciate the role of John McLean Harrington in Harnett County, the area where Campbell University is located. The students who participated in this project included Jessica Beall, Jay Berube, William Bratton, Brandon Bridges, Meredith Brunson, Brian Cadwallader, Zach Casteen, Christopher Caudle, Lori Crabtree, Mikaela Dalton, Lauren Dixon, Sarah Ferguson, Dinecia Renee Gates, Samantha Holvey, Melinda Jackson, Amanda Johnson, Renee Johnson, Brittany Judd, Kristen Hoogmoed, Rebecca Kinsey, Carole Laughton, Melissa Lilley, Harley Meaney, Sara McCarthy, Sara Mears, Natalie Moore, Tyler Olson, Astrid Rivera, Melissa Sheldon, Gregory Smith, Courtney Willey, Whitney Wood, Tyler Wood, and many other project cheerleaders. Finally, I acknowledge the valuable help of many readers, including my daughters, Shannon M. Ryals and Taylor Rae-Anne Smith, and my wife, Barbara Jean.

"With the exceptions of a very few pencil notations, the entries in the notebook had apparently all been made with a ball-point pen. The hand-writing itself was manuscript style, such as is currently taught in American schools, instead of the old, Palmer method. It was legible without being pretty-pretty. The flow was what was remarkable about the handwriting. In no sense—no mechanical sense—at any rate—did the words and sentences look as they had been written by a child."

—The character "Teddy" in J. D. Salinger's *Nine Stories*, writing in a small, 10-cent notebook.[1]

Table of Contents

Foreword by Roy Alden Atwood xiii

Preface: *Journaling, Blogging, and Neighborly Love,*
    by Quentin J. Schultze xvii

Introduction 1

1 The Context of Harrington's Life and Publications 5

2 The North Carolina Press Before and During the Civil War 17

3 Handwritten Newspapers Before the Harrington Papers 29

4 The Cultural School of Journalism History 37

5 The News, Literature, and Advertisements of *The Young American* 45

6 The News, Advertisements, and the Silent Partner of *The Nation* 61

7 Harrington's Other Newspapers 73

8 Why and How Harrington Handwrote Newspapers 89

9 Harrington as Writer, Businessman, and Politico 99

APPENDIX A: Photographs and Transcription of
    The Nation, first issue 111

APPENDIX B: Photographs and Transcription of
    The Young American, first issue 121

APPENDIX C: U.S. Census Figures of the
    Harrington Household: 1850–1880 187

Notes 191

Works Consulted 211

Index 219

Foreword

Printed newspapers may have dominated the news business for more than four hundred years, but the news is bound to no single medium. Drums, smoke signals, town criers, troubadours, court heralds, preachers, and prophets all delivered news for millennia before the first printed newspapers circulated. And people will likely continue to read newspapers long after the telegraph, radio, television, computer, Internet, and cell phones are challenged by the next yet-to-be-invented communication "revolution." The dominance and staying power of any news medium, however, is extraordinarily difficult to predict. False prophets once predicted that the "lightning lines" of the telegraph would utterly displace inky old newspapers. Today, a new generation of text-messaging web-wonks, who know almost nothing about the telegraph, is again spreading greatly exaggerated rumors about the demise of newspapers. Each new news medium may change the landscape of our public information culture, especially if it catches a big marketing wave, but it rarely sweeps away its older competitors. Yes, news has a long and curious history of flirting with both old and new communication technologies at the same time, while pledging its troth to none.

So if news can't be harnessed by any single communication medium, it should come as no surprise to discover that newspapers are not genetically bound to the printing press. Today's web editions of printed news have warmed us to the idea that newspapers can no longer be equated with printing technology of old. But were they ever equated historically? Is there any evidence that other newspapers have been published without the printing press by older communication technologies?

In the pages that follow, Professor Smith not only answers the latter question affirmatively, but unravels the story behind a series of newspapers that were written out by hand long after the advent of the printing press (not just before printing). Historians have long known that the Romans published some of the earliest "news sheets" in handwritten form. (These historians have resisted calling them "newspapers," as if somehow doing so would admit that there's a bastard in the modern media family lineage.) Journalism historians have acknowledged (again, almost grudgingly) that some of the earliest colonial American newspapers were in fact handwritten in Boston between 1700 and 1704. I suspect that to affirm the existence of handwritten newspapers in significant numbers *after* the advent of printing would undermine many a journalism historian's uncritical fideism in technological progress. Web-based newspapers can fit nicely within a theology of technological progressivism. Handwritten newspapers simply cannot. The very thought of handwritten newspapers rubs our technology-obsessed culture the wrong way. With all the technological advances out there, who in his or her right mind would *write* a newspaper *by hand?* The very thought is regressive, almost Neanderthal, technologically speaking. Yet, as counterintuitive and curious as they may be, the handwritten newspapers revealed in this study cannot be pushed aside as some antiquarian curiosity. Professor Smith offers here a compelling case that *handwritten* newspapers deserve a more prominent place in the history of American journalism and in our theories of communication technology.

Professor Smith's engaging account of John McLean Harrington's handwritten newspapers sheds light on a handful of the literally hundreds of extant handwritten newspapers found in archives and libraries around the world. The Hungarian National Archives in Budapest, for example, proudly display the nineteenth-century manuscript newspapers published by that country's great Protestant leader for independence from Austria, Lajos Kossuth (1802–1894). When the Roman Catholic Hapsburg Emperor tried to thwart Kossuth's fledgling independence movement by outlawing printed newspapers, Kossuth ingeniously organized a modern-day "scriptorium" that produced hundreds of quite legal handwritten papers advocating independence. Kossuth would have chuckled at the now famous dictum "Freedom of the press only belongs to those who own one" because, as the Hapsburgs quickly learned, newspapers and freedom of expression are not bound to the printing press. Even today some people groups with unique or complex language systems, which have no typescripts, typewriters, or computer fonts, still write out their newspapers by hand and then photocopy them for distribution. *A Free Press in Freehand* throws open a window to this latter-day manuscript tradition for all to see. Handwritten news did not die with the invention of the printing press or, even in our own age, with the television or the computer.

Professor Smith's careful work and helpful analysis of the Harrington newspapers, *The Young American* and *The Nation,* provide a much-needed and belated addition to the canon of journalism history. It is fitting that these *handwritten* newspapers should be given their due at last and honored histori-cally in a *printed* book that was originally produced with *handwritten* notes and then typed out on a computer. No doubt it will eventually end up in an *electronic* edition someday. Journalism history, like news itself, has a curious way of messing with our technological assumptions. My hope is that Profes-sor Smith's book will spark each reader's curiosity and resolve to challenge the dominant journalism history paradigm by digging more deeply into the fascinating tradition of handwritten newspapers.

ROY ALDEN ATWOOD, PH.D.
President and Senior Fellow
New Saint Andrews College
Moscow, Idaho

Preface

Journaling, Blogging, and Neighborly Love

In the parable of the Good Samaritan, Jesus tells of an unlucky traveler who was minding his own business along a country path when he was suddenly jumped, robbed, beaten, and left for dead. After the thugs skedaddled with their booty, a couple of religious travelers individually came upon the scene but just ignored the poor guy. Then along came the compassionate Samaritan who took the unfortunate victim to an inn and compensated the proprietor. The Samaritan even promised to cover additional care expenses.

This well-worn parable is one of the most widely circulated news accounts in the history of the Western world. Even if it is fictional, it is telling. We all read in the news about the same three kinds of characters: the wounded, the indifferent, and the compassionate. Most news reports cover the people whose oxen are getting gored, the people who seem to be doing the goring, and whether or not anyone cares enough to address the situation.

We all dwell in the gap between the way we would like the world to be and the way that it actually is. We dream of a better world—such as a healthier community or a more supportive workplace—and then we tune in the daily news for another sobering dose of reality. Or we personally do a good deed only to discover that someone in the meantime has gored our ox. When it comes to the newsworthy reality of the human condition, all of the academic arguments about whether news reports reflect or shape society are relatively insignificant. It doesn't take even a newsroom intern to recognize that the world is deeply broken, and that such brokenness extends all the way up to the supposedly great powerbrokers of the planet, and all the way down to the weakest persons. We are broken people living in a highly dysfunctional world.

This book is about someone who self-consciously dwelled in this gap and wanted to become a Good Samaritan. He sought to be a journalist working on behalf of his own community in rural North Carolina as the Civil War loomed and political fissures threatened to divide families and counties as well as nation. John McLean Harrington felt called to pay attention to the world around him, to reflect on it, and to share his observations and thoughts with citizens across his divided county. "We can promise nothing in the beginning of our enterprise," he told readers in the inaugural issue of one of his papers, "but will spare no pains to please. Our paper is intended for a repository of Pure Literature, Poetry and general news information and as a past time for myself to jot down my thoughts as they may come to the surface" (*The Times.*, October 17, 1867). The "we" was probably just him—except possibly for a younger brother turned factotum. Harrington was like the Samaritan coming upon a terrible, potentially tragic scene—from the plight of slaves (his family had them) to the economic exigencies of farmers, and from political corruption to drug addiction, including his own deepening dependence on alcohol. As the area postmaster, he got to see and hear about the real-life dramas arriving over the transom; he worked at the postal network hub before the telegraph came through town, and long before Ethernet and wifi linked the county to the world. Like the Samaritan, he felt compassion; he suffered with fellow citizens. While the Samaritan also had financial resources, Harrington had a fine education, a quick wit, and a talent for penning evocative prose—including a flair for handwriting itself. Perhaps even more than such resources, Harrington had at least one major, essential trait: he was literarily compulsive. He simply had to write. Period. He would have been a barmy tweeter on Twitter, firing off more insightful tidbits than any normal person could even imagine.

Many of today's bloggers seem to be created in the image of this North Carolinian. Who in the world are all of these folks posting prose faster than most of us can read it? Who has the time? The energy? The determination? The compulsion? Why do they blog? Does anyone beyond a few friends really care about what they have to say? We could ask the same questions about Harrington, the paper blogger. Fortunately for those of us trying to decipher media history, Professor Michael Ray Smith does ask these questions about the prolific and eccentric Harrington. In the process, Professor Smith sheds light on today's blogosphere as well as yesterday's news reporting.

If the analeptic growth of the Internet has demonstrated anything about human nature—other than humankind's insatiable quest for sundry erotica—it is that countless individuals feel a need to express themselves. They want their thoughts to be noticed. They want their feelings and sentiments to matter to others. Moreover, they want to use their keyboards to try to figure out what they themselves are actually thinking, feeling, and doing in life. They even want to compare their conclusions with those of others, especially well-known others in politics or entertainment. One solid criticism of someone else—especially someone supposedly successful—can make an everyday blogger feel much better about herself or himself. If we who blog are lucky, a few other lonely bloggers might harmonize with our voice so that we together can feel camaraderie as we shuffle around in the gaps of life, firing salvos at the demons we spot poking their pointed noses into news dramas. Oh, the techno-splendor of online pot shots! Yes, Harrington takes a few good ones with his fiery pen. He even has the nerve to publish a pointed rejection note to a dear woman who submitted a mediocre manuscript for publication in one of his papers. Couldn't he have just sent a personal letter to the poor lady? I frequently ask myself the following question when reading blogs: Couldn't the writer just carry on privately with the recipient of the attacks? Why must such stings be public?

As Professor Smith makes clear, Harrington's work is not historically important merely because he handwrote so many copies of so many of his own various papers. Harrington's journalism is also important because it provides us with a body of blogs leading up to and during the Civil War. Harrington was a journalist more than just a reporter. He journaled about the breached world around him and—less overtly—the bedeviling cracks in his own mind and heart. He lived geographically, metaphorically, and psychologically between North and South. He angled between cosmopolitanism and provincialism. He practiced reporting in a style that would have been somewhere between the *New York Times* and Twitter of his day. He shuttled back and forth between hard news about politics and soft news about interpersonal relationships. Moreover, he recognized the personal in the national, and the national in the personal. Professor Smith persuasively argues that Harrington's fiction frequently was parabolic, a poetic means of addressing the widening crevices in Southern culture and society.

Why did Harrington believe that anyone would pay for handwritten copies of his hometown paper? Today, that kind of faith would be like assuming that someone would pay to subscribe to a blog. A few people will subscribe to an online news blog that is fashioned like a paper, but gaining enough legitimacy as a blogger is not easy. Journalists of Harrington's day worried more about paying their bills than gathering enough news or forming expressible opinions, especially because it was so common and even accepted to lift news from other papers. Most journalists had to pay printers, too. Unless a political group was willing to become their patron—in return for politicized coverage, no doubt—or advertisers were feeling particularly wealthy—hardly the case in the South as the Civil War unfolded—these reporter-journalists were, like monks in the ancient scriptoria, facing vows of poverty. This was even more true in rural areas, such as Harrington's Harnett County, apparently the last North Carolina county to reap the benefits of mechanically (vs. hand-) printed newspaper.

The advertisements in Harrington's papers remind me of the silly ones that pummel online visitors to some of today's major blog sites. Even if the blogosphere is technologically sophisticated, it certainly is not aesthetically refined. Harrington would be at home on WordPress, Blogger, or even Facebook, with ads by Google and the latest patent medicine and weight loss peddlers.

The magic in Harrington's labors is the thrill of being in complete control of news production and distribution—the same buzz that has seduced so many contemporary bloggers who have no interest in being shackled by a news institution regardless of the instant legitimacy to be gained. Harrington had read other papers, most of them undoubtedly printed on movable-type presses. He knew what "the news" should more or less look like and how it should read. His classical education at a nearby academy undoubtedly gave him the intellectual equipment needed for parsing conventional news practices. Still, his own news-creation and news-distribution concept was regressively revolutionary. Harrington decided that he would be a truly independent journalist with pen, ink (preferably black, but red worked well when he couldn't get quality black ink), paper (both lined and unlined, perhaps depending on his mood or the extent of his intoxication), and a wooden ink stamp for a common masthead. Handwritten newspapers have a long and interesting history, as Professor Smith accounts, but nevertheless the shear, outlandish ambition of Harrington is itself worth contemplating. Yes, he probably was a bit daffy—"eccentric," to be kind. But he was also a proponent of a truly free press—as free as the lone blogger saying whatever she or he wishes without having to depend on anyone else's network server.

The ironies of Harrington's free-blogging story are abundant. Here was a guy dwelling seemingly in the middle of nowhere whose own county ends up hosting one of the last major battles of the Civil War. Here was a guy who would try to launch a newsy literary journal for many readers who probably had never seen such a thing. Here was a guy who admired the *Saturday Evening Post* and actually imagined himself serving his community with similar content, all of which he had to compose himself or borrow from other publications. He refused to become just what today is called an online news "aggregator" who doesn't produce original content (e.g., Matt Drudge); he wanted personally to write as much of the content of his papers as possible. Again, he took this as his calling, not merely as a job or occupation, so he was less concerned about the ironies than the regular output.

One of Harrington's later taglines for *The Nation* captured both what he aimed to accomplish and what most journalists and bloggers essentially practice: "With pleasure or displeasures to friends or foes [sic] we sketch the world as it goes by." In fact, that tagline is a better definition of journalism and reporting than I have read in some academic papers and journalism textbooks. Since Harrington handwrote his papers, the word "sketch" is especially fitting. In addition, a sketch is not fine-tuned or even particularly delicate. Sketching is somewhat improvisational and impressionistic. News bloggers are primarily sketchers even when their output is more impressionistic and psychological than realistic and sociological.

Harrington also performed like a blogger in the ways that he launched and folded publications at will. He would get a notion for a new publication and run with it. How about a literary journal with international news? How about a local newspaper with war coverage? How about a national paper peppered with local anecdotes and human interest stories? He gave them all a try—and then some. He mixed and matched genres. He might decide after a couple of issues that a particular periodical was a bust. Or he might proclaim some great new feature in an upcoming issue and then never publish that or any other forthcoming issue of the paper. I just visited the blog of a dear colleague who has not posted a new item for six months. Before then he was cranking out two or three missives weekly. I discovered why: He's writing instead for a different blog site with some friends. No one knows how long that will last—not even him. The blogosphere is filled with faded ambitions as well as good intentions. Harrington's work reflects both.

Bloggers make mistakes. So do journalists. Neither group is too inclined to admit them. Harrington dealt with mistakes by editing his prose along the way, from copy to copy of each issue. He didn't have a blogger's ability to revise the original version and republish it as if the first version never existed. Online newspapers sometimes do make and date copy changes as a means of correcting errors. Harrington made some copy edits in ink by crossing out or adding words—for the reader to see. But it would be fascinating to review a hundred copies of one issue of one of Harrington's papers to see what he actually changed—just as it would be interesting to access the *New York Times'* internal database to review pre-published versions of news stories.

Years ago as a teen in Chicago, I remember perusing different editions of the same newspapers on the mini newsstand in the local drug store where I worked. Stories changed from edition to edition. Sometimes the story was exactly the same but the headline or placement of the story changed with editions. Long before I ever imagined studying media, I thereby gained a sense of the fluidity of news. That, along with the predictably partisan editorials in the three or four different Chicago dailies (my father was devoted to the middling *Chicago Daily News* and suspicious of the right-leaning *Chicago Tribune*), taught me how sketchy journalism actually was in spite of journalists' self-proclaimed objectivity. Like many news bloggers, Harrington was refreshingly transparent about his biases if not always his errors.

Professor Smith aptly refers to Harrington's handwritten newspaper legacy in terms of holography—documents written wholly in the handwriting of the individuals whose signatures they bear. Like a "signed" blog post whose lone author is obvious, each copy of Harrington's papers conveyed a distinct, letter-like personality. His handwritten papers returned journalism to its roots in the personal journal—like a daybook in accounting, a ship's record, or a personal diary. We humans believe that such records can serve as telling clues to a larger story, such as the tale of a business venture, a voyage, or a personal life. Informed by some secondary sources, Professor Smith delves as deeply as he can into Harrington's extant prose in order to paint a picture of the man. The resulting portrait is not altogether clear. Perhaps he was bored and frustrated. Maybe he suffered from bipolar depression, which stimulated the mania and melancholy evident in both his prose and his abrupt starting and stopping publications (that's my thoroughly amateurish guess). All such speculation is part of the mystery of the anxious man behind the deft penmanship. Since we are not likely to find any additional historical records on the matter, we will have to make do with what we already know.

Nevertheless, it seems to me that Harrington's most worthy legacy is his desire to serve the readers of his community. He recognized and accepted that calling. He admitted to himself and to his readers that for all of the goodness in Harnett County and the world there were also problems that needed to be addressed. Like the Good Samaritan, he felt compassion and decided to pitch in rather than to pass by. He knew that he would not make a very profitable living at it, and that technology could not ensure that he served the community well. In one sense, his calling to handwrite newspapers was folly. In another sense, it was simply his way of living an honest life of mostly humble service—a means of participating in the comedy of grace even while the darkening clouds on the horizon indicated that a tragic storm was brewing. Harrington wrote in *The Young American*, "An editor in Iowa has become so hollow from depending on the printing business alone for bread that he proposes to sell himself for a stove pipe, at three cents a foot." Somehow Harrington managed to put bread on his table and brew in his glass, and even satisfy his literary soul without selling out to the highest bidder. No doubt many bloggers, caught in technological if not commercial spells, would wish to do so well.

QUENTIN J. SCHULTZE, PH.D.
Arthur H. DeKruyter Chair
Calvin College
Grand Rapids, Michigan

Introduction

I n "The Overcoat," a short story by Nikolai Gogol (1809–1852), the main
character, Akaky Akakievich, is a clerk who copies text for a living. Akakievich loves the job so much that he likes to spend his free time handwriting copies of texts, and he falls asleep giddy with the idea that in the morning
he will begin his handwriting work afresh. At one point in the story, the nar-
rator explains Akakievich's love of handwriting: "It would be hard to find a
man who so lived for his job. It would not be enough to say that he worked
conscientiously—he worked with love. There, in his copying, he found an
interesting, pleasant world for himself and his delight was reflected in his face.
He had his favorites among the letters of the alphabet and, when he came to
them, he would chuckle, wink and help them along with his lips so that they
could almost be read on his face as they were formed by his pen."[1] This account
reminds me of John McLean Harrington, who also made a career of handwriting. Although Akakievich is a fictitious character, his devotion to handwriting
reflects Harrington's real-life commitment as a nineteenth-century journalist.

Shortly before the Civil War, the son of an affluent Southern family began
a journalism career unlike any in his community, his state, or perhaps even
the nation. Journalist John McLean Harrington (1839–1887), also known as
"John McL," and "McL," worked as a bookkeeper, surveyor, educator, sheriff,[2]
and postmaster in a community located about thirty miles south of Raleigh,
in Harnett County, North Carolina.[3] This book explores Harrington's *The
Nation,* a newspaper, and *The Young American,* a literary journal that contained news. Both were handwritten in 1858.[4] With the completion of the

first trans-Atlantic telegraph cable in that year, the world felt united in a new way, and the occasion was greeted by bonfires, fireworks, and pageants on both sides of the Atlantic.[5] In Europe, Victorians, overcome by sewage odors from the Thames, built massive sewers, a monumental public works project for the time. Meanwhile. Abraham Lincoln debated Stephen Douglas as the divided United States moved toward Civil War.

In 1858, Harrington's *The Nation* was stridently pro-Democratic and hinted at the nation's collapse, but it also featured lighter fare such as jokes and marriage announcements. Harnett County historian Malcolm Fowler described the newspaper as an early version of the *Kiplinger Newsletter*.[6] The handwritten newspaper included paid advertisements along with local, state, and national news, including some references to the growing uneasiness over the future of slavery. *The Young American,* with a circulation of one hundred subscribers,[7] included news, quips, original fiction, poetry, and paid advertisements.

Harrington's work reveals a reporter-publisher who embodied the concept of the personal journalist. He was committed to a partisan cause and willing to promote it without benefit of a movable-type printing press, although they were available as early as the mid-fifteenth century.[8] The printing telegraph was also available at the time, but went unused by Harrington.[9] In his career, Harrington edited seven handwritten publications over the course of eleven years. He suspended his work during a portion of the Civil War, living where the last major campaigns were fought in North Carolina's Harnett and Sampson counties. The Union and the Confederates fought their next-to-last battle on March 15 and 16, 1865, in Averasboro, about twenty miles from Harrington's home. In that mission, General William J. Hardee's Confederate Army fought to delay Union General William T. Sherman's march north from Atlanta.[10] The last battle of the Civil War, and the largest fought in North Carolina, took place just a few miles away in Bentonville, part of adjacent Johnson County, on March 19-21, 1865. Harrington did not publish during 1865, so he was unable to cover these major tactical offensives, but he resumed his handwritten publications with *The Times.*—a newspaper with an odd period in its name—which ran from October 17, 1867, to April 2, 1869. This book refers to his later journalistic work but does not cover it in-depth. I explore primarily Harrington's publishing before and during parts of the Civil War.

Harrington is worthy of study because of his unusual experiment in freehand publishing and because of the various aspects of his life and character evident in both his public and private lives. Harrington was:

A courageous dilettante journalist who both learned from others and followed his own creative impulses and professional sensibilities.

Democrat. Republican. Personal journalist. Innovator. Harrington was a figure of intrigue, the kind of writer who was not trained formally in the news business but who successfully modeled the conventions of the day. He reprinted articles from other periodicals and inserted his whimsical observations along the way. He did not pioneer any breakthroughs in the press, but his desire to publish by

FIGURE 1. John McLean Harrington
Courtesy of Mrs. Geneva Harrington Cameron

handwriting his work is so novel that it demands attention. Harrington has been called an eccentric and a man who knew no political party loyalty. Yet he contributed a service to his community by providing a voice when no other newspaper existed for his rural area. He worked without benefit of counsel from a veteran journalist. There was no mentor to explain what kind of articles community newspapers commonly published or how to unite a community through the medium of a shared periodical. While brief and unpolished, his work helped his rural community gain a better sense of itself and feel more connected to the world at large.

An unsung hero who accomplished much while learning to navigate between his own public and private lives during socially, culturally, and politically complicated times.

No press association recognized Harrington, and his newspapers have never been on display as examples of journalistic excellence. Yet Harrington demonstrated a commitment to his craft that suggests what is most desired in the work of a journalist. He sifted the news and presented it in an arresting manner with commentary and humor. In a sense, he was ahead of his time by anticipating the fashion of a citizen journalist; he weighed in on the issues of the day because of an irresistible need to be heard. An amateur, Harrington wrote to delight himself first, then others. For this reason, John McLean Harrington could be described as the dilettante editor of Harnett County.

Though he received no accolades, Harrington published his handwritten newspapers over the course of several years. His first publication, *The Young American,* began in January 1858 and was soon followed by a second newspaper, *The Nation,* during April of the same year. In late August 1858, Harrington suspended *The Nation* but persisted in publishing *The Young American.* Harrington's work revealed a reporter-publisher who embodied the concept of a personal journalist, committed to a partisan cause and willing to promote it without the benefit of a printing press. He used his work to support the Southern cause during the Civil War years even though he later supported the Union. Harrington, who lived from 1839 to 1887, edited a total of seven handwritten publications during his eclectic career. The year he died, the first printed newspaper began in Harnett County.

A highly independent journalist who supported the free press using freehand writing.

Harrington exemplified the notion of a free press. He did not let the lack of a printing press keep him from publishing, but instead freely hand copied and distributed his publications partly as evidence of his support for a vigorous free press. In the process, Harrington depended on no other vendors to make, circulate, or run his operation. He may be one of the nation's earliest and best examples of the independent journalist, taking freedom to a new level with his commitment to a free press using freehand to launch and discontinue periodicals at will.

Though his work has not been widely recognized, Harrington was committed to the cause of a free press, even when it required the tedious work of writing by hand. In the pages that follow, I examine questions about the production and distribution of a handwritten newspaper in the political, social, and economic milieu of the rural South before and during the Civil War. In many ways, Harrington might even be considered one of the first off-line bloggers who controlled the design as well as the content of his personal musings about public life.

The Context of Harrington's Life and Publications

SLAVERY

The issue of slavery colored all areas of life during the period from 1858 to 1869 while John McLean Harrington was handwriting his newspapers. Slavery affected legislation such as the Compromise of 1850, led by U.S. Senator Henry Clay. This legislation temporarily warded off sectional strife by admitting California as a free state and applying the policy of popular sovereignty to the land acquired from Mexico. Slavery also dominated the struggle over the Kansas-Nebraska Act of 1854, which allowed these territories to maintain the use of slaves; for all practical purposes, however, the law overturned the Missouri Compromise and created renewed national strife.

Slavery served as the central character in the most notorious novel of this period, Harriet Beecher Stowe's *Uncle Tom's Cabin*. In 1852, the book sold 300,000 copies and rallied anti-slavery sentiment.[1] By 1854, the antislavery movement became the centerpiece of the Republican Party and inspired many supporters, some who thought slavery hurt business and others who considered it immoral.[2] In May 1856, New York abolitionist John Brown carried out a midnight execution of proslavery settlers in Kansas, shocking the nation.[3] And in 1857, the U.S. Supreme Court ruled that Missouri slave Dred Scott was property and therefore had no standing before the courts. The high court also ruled that the Missouri Compromise was unconstitutional "because it was illegal for Congress to deprive an owner of property—in this case, a slave—without due process of law."[4]

While slavery was the overriding issue during Harrington's time, Southerners were not unanimous in their opinion of it. In particular, North Carolina differed from its Southern neighbors.[5] About one third of Virginia families owned slaves, and half of the families in South Carolina were slave owners, but only about one in four North Carolina families owned slaves.[6] Yet even with a smaller proportion of slave-owning families, North Carolina still included a significant number of slaves. By 1850, the state contained 580,491 Caucasians and 288,548 slaves, and by 1860 the numbers had jumped to 661,563 Caucasians and 331,059 slaves,[7] making the enslaved population a crucial part of the state's economy.

The value of slaves for tax purposes (ad valorem) was among the top issues in North Carolina during the 1850s. North Carolina legislator and Whig Moses A. Bledsoe created an organization to fight the inequalities arising from what he considered to be the privileged position of slave property.[8] The Whig party dissolved over the question of slavery, but during the anti-Jackson years the Whigs supported tariffs and a strong Congress. Slaveholders benefited most from railroads and other improvements, yet they contributed less than their fair share to reducing the public debt.[9] It would have been in the best interests of all to tax slaves as persons because it would reduce state debt.[10] The Whigs kept the issue of taxation prominent, but North Carolina Governor John W. Ellis, elected in 1858 and re-elected in 1860, gained support with his idea that taxing a poor person's oven, pots, and chickens was unfair, and he lobbied for exceptions.[11] Since 1830, Andrew Jackson Democrats had resisted the idea of government interference in the lives of farmers; however, Whigs who opposed Jackson sought government assistance for projects such as road construction, sewage drainage, harbor and river dredging, and other internal improvements which were desperately needed in rural North Carolina.[12]

By the time of the Civil War, most residents of Harnett County were poor farmers who grew corn, sweet potatoes, and peas.[13] About 1,000 of the 1,600 men of military age enlisted in the Confederate Army.[14] To keep the farms going, most families depended on slave labor. According to the 1860 Census, 8,069 people lived in the county, thirty percent of whom were "non-white."[15]

THE HARRINGTON FAMILY AND SLAVES

The Harrington family was part of the more affluent tier of Harnett County society that depended on slave labor. According to the October 11, 1850, U.S. Census, John McLean Harrington, ten years old at the time, lived in a household with nine slaves.[16] In 1860, when he was twenty, his family owned fourteen slaves and he owned ten. By 1870, when the War Between the States was over, John Mclean and his family had only seven non-family members listed as part of their household.

The 1870 U.S. Census listed John's father as sixty-three years old and noted that he was a farmer and former state senator. John's mother, Margaret, was listed as fifty-four years old and described as "keeping house."[17] The listing indicated that thirty-year-old John McLean was an assistant U.S. marshal. Other listed household members included: James, age twenty-one, described as working on the farm; Sion, age nineteen; and David, age sixteen, noted as "Do" (which may be an abbreviation for a "domestic."). The last entry for this family, written by John McLean Harrington as assistant marshal for the census, includes the name Louis, age eleven, mulatto; and Sarah, age eleven, black. Since this U.S. Census is post-Civil War, it's impossible to know the role of the others in the Harrington household (See Appendix C for the complete U.S. Census figures for the Harrington Household from 1850 to 1880).

A scribe for all seasons, John McLean Harrington is listed as the enumerator who collected the U.S. Census figures for Upper Little River Township of Harnett County. His ornate signature appears on the U.S. Census figures of July 9, 1870, and June 17, 1880. Harrington died before the next U.S. Census in 1890 at the age of forty-seven, on April 3, 1887.[18]

HARNETT COUNTY DURING THE TIME OF
JOHN MCLEAN HARRINGTON

Harrington lived in the Piedmont section of North Carolina in Harnett County, established in 1855. This impoverished region is where Harrington published his papers. Buffalo Springs, located near the village of Harrington, "was a thriving little hamlet centering about the turpentine industry" in Harrington's day.[19] In addition to the harvesting of turpentine, barrel making proved to be one of the few profitable commercial industries in the Buffalo Springs and Harrington areas of Harnett County. Journalist Harrington referred to barrel making in a display advertisement for 20,000 white oak staves on page two of his maiden issue of *The Young American* in January 1858. Buffalo Springs and the surrounding area had faded with the arrival of the Western, or Coalfield, Railroad, and the Salem Plank Road.[20] The shaky economics of this period added to the instability of attracting and retaining a reading audience willing to pay to receive news—even crucial news about the financial health of the community.

THE PUBLICATIONS OF JOHN MCLEAN HARRINGTON

Harrington was the first person to attempt a newspaper in Harnett County. He published his newspapers from his home in Buffalo Springs, a town also known as "Harrington," from 1858 to 1869. In 1858, seventy-four newspapers were officially listed as circulating in North Carolina,[21] not including Harrington's handwritten newspapers. By the end of his career, he published 302 issues of newspapers and periodicals under varying titles. Table 1 summarizes the publications.

Duke University's collection includes the surviving issues of seven Harrington publications. *The Young American,* Harrington's first periodical, was a type of literary magazine that also contained news, short stories, and

TABLE 1
HARRINGTON'S PUBLICATIONS

Name	Date	Location	Number	Number Surviving
The Young American	January 1858 to December 1858	Harrington and Buffalo Springs, N.C.	12	8
The Nation	April 17, 1858 to September 8, 1858	Harrington, N.C.	21	16
Weekly Eagle	April 20, 1860	Harrington and Pine Forest, N.C	1	1
Semi-Weekly News	July 20, 1860 to August 13, 1860	Harrington, N.C.	6	5
The Weekly News' Advertising Sheet. Monthly.	February, March, April 1861	Harrington, N.C.	3	3
The Weekly News	June 7, 1860 to March 2, 1864	Harrington, N.C.	182	153
The Times.[22]	October 17, 1867 to April 2, 1869[23]	Harrington, N.C.	77	68

The John McLean Harrington publications are based on the originals from the Rare Book, Manuscript, and Special Collections Library of the Perkins Library at Duke University, Durham, NC, microfilmed in 1998.

poems by Harrington and other authors from central North Carolina. The publication measured eight inches wide by ten inches long and consisted of a single column. Within four months, Harrington began another handwritten paper, *The Nation,* a weekly that focused on state and local news with a strident pro-Democrat slant. *The Nation,* typically four pages, was written on one sheet of paper, measuring eight inches wide and twenty-four inches long. It was penned on both sides of the paper and folded in the center to create a page eight inches wide and twelve inches long.[24] *The Weekly Eagle* followed shortly after *The Nation,* and it focused on political news. Harrington's other publications—*The Semi-Weekly News, Weekly News, The Weekly News' Advertising Sheet. Monthly.,* and *The Times.*—were published after the Civil War.[25] *The Times.* was used to mildly criticize Harrington's newly united country for too much government while also praising it as the best of all nations. Harrington might have played a role in his younger brother's (Sion) publication of *The Leisure Hour*—which creatively employed the word "leasure" but lasted only two issues.

Harrington's newspapers demonstrated a variety of page sizes, and publication ranged from twice a week to monthly. He wrote *The Nation* in red ink on April 17, 1858, and blue ink with some red highlights on April 24, 1858. Sometimes he used lined paper, such as in the April 1, 1858, issue of *The Young American*. He also used unlined paper in the January 6, 1863, issue of the *Weekly News*. The *Weekly News*, which began as an 8 × 10″ publication in January 1863, but became progressively smaller over time. It was 6 × 7″ by the issue dated September 2, 1863, and 4 × 8″ in size by the one dated January 24, 1864.

Harrington's publications contained articles on disparate topics ranging from recipes to news of the Civil War. In addition to *The Nation* and *The Young American*, in 1860 Harrington began publishing *The Weekly Eagle*, but he suspended this periodical when paper became scarce. Like his other newspapers, *The Semi-Weekly News, Weekly News, The Weekly News' Advertising Sheet. Monthly.,* and *The Times.* all included traditional newspaper content. Harrington's last handwritten newspaper was an issue of *The Times.* dated April 2, 1869—eighteen years before his death. Some of his personal correspondence is available at Duke University's Rare Book, Manuscript, and Special Collections Library, and various letters addressed to Harrington are part of a collection in a private printing.[26]

In the July 7, July 14, July 21, August 4, August 11, August 18, August 25, and September 1, 1858, issues of *The Nation,* editor John McLean Harrington wrote, "With pleasure or displeasures to friends or foes [sic] we sketch the world as it goes." This slogan emphasized Harrington's approach to recording life in his community. While untrained as a journalist, Harrington sensed the need to provide a snapshot of the highs and lows of his neighbors' activities, particularly the politics of the region.

HARRINGTON'S LIFE

Harrington was born on November 2, 1839, one mile south of Mt. Pisgah Church, a Presbyterian congregation founded in 1834 in rural Harnett County, North Carolina.[27] He died on April 3, 1887, at the age of forty-seven.[28] He is buried in the Mt. Pisgah Presbyterian Church cemetery, 128 McArthur Road, Broadway, North Carolina, in western Harnett County. Still standing, his headstone is close to the road. As of 2011, this area remained undeveloped and sparsely populated. The surrounding vicinity is a part of what is called "The Sandhills"—an area characterized by poor sandy soil, not well-suited for any large-scale agriculture. This area was traditionally the poorest, most rural, and least populated part of Harnett County. Only with the influx in 2011 of military personnel stationed at nearby Fort Bragg did the area start to lose its isolated rural character.

John McLean Harrington was the son of James Stephen (1806–1888) and Margaret McLean Harrington (1816–1884). James served as an elder of both the Barbecue Presbyterian Church and Mt. Pisgah Presbyterian Church,[29] and as the Cumberland County member of the House of Commons from 1861 until 1865.[30] He was also a member of the Harnett County finance committee from 1858 to 1865, and served in the House of Commons in 1866.[31] In 1868, he served in the North Carolina State Senate.[32] In addition, James was elected to the Harnett County Board of Commissioners for most of his adult life. Following in the footsteps of his father, John McLean Harrington would grow up to monitor politics and seek political appointments, though the manifestation of his civil service would best be seen in his handwritten periodicals.

John McLean Harrington was born in a log house.[33] This Harrington was considered brilliant,[34] a child prodigy who graduated from Pine Forest Academy, a private school that began in the 1840s and served as both a school and a meeting place for the Masonic lodge.[35] He graduated at the age of twelve[36] and went on to study at Archie Black's Academy at Haywood near Moncure, North Carolina, in Chatham County. He may have also studied twenty miles south of his home in Fayetteville at Donaldson Academy.[37] At the age of fifteen, Harrington became a teacher at Pine Forest, where he was paid $154 and five pairs of socks for a three-month term.[38] At that time, public school teachers earned $15 to $30 per month. He also worked as a surveyor.[39] In addition to writing fiction and prose, Harrington served as president of the Pine Forest Debating Society during 1869.[40]

In 1857, Harrington worked as a bookkeeper for J. & D.G. Worth, merchants,[41] and for naval store[42] operators at Buffalo Springs, two miles east of Spout Springs.[43] Buffalo Springs, now defunct, is sometimes listed as Pineview, located ten miles south of Broadway, North Carolina, a tiny town of about three hundred that still exists today. Harrington worked for T. C. and B. G. Worth, a turpentine-commissioned merchant headquartered in Wilmington,[44] likely the same as the aforementioned Worth business. Harrington avoided military service during the Civil War because of his position as postmaster at his family's Harrington Post Office,[45] the same wooden building where he lived and published.[46] In 1944, the *Harnett County News* noted that the

FIGURE 2. John McLean Harrington, the tallest man in the back, taught at Pine Forest Academy, where he once studied as a student. *Courtesy of Geneva Harrington Cameron*

derelict structure of the post office could be seen off a rural road, aptly named Harrington Road.[47] The building was razed in the 1970s and today the area that once was home to so much handwriting is a grassy area bounded by a dirt road and a farm pond.[48] Harrington's various roles prepared him to be a journalist who knew firsthand the hardships of life in the rural South. His work as a postmaster gave him ready access to newsy information whenever residents collected their mail. In addition, Harrington could monitor the content of periodicals in the U.S. mail and glean information and ideas from them as he tried his own hand at journalistic prose.

Even if he had not been the postmaster (sometimes referred to as "sub-postmaster"), Harrington still might have avoided the draft because Confederate newspapers typically were allowed to have one editor who was exempt.[49] Never married, Harrington was considered an attractive man with a dark complexion.[50] He dated many women and reportedly claimed that he "never succeeded in fooling one of them into the bonds of matrimony."[51] An active Mason, Harrington rose to the position of leader, or master, of his lodge, which met at the schoolhouse.[52] While celebrated in his community, Harrington was not well known outside the county, and his popularity sagged when he did not leave home to serve in the Civil War[53] in spite of friends who urged him to join the service.[54] According to the Adjutant General's Records of North Carolina, however, John McLean Harrington served in the Confederate home guard as 1st Lieutenant for Upper Little River District, Fifty-Second Regiment, North Carolina Militia in Harnett County. Harrington's name is listed in the "Roster of Officers of the Militia of North Carolina," which includes entries for 1861–1862 and 1864.[55] Following the war, Harrington and his prominent father left the Democratic Party and joined the Republican Party, which did not endear either man to the community.

In a letter of September 3, 1866, to James S. Harrington, John McLean's father, William Woods Holden, North Carolina's provisional governor under President Andrew Johnson, called for a meeting of loyal Union men in Raleigh.[56] The letter said a convention was planned for September 20, 1866. Holden wrote, "Please spread this information among Union men as far as possible. Come yourself, and urge others to attend."[57] The letter suggests that the elder Harrington was a Union supporter; if so, John McLean's sympathies by that time were the same as his father's. On June 30, 1865, Holden recommended John McLean for a presidential pardon from Johnson because John McLean was considered a Confederate official due to his position as a postmaster.[58] In his letter to Johnson, John McLean requested amnesty based on a May 28, 1865, presidential proclamation. Using the third person, John McLean wrote that he "had always been a consistent Union man and has never been in the military service of the Confederate states or voluntarily aided in the rebellion, that his acceptance of the position of sub-postmaster was in order to evade military service and petitioner asks that a special pardon may be granted to him and that he may be taking the oath of amnesty."[59] On June 27, 1865, John McLean Harrington signed his name to pledge support to the Union of the United States of America. The document recorded Harrington as fair in complexion, with dark hair and hazel eyes, six feet tall, and twenty-five years old.[60] Harrington solemnly swore in the oath that he would "abide by and faithfully support all the laws and proclamations which have been made during the existing rebellion with reference to the emancipation of slaves."[61] Harrington did not record his profession as a postmaster, teacher, or publisher, but as a farmer.

By June 22, 1870, Adjutant General A. W. Fisher issued General Order No. 6, which reorganized the state militia using strong Unionists and prominent native sons, including John McLean Harrington.[62] The order, published on July 6, 1870, in the *Weekly North Carolina Standard,* Holden's old Raleigh newspaper, listed "John McL. Harrington, Harnett," as Brigadier General of the Thirteenth Brigade. This appointment firmly established Harrington as a Unionist.

Throughout his career as a journalist, Harrington probably left readers wondering about his real intentions, desires, and loyalties. At times Harrington told his reading audience that he would begin a new publication or continue an existing one, but then would do neither. He talked of a partner but never revealed the colleague's identity—if he indeed had one. He discussed the evil of drinking but died an alcoholic. He served as a member of the Confederate militia only to swear an oath that he would always remain a loyal Unionist. Perhaps Harrington tended to do or say whatever was expedient or expected at the time. Maybe he was himself just conflicted in numerous ways.

HARRINGTON AND POLITICAL PARTIES

As a journalist with the heart of a dramatist, Harrington evoked the pathos that can be missed in the tedium that often dominates rural life. Consider a letter he wrote to President Andrew Johnson. He addressed his request for a pardon to "His Excellency, Andrew Johnson, President of the United States." Harrington said he worked as a postmaster to evade military service, but at age twenty-six, he wrote Johnson that he was willing to support the Union. Already at age eighteen, Harrington had adopted the pose of a reformer who could be zealous for a cause even if he later seemed a bit unsure of his genuine convictions.

In a May 15, 1880 letter, John McLean wrote Gen. F. A. Walker, superintendent of the federal censuses of 1870 and 1880 and later the president of the Massachusetts Institute of Technology. In his letter, Harrington requested that he be allowed to work on the 1880 Census, as he had already served on the 1870 Census as the recorder for the Upper Little River District. Harrington stated that he was afraid that his status as a Republican caused him not to be approved for the post. In his May 15, 1880, letter to the Honorable F. A. Walker, Harrington, at age forty-one, stated, "I made application for this township (Upper Little River) in the Census for this year but being a Republican I am afraid Col. Stanford will not recommend me though

FIGURE 3. Harrington's tombstone in the cemetery of Mt. Pisgah Presbyterian Church. The lower half of the stone reads "At Rest." *Photograph by Michael Ray Smith*

Rep. [Daniel L.] Russell said he would do all he could for me."[63] Harrington had been responsible for the county at the 1870 census. By 1880, Republicans held sway on the national level, but Democrat Thomas J. Jarvis occupied the North Carolina governor's mansion. By 1880, being a Republican was a liability rather than the asset it had been just after the Civil War, according to Sion

Harrington, a historian and descendant of John McLean Harrington. During these later years, Harrington began to drink excessively and his mind deteriorated.[64] Harrington died on April 3, 1887, just a few months before the launch of Harnett County's first machine-printed newspaper, *The Dunn Signboard*.[65]

NEWSPAPERS THAT FOLLOWED HARRINGTON'S HANDWRITTEN ONES

Subsequent to Harrington's handwritten newspapers in Harnett County, North Carolina, other journalists were inspired to begin newspapers with the aid of a printing press. *The Dunn Signboard* was among the first of these papers, edited by J. D. Brooks and published by N. R. Richardson until December 16, 1887.[66] The newspaper went through a series of publishers that included D. N. Farrell from December 23, 1887, until May 17, 1888. That publication went out of business around 1888 and was replaced by the *Harnett Courier*, edited by David Henry Senter and Charles T. Stewart and published by Joseph T. Stone.[67] The *Courier* ran until sometime in 1889.

The next Harnett newspaper was the *Central Times*, published in southern Harnett County in the town of Dunn.[68] The paper began on February 26, 1891, was edited by E. F. Young and G. K. Grantham, and was published by Grantham and J. P. Pittman. On March 27, 1895, the title was changed to the *County Union* and the publication survived until 1899.[69] In 1901, the *Democratic Banner* began. This newspaper was followed by the *Cape Fear Enterprise*, a publication that moved from Holly Springs to Angier on May 31, 1901.[70] *The Weekly Guide*, another Dunn newspaper, began circulating in 1903 under Pittman's leadership. In 1903, John Tyler McLean founded the *Cape Fear Pilot* in Lillington, part of central Harnett County.[71] The newspaper record is unclear with many publications coming and going, such as: The *Dunn Enterprise*, 1890; *The Little River Record*, 1899–1916; *Tobacco and Manufacturers' Guide*, 1902–1918; *Reporter*, 1902–1905; *Harnett Leader*, 1911–1912; and *Dunn Dispatch*, 1914–1978.[72] In 1950, Hoover Adams founded the *Daily Record* in Dunn. Today the *Daily Record* has one of the highest rates of newspaper penetration in the nation.[73] But from the period before the Civil War until shortly thereafter, there was only one active journalist in the area: John McLean Harrington.

The North Carolina Press Before and During the Civil War

2

THE PRESS IN NORTH CAROLINA
1815–1835

The North Carolina press in the decades leading up to the Civil War was mediocre on its best days. Only ten newspapers were known to circulate in 1811.[1] Between 1815 and 1835, no more than thirty newspapers, most of them weeklies, operated.[2] According to the 1825 Fayetteville *Carolina Observer,* only 75,000 copies of newspapers circulated throughout the entire state.[3] The newspapers tended to be four pages long, and most of them contained non-news content, including lottery advertisements, lists of current prices, court orders, notices of rewards for runaway slaves, and notices of sales for taxes.[4] Much of the news that was published came from such sources as other periodicals, stage drivers, friends of the editor, and members of the United States Congress. Also, the news that was included tended to be weeks old. The common content was an editorial, usually found on page one and continued inside the newspaper.

Collecting subscription fees proved difficult, and payment could take the form of bartering with farmers, some of whom paid with produce. Among the conventions of the day was the custom of sending "a slice of wedding cake for the insertion of a wedding notice."[5] Most editors supplemented their publishing incomes with stipends from occupations such as postmaster, lawyer, elected official, or clergyman.[6] Many worked in commercial printing and some even supplemented their meager incomes by peddling "worm-destroying lozenges and other medicines."[7]

Partisanship colored the North Carolina press of this period. Prior to 1815, the editors tended to support Federalist politics, but by 1828 the majority of the state's newspapers backed Andrew Jackson, anti-Federalist and president of the United States from 1829 to 1837. In 1832, the North Carolina press split between support for Jackson and for Martin Van Buren, who would become U.S. president from 1837 to 1841. Despite the controversy, the state's newspaper "editors of this period show a disappointing lack of interest in state and local political affairs."[8]

Not far from John McLean Harrington's home was the Fayetteville *Carolina Observer*, started in 1816 and sold to John McRae in 1823. It was ranked among the top ten newspapers in North Carolina. By 1829, McRae sold the newspaper and the new owners of the *Carolina Observer* joined others in the state in opposing Jackson.[9] While Fayetteville is situated twenty miles south of the location of John McLean Harrington's home, Harrington did not avail himself of this nearby printing press. Still, the layout and content of the Fayetteville newspaper can be seen in Harrington's aesthetic approach, which featured small headlines, crowded layout, and news articles displayed in no discernable order.

Among the most outstanding journalists of this period was Joseph Gales, who published the Raleigh *Register* as early as 1799.[10] Gales worked in Raleigh, thirty miles north of Harrington's home, as state printer and commercial printer.[11] As an active printer, Gales published reports of court cases, a manual of laws, and a two-volume set of laws for North Carolina.[12] In addition, he printed materials for Baptist associations, the Raleigh Female Tract Society, and the North Carolina Bible Society. He printed music for the Moravians, along with sermons, including one by his son-in-law, Anthony Forster.[13] Gales additionally printed his wife's novel and a book of poetry.[14] This literary streak matches Harrington's tendency to publish short stories, poetry, and non-news content in his handwritten work from 1858 to 1869.

Gales is best known for his editorial support of law and order, and he may have initiated the idea of "society news."[15] In 1831, Gales called slavery a great evil but noted that he was not an abolitionist, adding that he feared an uprising of Blacks.[16] He promoted the cause of a gradual colonization of American Blacks in a return to Africa, and he supported the American Colonization Society, which purchased land on the West African coast in 1821 for the settlement of free Blacks.[17] Although Gales retired in 1833, the *Register* might have been "politically the most important paper in North Carolina before 1824."[18] The newspaper set at least one ethical standard by avoiding name-calling and personal attacks on anyone with whom the editor disagreed.

THE PRESS IN NORTH CAROLINA 1835–1861

Between 1833 and the Civil War, the newspaper established itself as a true mass medium throughout the nation.[19] Between 1835 and 1861, however, the presses of North Carolina were still few in number and produced lackluster editorial efforts. By 1851, forty-four newspapers were known to circulate, and by 1858 at least seventy-four existed.[20] The editors of the period had marginal journalistic ability and spent as much time trying to collect from delinquent subscribers as they did publishing.[21] Although periodical subscriptions were available from the earliest days of the United States, by 1828 they were sold primarily to a handful of men interested in government, politics, and business.[22] In Harrington's case, most of his subscriptions were $2 in advance per year. In comparison, the North Carolina *Chronicle* or Fayetteville *Gazette* cost $3 annually.[23]

With North Carolina's illiteracy rate at thirty percent, finding a reading public presented a challenge to editors.[24] The growth of newspapers was painfully slow. By 1844 the editors tended toward partisanship, with the Whig party sponsoring twenty newspapers and the Democrats sponsoring seven. As the time of the Civil War approached, the Whig party newspapers were replaced by Democratic organs, and by 1859 the number of Democratic newspapers had increased to eighteen.[25] Between 1835 and 1860, the *Standard,* published in Raleigh, gained a reputation as the official Democratic party mouthpiece.[26] In 1860, the *Standard's* weekly circulation was more than 2,500 and its semiweekly circulation 400.[27]

Throughout the period leading to the Civil War, Raleigh was home to many failed newspapers, but the one that remained vibrant was the *Standard,* which began in late 1834 but took some time to get established.[28] Thomas Loring of Massachusetts led the *Standard* and urged an ethical code among editors that included the use of respectful language among leaders in state politics.[29] By 1843 Loring lost favor with Democrats, and William Woods Holden of Hillsboro (now Hillsborough), North Carolina, assumed control of the *Standard* in that year.[30] When he died in 1892, his readers regarded him as one who, for his twenty-five years editing the *Standard,* could "kill or make alive" those involved in Tar Heel politics.[31] Holden used the newspaper's Democratic influence to ridicule his former party, the Whigs.[32] Though Holden had once identified himself with Whigs, he had no trouble changing sides to become a Democrat.[33] By 1850 Holden had advanced the *Standard* from a weekly to a semi-weekly publication and used it to build up the Democratic Party.[34] He considered himself a man of influence and once boasted that he, as an editor, had made the Democratic Party.[35]

No one seemed to balk at the fact that in North Carolina the *Standard* and other newspapers freely copied material from each other. However, relations could get acrimonious regarding politics. For instance, in 1844 the *Standard* sparred with the *Mecklenburg Jeffersonian* over John C. Calhoun's fitness as a presidential candidate.[36] The *Jeffersonian* stridently supported Calhoun and insisted that the rest of the state do so as well. In response, Holden accused the *Jeffersonian* of being lukewarm toward the Democrats. Sixty miles south of Raleigh, the *Fayetteville North Carolinian* attacked the *Standard*[37] and in 1845 accused Holden of treason.[38] Hostility between North Carolina newspapers was the rule,[39] although polite conventions often existed, including the practice of welcoming a new publication, regardless of party. The *Standard* sometimes even praised the talents of a Whig editor—especially if the editor died or gave up the publication.[40]

The decade before the Civil War included more of the same pedestrian reporting by the North Carolina press.[41] The number of Northern periodicals far exceeded those in the South, and the Northern papers offered more timely news presented in a more arresting manner.[42] While the newspapers in North Carolina increased from forty-five in 1850 to seventy by 1860, editors continued to complain that subscribers did not settle their accounts.[43] A typical example of acceptable circulation figures in 1850 is the *Standard* count of 1,500 subscribers.[44] Sagging circulation and wayward subscribers took their toll. The *Rowan Whig and Western Advocate* of Salisbury said in an editorial dated May 26, 1854, "Printer's accounts are said to resemble Faith, the substance of things hoped for and the evidence of things not seen." It hoped that the publication's "nearly one thousand of the best subscribers in the State, who are in arrears, will at once send us our dues."[45] Among the newspapers that adopted a "cash system" of paying in advance for a subscription was Raleigh's *Standard*.[46] Editor William Holden praised the cash system and claimed on July 23, 1856, an increase of "900 subscribers—almost 400 per month." Holden also profited from his work as the official state printer, considered a political plum, and in 1855 he produced 1,300 pages for the legislature, a feat Holden claimed cost him more than it had his predecessors.[47]

In good times and bad, publishing in North Carolina before the Civil War remained a difficult vocation and forced editors to give away advertising in the hopes of signing up clients for long-term commitments. Holden once gave the Koh-i-poor chewing tobacco company free advertising and praised advertiser P.F. Pescud's product "as the purest and finest article of the kine [sic] we have seen."[48] Holden had no such words for Northern advertising agents who placed notices for patent medicine but failed to pay for the service. He called them "vampires" who sucked the blood from the Southern press.[49]

Most likely reflecting other papers' stances as well, Holden's *Standard* supported the politics of free manhood suffrage, the 1857 proposal that a person did not have to own land to vote.[50] This issue was one of many that Whig editors of the period opposed, and by 1856, two years before Harrington began his handwritten newspapers, the Whig movement lost its attraction. During the 1850s, editors such as Holden used their editorial pages to deride candidates and policies they disliked. Holden wrote in the *Standard* in June 1853 that it was "a duty incumbent upon us all . . . to prevent the possibility ever of Whig success."[51]

By 1858, when Harrington started his first handwritten newspaper, Holden criticized any journal that did not endorse a strong Democrat to be the next governor of North Carolina. On December 23, 1857, Holden employed his *Standard* to chide the *Raleigh Register* for suffering bankruptcy along with the Whig party, by an illicit alliance with the Know Nothings, and for courting a new issue, one Holden called an "old broken down harlot—Miss Distribution."[52] This position, popular as early as 1853, involved distributing revenue collected under a tariff act in 1846.

In 1858, this issue of revenue dispersal, among others, served as the background for a gubernatorial race between Duncan K. McRae, a former Democratic legislator who once served in the U. S. consul in Paris, and Judge John W. Ellis, the son of a planter and a fervent opponent of abolitionists. Ellis won the race and served from 1859 to 1861. Harrington endorsed Ellis without commenting on the issue of tax revenue distribution. Oddly enough, editor Holden also ran for the Democratic nomination for governor in 1858, but lost to Ellis in the May primary. Ellis was governor when North Carolina seceded from the Union in 1861, but died in office that same year. Holden would eventually win office in 1865, becoming the thirty-eighth governor. He also served as the fortieth governor from 1868 to 1871. Although Holden once championed the rights of slaveholders, as the Civil War progressed he became an outspoken critic of the Confederate cause. After the war, he became leader of the state's Republican party and was appointed governor by President Andrew Johnson during the early days of Reconstruction.

By the end of his term, Holden was impeached and removed from office on charges related to his work to combat violence associated with the Ku Klux Klan. He was the first governor in the United States to be impeached and, worse, convicted.[53] During his days as editor of the *Standard,* Holden did not favor secession or, in his words, dissolution. He wrote in a June 11, 1860, editorial, "Disunion would be fraternal strife, civil and servile war, murder, arson, pillage, robbery, and fire and blood through long and cruel years."[54] During 1858, Holden used the *Standard* to highlight slavery and focus on the approaching 1860 presidential election while editors across North Carolina were debating the issue of taxation of slaves based on their economic value rather than as persons.[55] Because of the taxation issue, commonly referred to as ad valorem taxation of slaves, Holden's partner, Frank I. Wilson, who disagreed with the ad valorem idea, sold his part of the business to Holden.[56] All the while, Holden reflected the sentiment of the press throughout North Carolina in calling Republicans "unconstitutional and anti-slavery."[57] When the U.S. Supreme Court handed down the landmark Dred Scott decision in 1857, Holden and his *Standard* observed that "abolitionism has been stunned, faction and treason in both sections of the Union have been rebuked, and the Constitution has been restored."[58]

By early 1858, editors in North and South Carolina wondered if Congress would refuse to admit Kansas as a state because of its proslavery constitution, despite passage of the Kansas-Nebraska Act of 1854, which had said inhabitants could exercise popular sovereignty and choose to be either a free or slave state. Many feared an outbreak of civil war in Kansas.[59] On February 6 and 10, 1858, Holden used the *Standard* to question the sincerity of President James Buchanan's support of the proslavery Lecompton Constitution. Holden worried that not only Kansas, but also Minnesota and Oregon would gain statehood as free states and, before long, the South's power within the Union would wane.[60] As a result, Holden would sometimes use the *Standard* to promote antislavery sentiments and encourage North Carolina to align with the free states.

Holden's work later provoked controversy during the Civil War. Powerful sources, angry with press coverage of the Confederacy, sometimes sought retribution. Military punishment of the Southern press could be brutal, and the Georgia Brigade, unhappy with news coverage, once while passing through the capital destroyed the offices of Holden's *Standard* and the Raleigh *State Journal*.[61] Some historians even dubbed Holden "the father of secession"[62] for nearly getting North Carolina to secede from the Confederacy and pursue a separate peace with the Union.[63] Holden resembled Harrington in that each apparently "changed his political stripes to advance his own political ambitions."[64] While virtually all Southern editors were pro-Democrat, not all editors were pro-Southern rights or pro-Constitutional Union. During the war, Holden remained proslavery but changed his position when he accepted the leadership of the state following the Civil War.[65] As previously mentioned, Harrington also exhibited lukewarm support for secession in the prewar years and changed political parties following the Civil War.

THE PRESS IN NORTH CAROLINA DURING AND AFTER THE CIVIL WAR

By 1860, the peak of Harrington's publishing activity, the North enjoyed inexpensive newspapers and the burgeoning telegraph lines that ran along railroad tracks and helped to deliver news to a wider audience.[66] By contrast, the South, including Harnett County, had fewer rail lines and hence fewer telegraph lines than the North. The rail and telegraph advantage helped the North move troops and information with greater ease than the South.[67]

Throughout the nation, however, the press increasingly capitalized on the telegraph as a new way of understanding the process of newsgathering as well as the nature of news itself. No longer did all editors have to wait patiently for information to be delivered over the transom. News was becoming less "old news" than "new news"—the latest events and accompanying observations. Using speedier means of gathering and distributing information and opinion, editors redefined news. News ceased to be only "whatever accounts came to hand," and increasingly came to be "what's new."[68] This change caught on, and "Americans learned almost everything taking place outside their communities from newspapers."[69]

Moreover, this change contributed to a growing emphasis on selling news as a commodity rather than simply using news to distribute timely information or to advance partisan opinions. Editors might have political agendas, for instance, but they also had to support their work financially if they did not have other paying jobs, personal wealth, or patrons. As today, conflict as well as timeliness could attract readers and presumably subscribers and advertisers. Journalists had to be storytellers if they expected to attract audiences. They had to identify if not create some social conflict for the sake of publishing engaging stories. Perhaps this tendency is one reason why the various papers were not above borrowing and reprinting each other's words in order to instigate or at least fuel existing regional friction.[70] Press-fueled social conflict was probably reflected in the rhetoric of the *fire-eaters*—those extreme proponents of slavery who were "intent on protecting and promoting their region's interests even if it meant sacrificing the Republic."[71]

In the South, the press, while the most important medium for disseminating news, rarely excelled at speedy or even comprehensive local and state coverage.[72] Despite this shortcoming, the Southern press proved to be the medium of choice in the clamor for secession. As the debate over slavery grew more passionate, papers such as the Richmond *Examiner,* the Jackson *Mississippian,* and Atlanta *Daily Intelligencer* called for the South to declare its independence and secede from the United States.[73] The Southern press shared a reason to be ideological rather than just commercial.

Among the slave states that resisted this drive for secession was North Carolina. Nationally, the issue of slavery haunted Lincoln during his painful term as president. He gradually came to believe abolition was a military necessity essential to preserving the Union. In his effort to save the Union, Lincoln generated the Emancipation Proclamation, a challenge that enraged the Southern press. In rural North Carolina, Harrington had publicly rejected secession during the years before the war. His writing in 1858 was proslavery, but muted. Probably because slavery was a key part of life in his own community, Harrington joined others in criticizing "Black Republicans" and supporters of slave rights. Nevertheless, Harrington's sentiment on this topic was mild compared to other topics he addressed and compared to other area writers. Holden's *Standard* more stridently insisted that it would not submit to Black Republican rule.[74] At the time, newspapers in the Piedmont region of North Carolina existed primarily for political reasons, including support of the Democrats and opposition to "the parade of organizations opposing the Democrats including the Whigs, 1850–1854; Americans, 1855–1856; American-Whigs, 1857–1858; and Opposition, 1859."[75] Harrington was partisan, too, but not exclusively or even primarily. Along with the new definition of news emerging in the urban North, Harrington was developing a broader notion of news even within his highly partisan, largely rural culture.

While some reporters in the North and South did use parody, propaganda, or outright deceit, a new wave of business-minded editors like Horace Greeley of the New York *Tribune* sought to be fair minded if not objective.[76] He and Charles Dana excelled in their coverage of Ulysses S. Grant, the Union general most responsible for the Northern victory. In order to increase circulation, Greeley continually experimented with his newspaper and often focused on news in rural areas, where he found eager readers.[77] In addition, he promoted the notion that his newspaper would tolerate no factual errors, hiring Dana as the *Tribune's* managing editor to implement this policy.[78] Presumably such a policy would also help Greeley and other editors pacify angry readers or news subjects. When Civil War generals became disgruntled over the press's mistakes or excesses, they could make a journalist's job especially difficult. General William Tecumseh Sherman endured a stormy relationship with journalists, many of whom considered him insane.[79] Sherman castigated reporters for publishing his battle plans, calling them "dirty newspaper scribblers who have the impudence of Satan."[80]

Like others in the Piedmont, Harrington followed the trend of the day to include "locally written fiction either in serial or capsule form; selected and/or locally written poetry; humor, medicinal aids; books reviews; and essays on religion, agriculture, education, and temperance."[81] Editors, including Harrington, encouraged members of the community to contribute literary submissions.[82] The journalistic trends of the 1850s included a chaotic layout without much effort to guide the reader from one item to another,[83] and Harrington followed this convention as well.

Nevertheless, the city press was often very different from Harrington's rural newspaper, and frequently included political propaganda. Among Lincoln's supporters was Assistant Secretary of State John Hay, who sent dispatches to sympathetic newspapers to promote Lincoln's actions as part of the North's propaganda machine.[84] One of Hay's humorous dispatches of 1881 ridiculed the Rev. Marble Nash Taylor, a politician from the Outer Banks of North

Carolina, and Charles Henry Foster, a North Carolina newspaper editor. In 1861, Taylor and Foster tried to reinstate federal authority in the eastern part of the state, with Taylor as provisional governor. President Lincoln and the Congress, however, disavowed the efforts of the two men. Hay wrote, "The Reverend Marble Nash Taylor closes my list of remarkable parsons who seemed to find politics a hard road to travel. This is the highly respectable party who recently elected himself Governor of North Carolina, and a young reporter, named Charles Henry Foster, Congressman from the Hatteras District." He added that the "Provisional Government of North Carolina is considered a very good joke. Imagine a half-dozen barefooted fishermen calling a moonlight meeting on Bloody Island, and establishing a Provisional Government for Missouri, and you have a fair idea of the brilliant Gift Enterprise of Mr. Taylor and Mr. Foster."[85]

The war itself confronted the Southern press with many unique and trying situations, particularly the chronic ink and paper shortages along with technological limitations.[86] Among these challenges were "wartime scarcities and skyrocketing costs of paper and other printing materials, the increasing obsolescence of presses and typographical equipment."[87] These scarcities caused by the war "limited the effectiveness of the Confederate press and caused subscription rates to soar to heights undreamed of at the beginning of the war."[88] Production became such a problem that the South "could not produce nearly enough paper to meet even the section's peacetime needs, and it was not possible to smuggle enough through the blockade or to accelerate domestic production sufficiently to meet the wartime demand for newsprint."[89] Harrington's wartime work was hampered by lack of paper and other shortages.[90]

During the Civil War, both the Northern and Southern presses struggled to publish, but the problems were particularly acute in the South. The North used military occupation to control information. Northern military officials confiscated most of the South's resources, making it nearly impossible to successfully operate a newspaper. The Union "frequently used equipment taken from printing plants in the Confederate towns that they captured to print newspapers for the soldiers."[91]

Limited manpower for reporting and printing created another roadblock for the Southern press. Of the eight hundred or so printers "who made up the entire printing force of the Confederacy in 1863, at least seventy-five percent either had been or were in the army by June 1864."[92] Those left behind were often untrained in the publishing and reporting roles they assumed. Of course, the lack of a printing press did not hinder the handwritten work of Harrington, but some paper shortages were unavoidable during the conflict.

3

Handwritten Newspapers Before the Harrington Papers

HANDWRITING AS A SPECIAL COMMUNICATION ACT

Handwriting is largely a bygone activity gaining attention only when it comes from the hand of a prominent figure. Nonetheless, handwritten correspondence suggests a level of intimacy not found in the uniformity of printed or even emailed letters. As with a person's signature, the style and cast of handwriting create an effect unlike anything produced on a press. The message's unique appearance adds to its meaning, a feature that cannot be accomplished with a printed message designed to look the same each time it is reproduced.[1] The recipient of a personal letter enjoys this kind of unique message right down to the feel of the paper as it is unfolded.[2] Harrington and other handwritten newspaper publishers expected to influence multiple readers, as do present-day bloggers who share personal impressions for the entire world to read. But Harrington provided a different, more handcrafted kind of multiple-message system that appealed *visually* as a modest work of art, *tactilely* as idiosyncratic surface impressions made by pen points, and *aromatically* as distinct smells created by handwriting rather than printing inks.

As "news artists," Harrington and other handwritten newspaper publishers probably maintained at the time the most personal form of journalistic communication. Like print journalists, they could be highly committed to informing readers and serving their communities—as well as to making a living. But their level of personal commitment to their work had to be enormously high since they also had to produce multiple copies by hand. For them, producing a newspaper was not primarily a matter of generating circulation or establishing political influence. They were personally vested in their labor as news artisans. They personally used a wide range of talents and resources to create particularly rich journalistic expression. Like other journalists but perhaps more passionately, they sought a means of creating a "a semantic reality"[3] rather than merely words on the page. Harrington and similar craftpersons personally connected with their communities and helped to forge a shared sense of identity, belonging, and responsibility for their shared public lives. Like handwritten letters, handwritten papers deepened the personal connection between writer and reader, thereby enhancing the semantic sense of collective life.

Harrington personally created this shared semantic reality with his handwritten copying, an ancient approach to communicating with its roots in the noble vocation of manuscript writing carried on by ancient monks largely prior to the printing press. Perhaps writing even the news in longhand is something vocationally like the work of ancient monks who devoted their lives to copying scripture for distribution. Copying news stories is not so directly religious, but it nevertheless requires a selfless devotion to handcrafting and disseminating words as "news" about and for a particular community's semantic reality.

THE DEFINITION OF A NEWSPAPER

Historians differentiate between the *stipulative* and *lexical* definitions of the word "newspaper."[4] Stipulative, or working, definitions create a formal category as to what constitutes a newspaper. For example, scholars use such definitions to determine whether a periodical is truly a newspaper rather than a literary journal or an advertising sheet (such as a modern-day "shopper"). Stipulative definitions do not necessarily connect to the "vast range of past meanings previously associated with the terms to be defined, but are imposed by the authors or researchers using the terms."[5] In other words, stipulative definitions may not help people understand how others defined and used "newspapers" in a specific historical context.[6] By contrast, a lexical definition—such as one of the many definitions often found in a list from a people's own everyday dictionary—can more accurately define a newspaper in the way people of Harrington's community would understand and apply the term in their own historic moment, "regardless of its present-day utility or application."[7] The historic record shows that Harrington's papers were meant to be experienced as newspapers because their content and style were similar to those of the printed productions available during that period. Like prisoner-of-war newspapers[8] and shipboard newspapers,[9] Harrington papers were "real" newspapers though handwritten. They were not merely personal letters or just artistic expressions, but artistically personalized newspapers meant to be read as news.

The handwritten press appeared in Rome in 59 B.C. when the *Acta Diruna* (Events of the Day) circulated.[10] This daily handwritten news sheet reported political happenings, executions, and even athletic contests. The handwritten press took many forms over the next two millennia. As late as 1566, a handwritten news sheet called a gazette was distributed in Venice. It wasn't until 1665, nearly one hundred years later, that newspapers began being printed on a press in England.[11] In colonial America, printing press technology could be found as early as 1690, when Boston bookseller Benjamin Harris printed the first and only copy of *Publick Occurrences Both Forreign and Domestick*. Boston is also home to one of the earliest handwritten American newspapers, *The Boston News-Letter*.[12] John Campbell handwrote the successful *News-Letter* from 1700, when he became Boston's postmaster, to 1704, when he had it printed to save production time.[13]

Although printing presses existed as early as the fifteenth century, handwritten newspapers persisted.[14] With printing technology readily available, why anyone would handwrite a periodical? Often publishers did so for expediency, such as when a press was not readily available or a journalist wanted to challenge the town's printed newspapers.[15] Handwritten newspapers sometimes simply preceded printed newspapers.

In other instances, handwritten newspapers possessed a mystique that proved attractive, endured over the centuries, and even inspired printed imitations. In seventeenth-century England, the design of *Dawk's News-Letter* of London was inspired by the handwritten newspapers of the day.[16] In the same century, the editor of a handwritten newspaper was chosen to start a printed newspaper, the *Oxford Gazette*, which later became the *London Gazette*.[17] While 1842 marks the earliest handwritten newspapers identified in the American West, examples of handwritten newspapers can be found across the nation throughout the eighteenth and nineteenth centuries.[18]

A kind of handwritten newspaper is even published today in Channai, India. *The Musalman* is a daily newspaper handwritten before being produced on a printing press. The purpose of handwriting the text is more about keeping tradition alive than about economics. The Muslim-oriented newspaper uses the ancient art of Urdu calligraphy in expressing news stories, verse, and devotional content.[19] This type of literary practice is not person-specific, but it is a highly personal in the sense of representing the semantic mode of a particular preindustrial tradition.

In some cases, a handwritten artifact was one part of a more mechanized transition to a printed product. For instance, some newspapers were handwritten and then mimeographed. This was the case of *Neya Powagans*, a publication of Calgary, Alberta, started in the twentieth century and still produced in the 1990s.[20] The approach is similar to the method used by *The Musalman*.

THE HANDWRITTEN PRESS AS LEGITIMATE NEWSPAPERS

The handwritten paper is no less a newspaper than a printed one. It must and does serve communities in the ways that printed papers serve them.[21] Records of handwritten newspapers include those from Iowa,[22] Nevada,[23] and other American territories.[24] As of 1993, there was evidence of 118 handwritten periodicals in North America.[25] A handwritten newspaper can be considered a newspaper by virtue of its content, style, frequency, and circulation—all of which Harrington's publications demonstrated with his small, perhaps isolated, readership in rural North Carolina.[26]

Numerous handwritten publications existed in the United States before Harrington's. These included *The True Blue,* a publication read by inmates which even included an article on a ball to be held April 21, 1842, to celebrate the Battle of San Jacinto;[27] the *Barometer,* California, 1849; *The Emigrant,* California, 1849; *The Petrel,* California, 1849; and *The Shark,* California, 1849. Between 1849 and 1851, passengers and sailors published five handwritten newspapers on ships out of Boston, New Orleans, and Sydney as they made their way to the gold fields in California.[28]

Handwritten newspapers could be distributed in numerous ways. They were posted in a public place such as a store or church, shared like chain letters, or read aloud to an audience. In most cases, handwritten newspapers were temporary and meant to be proofs for a printed edition. The available evidence suggests that most publishers produced no more than one or two handwritten copies of any given issue, so most of the papers were likely published by one or more of these methods.[29] Harrington may be the major exception since his newspapers' circulations numbered up to one hundred,[30] although the only copies that survived are in likely incomplete university library collections.

HANDWRITING AS A NECESSITY IN LIEU OF A PRESS

The typical reason for a handwritten newspaper, both in the United States and around the world, was that the journalist lived in a harsh environment or faced some other challenge, but was still committed to producing a newspaper. Handwritten newspapers could be found in Melbourne, Australia, in the nineteenth century.[31] In fact, the first nine editions of *The Melbourne Advertiser* were handwritten beginning January 1, 1838. The newspaper was suspended until it obtained a license, and it resumed publication in February 1839 as the *Port Phillip Patriot and Melbourne Advertiser.*

In 1839, the Chinese handwrote newspapers using translated articles from foreign newspapers.[32] The articles included opinion pieces by foreign journalists on the opium eradication campaign. In 1999, a set of these handwritten newspapers went on display in Nanjing, the capital of east China's Jiangsu Province.

The West had more than its share of handwritten newspapers as well, most of which lasted only a few issues. As early as 1845, Charles Edward Pickett wrote a newspaper in longhand on foolscap and gained the distinction of establishing the first English newspaper in the Pacific Northwest, specifically Oregon.[33] Pickett, of the famous Confederate charge at Gettysburg, was cousin to Charles Edward Pickett, a man known for his orating and philosophizing. Charles was involved in politics and wrote in the *Flumgudgeon Gazette and Bumblebee Budget* about the Oregon frontier, using pen, ink, and foolscap. The newspaper's name "implies persiflage."[34] Pickett produced twelve issues of the newspaper, sending one of each edition to President James K. Polk (1795–1849). The newspaper contained humorous accounts of the Provisional Government's Legislative Committee, which Pickett characterized as a theater of tragedy, comedy, and farce. Pickett also used his newspaper to feud with Dr. Elijah White, a subagent for the Native Americans west of the Rocky Mountains, and succeeded in having the man dismissed from office.[35]

The content of the *Flumgudgeon Gazette and Bumblebee Budget* newspaper proved to be as unconventional as the practice of handwriting a newspaper. Its stated mission was to be "devoted to scratching and stinging the follies of the times."[36] Written by Pickett, who called himself Curltail Coon, the newspaper's nameplate featured a raccoon saying, "Don't stroke us backwards! There is enough villany [sic] going on to raise our bristles without that."[37]

At that time, as many as five handwritten newspapers were published in the frontier town of Washington, located in southeastern Iowa. Among them were the *Washington Shark*, the *Domestic Quarterly Review*, and the *Quarterly Visitor*.[38] While handwritten, these newspapers included the same content as a machine-printed newspaper. In 1856, two years before Harrington began his papers, a handwritten newspaper circulated in Wilkesboro, North Carolina, about 140 miles from Harrington's home.

In 1857, a handwritten Nevada newspaper called *The Scorpion* reported that it offered the news of the day.[39] It came out monthly with amusing caricatures, and it was read by prospectors, opportunists, and adventurers.[40] In Colorado, *The Rocky Mountain Gold Reporter and Mountain City Herald* handwritten newspaper began August 6, 1859, 104 days after the *Cherry Creek Pioneer* handwritten newspaper began in the Rocky Mountains.[41] From 1857 to 1858, *The Hoilpum,* a handwritten newspaper in California, circulated among miners.[42] In British Columbia, the *Emigrant Soldier's Gazette and Cape Horn Chronicle* circulated as a handwritten newspaper aboard a ship for engineers enroute to Vancouver Island from England.[43]

From the 1860s to the 1880s, handwritten newspapers circulated in Utah and might have been common in frontier settlements.[44] These newspapers gave residents in extreme isolation a means of "recreating the cultural world they have known."[45] In other words, these papers, like their printed counterparts, helped readers locate themselves meaningfully in particular times and places.

The rise in handwritten newspapers in the western United States can be explained partly by the opening of the Pacific Coast frontier for miners, explorers, and settlers.[46] Some newspapers circulated aboard ships as part of the Gold Rush,[47] and by the 1850s at least two shipboard handwritten newspapers were circulating in the West.[48] By the 1860s, handwritten newspapers tended to be linked to mining camps, military posts, or prisons and settlements in Utah and Alaska.[49] The 1870s saw a surge in handwritten newspapers, many associated with the Mormon faith, but by the 1880s handwritten newspapers tended to focus on satire or be written for clubs and literary societies.[50] Perhaps literary societies filled the void at that time that the mass media and the Internet fill for audiences today, facilitating entertainment and interaction with others beyond the family unit. In the late nineteenth century, handwritten community newspapers could still be found in California along with the literary and mining camp periodicals.[51]

The early 1900s witnessed at least seven handwritten newspapers in the West, including two mining camp papers.[52] Utah accounted for the most handwritten newspapers, perhaps because of the value that Mormons placed on literacy and education even during a period when their geographic isolation prevented them from gaining the regular use of printing presses and other technology.[53] Handwritten Utah newspapers included the *Manti Herald*, which took strong editorial stands, including a call for the city to build a wall around Manti.[54] In the 1800s, *The Knowledge Seeker, Young Ladies' Thoughts,* and *The Evening Star* each kept the town of Hyrum, Utah, informed with up to ten pages of handwritten news.[55] In December of 1886, Kansas editor H.C. Banke told readers of his handwritten *The Redwing Carrier Pigeon* that because the paper had received disrespectful and personal contributions unsuited for publication the latest issue of the newspaper would be short of news.[56]

HANDWRITTEN NEWSPAPERS AS
EXPRESSIONS OF SHARED CULTURE

Printed newspapers of the Civil War still generally published news that arrived in the mail or was picked up by word of mouth.[57] Sources were slim and stories could not always be verified. According to standard journalism history, newspapers eventually developed through the course of the late nineteenth and early twentieth centuries from a biased "historical record of events" published "long after they occurred" into a more balanced, timely source of objective, current news, both domestic and foreign.[58] The publisher of the handwritten newspaper in the nineteenth century likely employed some of these developing professional conventions in order to claim "newspaper" status. Such a writer-publisher similarly exercised his or her editorial privilege to offer interpretative news and opinion, not just factual accounts. Eventually the more personalized or at least personally subjective "news" content would be relegated primarily to the opinion-editorial section of papers. The handwritten newspapers' editorial lines in the Civil War period were not as clear as they might be in today's mainstream press. But here again, history is not so clear-cut, particularly because it is not possible today to discern precisely how readers back then would have interpreted such distinctions between news and opinion.

Perhaps readers of handwritten papers have always assumed or expected greater editorial prerogatives than they would with printed papers—just as readers today might read bloggers differently than they view online newspaper reporters. As recently as 1954, Montreal's Sid Stavitsky produced the handwritten *Clark Street Sun* for three cents and provided more opinion than news. That project grew into a charitable organization with an annual budget of nearly $6 million,[59] making it one of the few handwritten publication ventures to make money.

In the twenty-first century, the handwriting of newspapers still occurs as a personalized combination of news and opinion. As late as 2004, an unemployed member of a daily newspaper in Baghdad resorted to penning a paper using scraps of paper he found on the pavement.[60] For this desperate writer, the content was the focus. His handwritten articles addressed political issues, including the U.S. occupation, and the kinds of topics that could have been found in the typical Iraqi press.

An online auction in 2008 featured a 9¼"-square handwritten newspaper called *The Prison Bee,* which eventually sold for $400. The seller said that the four-page periodical was written February 12, 1887, for inmates of New York's Sing-Sing prison. According to the seller, the newspaper copy read, "The Bee is issued in the interests of the gentlemen who are spending their retirement in the shades of S. S. State Prison. Amidst our general buzzing [sic] we seek to enlighten our fellow companions and if the Bee's humming cheers one moment of your time, we shall feel amply rewarded for our labors." The seller noted that the first page was devoted to international news, including the War in the Balkans and the riots in London. One inmate offered to sell "unique match boxes" and another inmate said he would teach "pugilism."[61]

All in all, the writers of handwritten newspapers often used extraordinary means because they were extraordinary people living in extraordinary times. Harrington was both extraordinary and "eccentric"—which might explain some of his motivations.[62] But it doesn't explain the specific form or content of his writing as a form of journalism rather than just literary expression. With 302 different issues of newspapers in his eleven years of editing, Harrington remains the editor with the largest output of extant handwritten periodicals, a rarity among the many exceptional people who have historically produced such newspapers.

4

The Cultural School of Journalism History

There is no single history of American journalism. In fact, historians disagree about how to interpret journalism history—just as they can disagree on what actually constitutes a newspaper. Just as journalists interpret events, historians interpret journalism.

THREE SCHOOLS OF JOURNALISM HISTORY

Nevertheless, American journalism history can be organized roughly into three interpretive approaches (or "schools"): ideological, professional, and cultural.[1] The ideological approach assumes that historians write from their own ideological perspective in interpreting facts.[2] For instance, some historians have emphasized "the unfolding advance of human liberty," represented in the history of the free press unfettered by government or other external controls.[3] Another group in the Ideological School includes the progressive historians who pit the free press against the forces of wealth and class.[4] A reaction against this camp, but still within the ideological approach, is the consensus school, which emphasizes that history—including journalism history—is marked primarily by agreement on fundamental principles of American life.[5]

The professional approach to journalism history assumes that the more modern the journalism practices, the more likely they will be considered proper.[6] This idea yields the development school, a historical approach that considers how the past journalistic developments contributed to modern journalism practices. The professional school views "the history of journalism as the continuing evolution of journalistic practices and standards."[7] It emphasizes professional over social progress, assuming that greater journalistic professionalism is itself necessarily in the interest of a free society.

The final and most complicated approach to journalism history is the cultural perspective. The Cultural School of communication history interpretation assumes "that impersonal social forces should be the focus in historical investigations; media are linked to their environment and sociological forces, and economics and technology interrelate with media."[8] This perspective assumes that media are shaped by the environment in which they operate and, in turn, shape the environment. Therefore, there is no single "journalism," but rather various types of journalism practiced in particular times and places. Cultural historians have been most interested in sociological, economic, and technological factors.[9] In Harrington's case, as in the case of newspapers in general, the news product (the "news" and the "newspaper" are both products) both influences and is influenced by the culture within which journalists practice. The Cultural School does not focus narrowly on the achievements of a person—a kind of history that is sometimes called the "great man" approach[10]—since journalistic notions of "progress" are bound to be different in various cultures, and since no single person can create a new form of journalism out of the blue.

According to this cultural perspective, Harrington should not be considered in isolation as an individual who single-handedly played a major role in affecting all journalistic media, or who alone created the concept of news or the practice of handwriting news. His work is worthy for the way it both adopts and deviates from the period's mainstream journalism while serving his own community's particular artistic modes of expression. In short, Harrington worked within a particular culture and—for good or for bad, well or poorly—adapted journalism to his own time and place. Thus, it is critically important to consider Harrington's work in his milieu and according to the journalistic practices and standards of the day rather than according to any ideological or professional assumptions that journalists and journalism historians might affirm in the twenty-first century.

The Cultural School provides a sensitive perspective from which to consider Harrington's work in the context of the cultural milieu in which he worked. As American sociologist Robert Park suggested early in the twentieth century, journalism is "the outcome of a historic process in which many individuals participated without foreseeing what the ultimate product of their labors was to be. The newspaper, like the modern city, is not wholly a rational product. No one sought to make it just what it is. In spite of all the efforts of individual men and generations of men to control it and make it something after their own heart, it has continued to grow and change in its own incalculable ways."[11] The cultural approach to journalism history, as used in this book, is founded on the premise that media such as a newspaper are part of their culture. Society's values and practices shape the development of media,[12] just as they did in the case of Harrington's personal journalism.

A complex combination of cultural forces shapes the media product. For instance, nineteenth-century businesses in the United States needed a vehicle to advertise their products and services, while at the same time citizens in local towns and cities sought news about their communities. In the tiny village of Buffalo Springs, North Carolina, the closest printed newspaper was in Fayetteville, nearly twenty miles to the south of Harrington's village. This vacuum helped Harrington gain an audience for his handwritten newspapers in a day when personal travel and cross-geographic communication were relatively slow by today's standards. The presence of Harrington's periodical provided advertisers with a more personal approach for getting their message to a local audience. In addition, it is unlikely that Fayetteville or Raleigh, nearly thirty miles to the north, would publish the western Harnett County news of weddings or obituaries, such as those found in Harrington's *The Nation,* or the locally-produced literary content found in his *The Young American.* In order to create newspapers for his area, Harrington became a journalist, businessman, raconteur, poet, and graphic artist. He learned from other papers, but also adapted journalism to suit his own abilities and to address the apparent interests of his community.

THE CULTURAL APPROACH AND HARRINGTON'S WORK

The 1850s still retained some of the early American commitment to political self-determination. In January 1858, Harrington was eighteen years old. Like his young country (his *nation*), he valued independence. In his cultural commitment to personal freedom of expression, Harrington anticipated twenty-first century approaches in opinion journalism—such as interpretative writing and blogging—by his frequent editorializing in his newspaper columns. In addition, at a time of uncertainty about slavery, Harrington offered his personal insight on social reform and Democratic policies throughout the twenty-one issues of *The Nation*. Lacking a printing press, the aspiring writer was not to give up, but to take up his pen and wrestle with social reality as he perceived it in his day. He hoped to use his independent voice to advance social change.

In order to be taken seriously, however, Harrington very consciously modeled his newspaper after the mid-nineteenth century mainstream print media. Newspapers of his period tended to reinforce a particular image of public life.[13] Publishers used their pages to create a shared association with readers and often used letters to the editor and guest commentary to animate collective social life—a trend that can be seen especially in William Lloyd Garrison's *Liberator* during the 1830s. In addition, these mainstream newspapers often opted for firsthand accounts and facts, including the chronology of an event, the crowd size, and other information seemingly based on detached observation.[14] The press of this period portrayed the world, at least in part, as it was presumed to be.[15] To convince readers that a newspaper was a worthy reflection of community and public life, it had to appear somewhat objective.

Once Harrington's coverage was seen as equivalent to the news of such legitimate printed papers, his own work would likely be viewed as legitimate as well. This is at least partly why Harrington adopted some of the news conventions of his day. His primary deviation from the norm was to handwrite his copy rather than produce it on a printing press. He was thereby able to provide news for a community that lacked its own local news voice. In this sense, he accomplished the feat by at least implicitly challenging the reigning technological approach. Indeed, Harrington succeeded without an office, without a staff, without a printing press schedule, and absent all the other accoutrements ordinarily used in printing a mainstream newspaper. He personally circulated legitimate news without creating a newspaper institution.

In addition to looking like a printed news periodical, Harrington's paper had to include news that reflected the existing public life of the community. Successful papers broadly reflected the shared norms of a community and helped contribute to a sense of affiliation and belonging.[16] Some of the press of this period still offered allegiance to political parties.[17] In fact, publishers often benefited from such allegiances through economic subsidies and a list of partisan subscribers. But newspapers still had to cover "the news" if they sought to be legitimate newspapers rather than just journals of comment and opinion.

Perhaps because of the manifest benefits of partisanship—after all, humans by nature prefer to have their values and beliefs confirmed rather than challenged—nonpartisan newspapers tended to read very much like the partisan ones.[18] It was inevitably the case that newspapers tended to borrow stories and perspectives from each other as part of the common public culture. Nonpartisan newspapers and their readers tended to understand themselves in terms of partisanship even if they were not exclusively or overwhelmingly partisan. The times were politically charged. Whether a particular newspaper was politically driven or not, news in the nineteenth century expressed a particular partisan-like reality for any audience seeking a way to understand public life. In addition, it is likely that the cash-strapped Democratic Party of Harrington's community could not help underwrite his newspaper regardless of his or any editor's desire to advance the dominant political party. Harrington probably had to be partisan in the sense of affirming some of the dominant values of his community. How else would he attract readers? How else could he gain subscribers? How else could he entice readers to consider his more literary content such as his poetry and short stories? Subscription revenues gave Harrington an opportunity to address nonpolitical topics—a common newspaper practice in his day. Communities cared about more than politics, but political news was often a community's most pressing interest, especially during the years leading up to and during the Civil War.

Harrington's greatest benefit from his own overt partisanship was demonstrated in his ability to capture his community's shared culture through the stories he selected and how he told them. In 1858, politics influenced discourse and was clearly understood as a natural and important part of life. Harrington as editor used his periodicals to advance not only his own values, but to express values that he borrowed from other periodicals and people of his area. Harrington thereby drew a circle around the political and cultural reality that he wanted to represent as part of the region's public life.

Like many publishers of his day, Harrington borrowed so heavily from the stock approach of others that his content suggests at least on the surface an unreflective repackaging of public life—with news that was little more than what one historians calls "a routine opportunity to reenact a basic vision of their common life."[19] But it is this very predictable quality of the news product that likely made Harrington's work so comforting to his readers. He presented a publication that looked and read in every way like an ordinary newspaper except that it was handwritten. In this way, Harrington contributed to the shared culture, not first by challenging it, but by producing "newsy" cultural artifacts (newspapers) that were unconventionally produced but nevertheless seemed familiar, normal, and legitimate.

Harrington's work presented the shared reality of his community, wherein he captured "contemporary reality by actually depicting peoples' lives and behavior."[20] *Harper's* editor Henry Mills Alden demanded that his writers present news as a human drama that nevertheless remained faithful to the facts. Although Harrington was the dilettante journalist of Harnett County, his work anticipated the idea of news that creatively explored themes and ideas suggested by journalistic facts.

One way that Harrington gained this credibility was by including in his papers personal references to himself. This style of journalism, along with his handwritten approach, provides a peek into the transitional period of the American press when partisan editors of the pre-Civil-War period gradually learned that taking sides could mean a loss of potential readers. In the later part of the nineteenth century, editors found that their newspapers could attract greater audiences if the content did not reveal an overtly partisan tone. Eventually a personal voice such as Harrington's would have been restricted largely to the editorial page. But at the time his voice gave him credibility as a lifelong, known member of the community.

A final cultural impact on Harrington's work can be seen in its reflection of the significance of the individual—especially the individual laborer—in the surrounding social and natural worlds. Surrounded by farmers and laborers who left their mark on the agricultural fields and pine forests of Harnett County, Harrington left his own mark via the newspapers he produced—including a uniquely personal style of presenting the news that suggested each person in the community made a singular contribution. His handwritten legacy could not be confused with the printed press in Raleigh or Fayetteville. Just as a portrait painter signs her art, Harrington provided his literal and figurative signature in every issue. Just as no two farmers were exactly alike, Harrington's literary culture was geo-culturally distinctive. Just as farmers in the region could not afford to use expensive, mass-produced agricultural machinery, Harrington employed his own very personal labor to cultivate news and literary journalism.

Aside from Harrington's obvious craftsmanship, his newspapers probably captured a deeper meaning within the social web of interaction.[21] Rather than using new technologies of the telegraph, available as early as 1844, or the printing press, available since the sixteenth century, Harrington resorted to the oldest of literary technologies to tell his narratives. Harrington produced a unique copy for each reader-subscriber. No two copies were exactly the same, just as no two personal conversations are identical. The personalized handwritten messages that Harrington circulated thereby probably contained a richer social weave than the content found in a printed newspaper. His handwriting could not achieve the visual standardization characteristic of type, which depends overwhelmingly on the literary text rather than the visual expression involved in the making (i.e., writing vs. printing) of the text itself. Harrington could use his pen to record a phrase in a way that suggested he was in a hurry, or in a line that was meant to possess a harsh tone by the thickness of the letters. Without telling his readers his opinion about the literary content itself, Harrington could use his handwriting as a novel visual language of its own that invited the reader to interpret Harrington's meanings.

THE CULTURAL APPROACH COMBINED WITH MEDIA ECOLOGY

The field of media ecology provides a useful lens through which to look at social interactions. Media and culture can be understood ecologically, with changes in news-disseminating technology altering the symbolic environment. The symbolic environment is said to be socially constructed, a "sensory world of meanings that in turn shapes our perceptions, experiences, attitudes and behaviors."[22] Marshall McLuhan challenged the idea that content is key in studying media; he instead focused on the medium.[23] The experience of reading a handwritten newspaper is far different from the experience of perusing a printed version—just as email is different than Skype, or just as reading the *New York Times* or *Wall Street Journal* on a computer screen at the office is not the same as reading one of them in a broadsheet format at a coffee shop. As McLuhan observed, since each medium emphasizes different senses, the regular use of one medium over the other conditions an audiences to register some stimuli and ignore others.

In Harrington's work, his rural society appreciated and was perhaps influenced by the tactile qualities of the handwritten periodical as opposed to the machine-printed periodicals that dominated the day. At first, the handwritten newspaper must have seemed a novelty for Harrington's readers, but over time they doubtless became acclimated to it as a part of the background of their lives. For them, the handwritten press provided a substantive pause in the rush to modernity and the advance of the new American national order that included an upheaval in agriculture and the loss of slave labor. Harrington's work could have provided his readers with a sense that the old order might continue and that the age of revolutionary or even evolutionary social change could be postponed.

The larger cultural and social norms of 1858 presaged the death of slave labor in America, a transition likely not appreciated by many Southerners at the time. Some in the society clung to the older tradition of the agricultural economy, just as Harrington clung to an older version of disseminating news. Harrington's methods were outdated by at least three centuries, but the act of handwriting newspapers was well within the cultural sensibilities of his community. The handwritten papers served as a metaphor for a community in denial. Many Tar Heels wanted to resist the coming tide of abolition and the economic change built on technologies such as textile mills, railroads, and telegraphs. In short, they were trying to resist modernity. Harrington shared the characteristics of his state's primary early nineteenth-century political leader, U.S. Senator Nathaniel Macon, who believed that if the people of the state were left alone they "would continue to raise boys and girls who would become men and women. These were the sorts of internal improvements he desired to see."[24] Harrington participated in this shared cultural vision that a bygone era could remain in existence by doing what one could without the curse and added expense of technology. Harrington may not have considered himself a Luddite, but his act of handwriting newspapers served as a symbolic indicator that the older ways were just as valuable, and perhaps even superior, to the newer ones. If nothing else, the older ways were more personal and more clearly tuned to local culture.

5

The News, Literature, and Advertisements of "The Young American"

Over the course of 1858, *The Young American* contained three sections: literary content, news content, and advertising content. Each section used cursive writing, which was about the size of a fourteen-point font. In many cases, the writing was ornate, but it would vary from time to time. The first issue ran twenty-eight pages, 8 × 12″ in size.[1] Harrington employed a continuous numbering system from issue to issue—as is the case for many modern journals and nearly all scholarly journals. For example, the first issue of *The Young American* ended with page twenty-eight, while the second issue began with page twenty-nine.

Some issues looked better than others. For instance, the March issue was one of the most difficult to read because words were smeared and blotted. On page eighty-two, Harrington apologized for the poor quality, noting that neither the paper nor the ink was up to his desired standard. Harrington said on page eighty-three that if he could not acquire better supplies he would resort to publishing in red ink—which he often used in 1858.

Harrington used graphic elements sparingly. A rare use of a drawing occurred in a display advertisement, appearing in November on page 292 and in December on page 314, where Harrington pictured a mortar and pestle to promote James A. Smith, druggist and chemist in Fayetteville, North Carolina. Another graphic he occasionally included was a hand with a pointing finger—presumably used to call attention to some item on a page. In April of 1858, on page 122, he published a hand pointing to jokes such as this one:

"Two well draped shoemakers being in company, [sic] were asked their profession by a very inquisitive personage. Says one of them, 'I practice the heeling art.' 'And I,' added the other [sic] 'labor for the good of men's soles.'" Harrington also used the pointed finger on page four of the April 24, 1858, issue of *The Nation,* also for a joke. It read: "A dreary joke, a coffin maker having apartments to let, posted his bill announcing the same for the coffin in his window, 'Lodging for Single Gentleman.'"

Harrington might have seen the pointed finger employed in display advertising in the *Fayetteville Observer. Semi-Weekly.*[2] A front-page advertisement on October 14, 1858, read, "Clothing! Clothing!! H. Graham." That advertisement included a hand with an index finger pointing to the words "Garments Cut in the Latest Fashion."

Harrington used a drawing of the North Carolina state flag on page two of *The Weekly News* on Wednesday, June 18, 1862. Occasionally, Harrington included the Freemasonry symbol to promote lodge meetings. For example, he used the symbol to promote a Pine Forest lodge meeting on page three of *The Times.,* November 7, 1867. The most elaborate visual element occurred on the front page of *The Times.* on Friday, February 19, 1869. Harrington placed line art of the North Carolina State House on the top of that page. It appears that the illustration was cut out of a machine-printed publication and pasted onto Harrington's newspaper—something like a news blogger who "borrows" an image from another website. Harrington does not include a credit line, just a note to his readers that those who have not seen the building will find the illustration interesting, and those who have seen it will confirm that Harrington is trustworthy in identifying it.

For his later publications, Harrington used an engraving to blot ink for the nameplates of his newspapers. For instance, *The Times.* included a blotted nameplate most likely from a woodcut carving.

Of the two publications Harrington produced in 1858, one was primarily literary and included some news, while the other was a partisan newspaper filled with local politics. The more literary *Young American* was the first of Harrington's handwritten periodicals, and he used it to promote his more partisan *The Nation* by placing display advertisements in the April, May, August, and October issues. Harrington wrote in April that *The Nation* would be connected to *The Young American* "in a manner" and *The Nation* would "be strictly Democratic" in its politics.

Harrington placed his masthead and editorial policy about midway through the maiden issue of *The Young American,* on pages fourteen and fifteen. He listed both Buffalo Springs, North Carolina, and Fayetteville, North Carolina, as his addresses. The masthead listed the cost per copy as twenty cents. He then listed the subscription price of two dollars in advance and offered an apology for the late delivery. Harrington added, "To tell you the truth, friends, we feel proud to look at our sheet. We think it is the best published in the old 'Rip Van Winkle' state[3] and you owe all this to us. We intend to devote ourselves to the advancement of pure and sound literature from fiction to amusement and we do not intend to let any subject go unnoticed. Our paper will give a true and fair statement of the politics of the day, but will not for the present take sides with any particular party but we expect to exercise the rights of a Freeman and vote for whom we please, and that is the way I hope every true friend to American freedom will do and also subscribe to The Young American—(Editor)."[4]

By June, Harrington praised his established publication, on page 164: "It has a good circulation through this state and a very fair circulation elsewhere." In the August issue, Harrington again lauded his work, writing on page 224, "We cheerfully recommend the Young American to the ladies for the many fine selections of poetry and also original selections, and as a young gentleman's magazine [sic] it can't be excelled [last word unclear]." On page 296 in November, Harrington wrote of his prospects for 1859, reminding his readers that the numbering system he used was evidence of "the mechanical skill with which it was executed." He went on to praise the content and the contributors, including the poet Elise and the contributions of Snap Jr., his pen name.

On page 316 of the last issue of *The Young American* for 1858, Harrington penned, "It was just as we told you in the commencement [sic] we said we would put this volume through and [sic] sure enough [sic] we have done it." He urged readers to renew their subscription to get "side-splitting jokes" in the January issue, which never materialized. Perhaps the joke was on the reader.

Probably because *The Young American* often was more literary than newsy, it sometimes ran out of material. In June of the first year of publication, Harrington wrote on page 164, "Nothing to write." He confessed, "How sad it is for a poor editor to sit pondering his brain in in [sic] vain to see if he can't find no item to interest his readers. That is the case with us just now. We have endeavored to find something that will interest our readers and if we have failed [sic] you will have to excuse us." On the next page, however, Harrington said his "devil"—presumably his apprentice or at least his assistant—offered his assistance on a slow news day. Harrington said his helper presented an off-rhyme verse about the lack of news. It read:

In vain you may look for an idea,
In vain you may simper and stew,
And after all it will turn out,
That you have nothing to write.

NEWS CONTENT OF *THE YOUNG AMERICAN*

Following the custom of the day even with the more literary papers, Harrington used news content from other newspapers to fill his periodical. Throughout the nation, weekly newspaper editors freely exchanged copies of their newspapers.[5] On page twenty-six of *The Young American's* first issue, Harrington praised the quality of *The Saturday Evening Post* and the *Fayetteville Observer. Semi-Weekly.*: "We could go on and on and enumerate more but will wait until next issue. Our thanks are [unclear] due to several of the Southern exchanges for sending in their paper in advance of our publication."[6]

The layout of Harrington's newspaper was similar to other community newspapers in the mainstream press. In practice, *The Young American* and *The Nation* used the same vertical layout and small headlines popular with the Fayetteville newspaper and other newspapers of the period. In 1858, the *Fayetteville Observer. Semi-Weekly.* circulated Wednesdays and Saturdays. It printed advertisements on the front page and short news articles from other newspapers on its inside pages, along with poetry and other light content. That publication used a six-column, four-page format. The *Fayetteville Observer. Semi-Weekly.* included the kind of quips Harrington employed in his own periodicals. For example, the September 13, 1858, issue of the *Fayetteville Observer. Semi-Weekly.* ran a note on page two with the headline "Ludicrous." It quipped about a clergyman who was reading to his congregation from a chapter of Genesis and found the last sentence on the page to be:

"And the Lord gave unto Adam a wife."
Turning over two leaves together, he found written, and read in an audible voice:

"And he was pitched without and within."
He had unhappily got into a description of Noah's Ark."

The *Fayetteville Observer. Semi-Weekly.* published display advertisements for runaway slaves as reported also on the front page in the issue for April 22, 1858. It ran an ad displaying the words "$50 REWARD" for "my man Jim." It also ran advertisements for "Negroes [sic] and land for sale." On page four of the September 2, 1858, issue, it reported "For sale thirty negroes [sic]" who "are all young, and in families, and [will] be sold in families or all together." In 1858, Harrington's papers did not contain these kinds of advertisements or reports, but he did liberally borrow content from other newspapers, including one in Fayetteville. On page three of its January 4, 1858, issue, the *Fayetteville Observer. Semi-Weekly.* offered a brief article reporting that "the editor of the North Carolina *Argus* announced in his issue of Saturday last, its suspension for three or four weeks, pending his negotiations for its sale." Harrington referred to a poem reprinted from the *Argus* on page nineteen of the first issue of *The Young American* in January 1858.

Harrington and other editors of his day not only reprinted information from other publications, but also keenly monitored others' circulation successes or failures. Sometimes they did credit other publications, but perhaps competing papers were not credited for fear of publicizing competitors' papers. The 1858 issues of the *Fayetteville Observer. Semi-Weekly.* never mentioned Harrington's work.

The news pages of the recently launched *Young American* were dominated by foreign news, possibly because such news suggested a more cosmopolitan and less provincial focus for what today might be called upscale readers. One of the most extensively covered foreign news stories was the *Leviathan*, a British steam ship that had been under construction since 1854 and was launched in September 1858 to much fanfare. Harrington mentioned the progress of the *Leviathan* in each issue. The ship was beset with problems, not the least of which was launching it safely. Harrington wittily alluded to Job 41:1, asking on page seventeen, "Can'st thou draw out Leviathan with a hook?" Harrington answered himself, "So far the answer seems to be as made by English science, 'We cannot over tame the artificial sea monster [sic] which our own hands have made.'" Harrington also noted that critics from Christian journals of the day were shocked that the British casually called the huge vessel *"Leviathan"* rather than its other name, *"Great Eastern."* Harrington continued his comments on page eighteen by suggesting that the irreverence and conceit of the ship builders hurt the launching efforts. In subsequent issues throughout the year, Harrington continued to discuss the launching of the *Leviathan.* In February, he reported on page forty-two that the ship was progressing in the move to launch. He further noted that the ship *Europa* arrived in New York from Liverpool. On the next page, Harrington mentioned the *Leviathan* a second time in another item, saying the ship had moved a few feet. In April on page 110, Harrington reported that the *Leviathan* had finally launched.

The news on page thirteen of *The Young American*'s January issue was reprinted from an undisclosed source. It concerned reports that President James Buchanan (1791–1868), the fifteenth president of the United States and a Democrat, sent the longest telegraph of record to England. The content of the message was not revealed.

The January issue also included random world news about Lucknow, India, and insurgent fighting and unspecified improvements in Hamburg, on page thirteen. That issue also offered an obituary of an editor of the *Wilmington Herald* on page eighteen, and a line from Harrington saying the British government could supply a Bible to everyone in the world with the budget it spends on intoxicating liquor. This comment may have carried some unconscious significance for Harrington, who likely died an alcoholic.[7]

In the February issue of *The Young American,* Harrington reported the January 5, 1858 death of Austrian Field Marshal Joseph Radetzky von Radetz, an opponent of Napoleon. Harrington also included a line about China on page forty-three, "Very little news is telegraphed now that will interest our readers." In April on page 114, Harrington reported that the "weather has been excessively hot for the last week or two" and that the fruit crop could be killed. He reported on page 139 of the May edition that war talk was brewing between Spain and the United States.

Harrington reported on the collision of British steamship *Europa* and the ship *Arabi,* in the August issue of *The Young American.* On page 212, Harrington also reported the success of the Atlantic cable connecting the continents of North America with Great Britain. Harrington alluded on the next page to the cable achievement, noting that nothing looked impossible now. He referred to the "fiery God" of the sun as "old Sol," and to the prospect that it was determined to "burn us up if he can." In an abrupt change in subject, Harrington concluded this section by noting that he could hardly breathe "let alone [try] to edit."

Local news was rare in *The Young American*, but page eighty-six of the March issue included a Harnett County obituary of a victim of scarlet fever. In April on page 117, Harrington wrote that Nancie (the spelling is unclear) Isabella, the youngest daughter of David and Julia A. Worth, died on April 2. In an unusual editorial comment, he wrote, "Oh, thou full [unclear] destroyer lay your ruthless hand lightly upon the afflicted family, scourge them lightly and may they be made to exclaim it is good that we are afflicted. Yet may I hear the parting sigh, it is a dread and awful thing to die."

An editorial on page 115 of *The Young American's* April issue told readers that Harrington would not support "any man who has his hands stained with the blood of his countryman for any office whatever." Furthermore, Harrington said he would not be pleased to see W.W. Avery of Burke, once a delegate to the Democratic convention in 1856, become governor. He wrote, "If Avery is governor, we aint [sic] satisfied, that's all."[8]

In the May issue, Harrington endorsed John W. Ellis for governor on page 141 and praised the delegates to the county convention. In August on page 213, Harrington included the local political news that Democratic gubernatorial candidate Judge Ellis won the election, and he reported that the legislature would be more Democratic in the next session. In other quasi-local news, Harrington published the kind of poetic personal notice whereby suitors used only their initials to send love letters to unidentified recipients, including this one from "A.M." on page 215:

A single trip? How light a thing,
To sway such magic art,
And bid each soft, remembrance spring,
Like blossoms in the heart!

THE LITERARY TONE OF *THE YOUNG AMERICAN*

Throughout 1858, Harrington published fiction and poetry along the model of the literary journals advocated by the region's intelligentsia. In 1854, poet and novelist Mary Bayard Clarke called for an emphasis on poetry in her anthology of North Carolina poetry, *Wood-notes,* and also used the idea of Rip Van Winkle as part of her rationale. She wrote:

> Come rouse you! ye poets of North Carolina,
> My State is my theme and I seek not a finer,
> I sing in its praise and I bid ye all follow,
> Till we wake up the echoes of "Old Sleepy Hollow!"
> Come show to his scorners "Old Rip" is awaking,
> His sleep like a cloud of the morning is breaking;
> That the years of his slumber, at last have gone by,
> And the rainbow of promise illumines the sky.[9]

In early issues of *The Young American,* Harrington derided the *Leviathan* shipbuilders for their hubris in calling the world's largest ship by an Old Testament word. In the Old Testament book of Job, a leviathan was considered a crocodile-type creature. Although Harrington found this reference irreverent, he published a submission by "Elise," a contributing writer, who praised the ship as a tribute to the triumph of engineering. Elise's poem recognized that many seek fame, but few attain it. Harrington seemed to appreciate the individual's need for recognition, particularly in the lonely work of publishing, but he denigrated work that challenged reverence for the divine, as in the case of referring to the largest ship of the day by a Bible appellation. Elise's ship tribute, a poem, was consistent with the other poetry Harrington included in *The Young American.* It rhymed, but offered little other literary creativity. Although the Harrington's published poetry "could not be considered of the highest caliber, it no doubt brought enjoyment to his readers, who seldom came in contact with the work of the Masters."[10]

As Harrington began his lyrical journal, he was working in a time when others shared his vision. For instance, Harrington used the bottom of page fifteen in his first issue of *The Young American* to note that North Carolina had shed its Rip Van Winkle lethargy, and he offered praise for the state's "good coal" and its independence "of the other states in almost everything." On page sixteen, Harrington also praised his first issue as "done up Brown," a slang term that meant one was doing something well, as in preparing meat to a satisfying cooked color. He praised his work as "done pretty well." Then he ended the page by reminding readers to pay their subscriptions.

As stated earlier, Harrington's work came at the end of a two-decade period between 1840 and 1860 when literary periodicals hoped "to enlighten the public mind."[11] University publications such as the Chapel Hill *Columbia Repository* and the Literary Society's *University Magazine* hoped to be literary forces to highlight academic and popular issues and to provoke readers to improve themselves.[12] Harrington had these kinds of high ambitions, but *The Young American* lacked the collaborative effort, financial resources, or institutional support needed to make it an intellectual power. The first issue of *The Young American* established a multi-part organizational structure with a short story that ran twelve pages along with poetry, humorous fillers, and some news and display advertisements. Except for the obituary of a Wilmington, North Carolina editor, the only local content was the display advertisements filling the last four pages of the thirty-page publication. The periodical served local readers by using literary content to creatively address the underlying moral and cultural sensibilities of readers in that area.

THE LITERARY AND MORAL CONTENT OF *THE YOUNG AMERICAN*

A short story dominated the first issue of *The Young American* in January 1858. Harrington said the incident was based on fact and called the episode "An Incident of the French Revolution." The story concerned Countess de Villeneuve de La Floret and a French officer's unrequited love. The officer, Pierre Duhem, vowed vengeance on the countess for her neglect of him. Duhem tortured her husband by hanging him on a barn while the soldier-citizens fired at his limbs to create a lingering death. Traumatized, the countess coped by imagining that her husband was on a business trip to Paris. The countess and her female assistant relocated outside of Paris to wait for the husband's return. Frustrated with his delay, the countess went to Paris only to encounter the solider-citizens ready to execute Duhem. Inexplicitly the countess pleaded for Duhem's life, but the commanding officer executed Duhem for theft and murder anyway. Then, in a twist, the countess broke from her feigned madness, cried, "Avenged. Avenged!" and died. The melodramatic story took twelve handwritten pages to tell, and by sharing it in his paper, Harrington established himself as a fiction writer worthy of the day. The short story was remarkably sophisticated for an eighteen-year-old writer. It had plot surprises, a polished vocabulary, and a breezy style. Harrington used more adjectives than would be customary today, but he was clearly a man of letters.

That first fiction piece set the tone for *The Young American* and differentiated it from *The Nation*, which rallied support for the coming primaries of 1858. *The Young American* used the conventions employed by other literary journals, publishing both artistic pieces and news. It especially reflected the approach of the national *Harper's Magazine*. For instance, on page twelve of the January issue of *The Young American*, Harrington included a joke about a child who mourned his lost kitten, Netty, drowned by his mother. The mother wondered if the child was overreacting, as if he had lost his father, and the child reasoned that another father was easy to obtain but Netty was irreplaceable.

POETRY, FICTION, AND OTHER LIGHT CONTENT IN
THE YOUNG AMERICAN

The poetry of *The Young America* used a traditional ABAB rhyme scheme, emphasized themes of fidelity and beauty, and highlighted earthy, rural topics. On page nineteen, Harrington included a poem by Finley Johnson about the sweetness of love; however, the best phrase followed that poem: "One line to fill this page." On page twenty-one, Harrington included this line: "Ranged on the hills, harmonious daughters swell the mingled tones of the home and harp and shell." Harrington repeated the line on page fifty-three of the second issue and randomly throughout the remaining issues. This lyrical line is followed in the January issue by a light-hearted poem decrying spitting on the floor: "They ought to live alone, far in some lovely moor, where the ladies could not see them, spitting on the floor." The longest poem, "Hard Times," was placed on pages twenty-four and twenty-five, lamenting the sad financial state of banks and merchants as well as the need for cash. It ended with these words:

"Hard Times! Hard Times! Was ever seen,
　Such hard times as hard as these?"
Times is the cry from morn 'til night,
　In which each one agrees:
A remedy I think I've found-
　Say how do you think 'twill do
Pull on your coat [sic] Roll up your sleeves,
　and work these hard times through!

The poetry and humor of *The Young American* were a mixture of hope, joy, and lamentation in the midst of somber times. On page twenty-three, Harrington included an item titled "Humorous" and wrote, "A little nonsense now and then is relished by the wisest men." Harrington also used a similar line in *The Nation*. On page four, in the first column of the April 24, 1858, issue, he wrote, "A little nonsense now and then is relished by the best of men."

In the midst of the grim financial conditions for residents of Harnett County in 1858, Harrington provided some light reading fare that could be used with polite company. The short story from the French Revolution was just shocking enough to provoke reader outrage at the atrocities of another land, but the terror was too distant to be of immediate concern to area farmers. On page twenty-eight, Harrington included an item called "Conundrums" and asked, "What part of a ship is a man like who supports a family? A—The main stay." Harrington proved to be an editor who provided content that was just witty enough for the average reader to find winsome.

Harrington began the February issue of *The Young American* with this line: "No pent up ethic contracts our powers, for this boundless continent is ours." Harrington used this tagline on the front page of subsequent issues. Following the table of contents in the February issue, an innovation from the first issue, Harrington repeated the slogan from the cover and added that the periodical was "devoted to the news of the day, sound literature, poetry, prose." He added that it would be "Independent in all things; neutral in nothing." He began Volume 1, Number 2 with the page numbering used for journals and listed the first article, "Rearing Boys," beginning on page thirty-two. "Rearing Boys" was a moralistic tale about a mother who allowed her son, Charlie, to be unsupervised. Charlie became progressively more rebellious until he was convicted of stealing and the mother was taken to a lunatic asylum. Later in the publication, from pages fifty-five to fifty-seven, Harrington included a long poem by Park Benjamin called "Cincinnati S(wine)" extolling the virtues of hogs. In "The Hoosier's Experience at Sea" on pages fifty-eight to sixty, an unknown poet described the travail of ship travel.

As a personal editor, Harrington retained his schoolmasterly role by warning others of vice. Although he did not suggest divine judgment for misbehavior, he used his fiction to highlight the American idea that uneducated people can still exercise good judgment and common sense. For instance, Harrington published a series of pieces by guest poets praising a virtuous woman—including "Lives" by Phil Henderson on page thirty-seven, and a poem about the benefits of an honorable life by Dr. [Elisha] Mitchell (no first name printed) on page thirty-eight.[13] On page forty-six, Harrington published a brief article titled "Editorial" that said, "This is the last rose of summer, Left blooming alone. Its lovely companions are, Faded and gone." In words of explanation, Harrington lamented that if the rose had a companion, it would have had some consolation. He wrote that people tend to take friendships for granted in middle age and are left without companionship. Instead of urging readers to practice friendship, Harrington reminded his readers that they, too, were "passing away." Harrington's work sometimes bordered on the maudlin even as it educated.

Breaking from the sober tone, Harrington published a series of aphorisms on page forty. They resembled Benjamin Franklin's folksy wisdom in his famous *Poor Richard's Almanac*. For instance, Harrington wrote, "'Did you ever see such a mechanical genius as my son?' said an old lady. 'He has made a fiddle out of his head and has wood enough to make another.'" Harrington also wrote this oddly humorous note: "Blessed are the orphan children, for they have no mothers to spank them."

On page forty-seven, Harrington told his readers that "The Drunken Husband," a story appearing on the next page, was his original short story even though he used the pen name Snap Jr. He told the story of an ill-fated marriage of a young woman to a promising attorney who took to drinking too much wine. The habit left the attorney broke and led to the tragic death of both husband and wife. Harrington ended the story four pages later with a warning: "Just see what drink has done—cut down a lawyer who would have been an ornament to his profession, and murdered one of the most intelligent and handsome young ladies that the world ever produced." The plot and the characters were not well developed, but the action provided a convenient excuse for Harrington to offer the kind of homespun moral insight that his readers would likely appreciate.

A novelty in the February issue of *The Young American* is the answer to a riddle from page twenty-five of the January issue:

RIDDLE

I often murmur, yet I never weep;
I always lie in bed, but never sleep;
My mouth is wide and larger than my head;

And much disgorges though it ne'er is fed;
I have no legs or feet, yet swiftly run;
And the more full I get move further on.
(Answer in next paper)

On page sixty-one in the February 1858 issue, Harrington wrote, "Answer to riddle in the January no. (River)." Throughout his publication Harrington included similar riddles, or what he called "charades."

From pages sixty-eight to seventy-four of February's *The Young American* was a light-hearted story about a love-struck couple bent on eloping. The bride's father foiled the midnight plan by trapping the suitor who tried to break into his barn. The farmer freed the suitor, gave him one hundred dollars, and the man then left the area. The daughter remained to marry another and enjoy a stable family life.

In April's issue, on pages 119 and 120, Harrington published the poem "Matrimony and Its Consequences," comparing marriage to digestion and noting that it takes its toll. While the work was meant to be witty, it contained an undercurrent of warning, like the piece about the foiled elopement. Marriage carries a cost of time, liberty, and wealth, Harrington warned. He never married and this warning might have reflected his own concern that marriage can be costly.

The novelty of *The Young American's* May issue was the serialization of "The Bridal Feast," a poem continued in each issue until October. This elaborate poem may be Harrington's best work. He told the story of newlyweds Gilbert and Rosaline, and Gilbert's secret love, Amethysta. Harrington used images of light to cast the scene in shadows and mystery. He also had an unknown speaker repeat the cry, "Misery." The July issue is unavailable and thus that episode of the poem is unknown, but the tone of the poem suggests that Gilbert's secret love was expecting a child. The action indicates that Gilbert deceived her, betraying her affections. Contrite, Gilbert confessed his guilt, while the brother of Amethysta planned to avenge his sister. However, the sister begs for Gilbert's life and the brother is content to curse Gilbert by magically aging him. Thereafter, Gilbert collapses either in exhaustion or death. The poem included forty-eight stanzas; about ten appeared in each issue.

Harrington employed the idea of light as a theme throughout the poem. Light was introduced in stanza three and reoccurred throughout the rest of the poem as an association with pain.[14] At the poem's end, Gilbert exhaust-edly drifts off to sleep as Amethysta whispers to him:

"For thee, though many a year
I'll shed the bitter tear;
Wherever thou mayest go,
I'll see and share thy woe,
And 'mid all pain and ill,
Pray for and watch thee still."

This poetry revealed Harrington's own understanding of the conflicted man, misunderstood by most, but suffering for his misdeeds.

Harrington continued the May issue with his light-hearted poem "Bobbin [sic] Around," on pages 142 through 144. He wrote of an unnamed woman who liked to go "bobbin [sic] around," concluding the poem with a line marked "Moral." He suggested that suitors should be cautious of women who go "bobbin around," presumably acting carelessly. Nonetheless, the repeated phrase "bobbin around" created a lively rhythm in the verse.

Harrington's in-paper discourse with readers and contributors reveals how all three parties interacted. On page 166 of June's issue, Harrington pub-licly responded to contributors. He told one contributor, "Try again. Per-haps you will succeed. Your communication did not suit the character of our paper. 'Oh, I Come to My Lover, My Love' is declined." On the same page, Harrington urged his male readers to send him more communications. On pages 169 and 170, Harrington scolded readers for not supporting *Stedman's Magazine*, which went out of business. "What are the people of North Carolina thinking about while they flood the North with money for worthless papers and books they could turn it to a better use subscribing for a paper closer to home." This line is very similar to an editorial column from the January 28, 1858, issue of the *Fayetteville Observer. Semi-Weekly*. The column, "A Word to Our Contemporaries," criticized the North Carolina press for alluding to *Harper's Magazine* and other newspapers and periodicals from the North. On page three of that issue, an editorial comment reprinted from the *Charlotte Democrat* said, "We are not at all selfish—we like to see others prosper, but especially do we want to see the press of the Old North State in prosperity; [sic] a thing that will never be as long as they continue to offer inducements, through their columns, to the people to subscribe for cheap publications at the North."

The June issue of *The Young American* began on page 156 with "The Recluse, On the Broken Bow," a three-page poem about unrequited love. The theme is repeated in that issue's "The Bridal Feast," which ran four pages. The issue continued with support for Governor Ellis, already established in the previous issue, and ended with the customary advertisements, including some for out-of-state vendors. The most humorous note from June's issue can be found on page 172: "A lady of Concord [sic] NC [sic] was lately granted a divorce on the complaint that her husband always slept with his back to her."

The August issue began with a poem by Elise, a writer Harrington said he would publish in his June issue. The poem on page 204 was titled "Give me Fame!"—a kind of yearning prayer to be famous. "Yes, grant me fame, for all my heart, and all my hopes, and I'll die content." On page twenty-four, Harrington thanked Elise for her contribution, "We will publish you anytime. . . ." Elise contributed a love poem in the November issue on page 289, which included these lines:

> I know it! I know it!
> Yes, Thou lovest me still!
> Thou cans't not forget it,
> Not even in death's chill.

Harrington did not always affirm contributors. He publicly wrote one contributor that the latter's work was "unfit for any respectable paper."

ADVERTISING IN *THE YOUNG AMERICAN*

The first advertisement of the January issue appeared on page twenty-seven and informed readers that the business of J. Worth Hans "dissolved" and the new business would be known as J.D. Worth. The next two advertisements on that page included announcements for commission merchants in Philadelphia and Baltimore. The following page featured advertisements for Dibble & Bunce of Wilmington and J. & D.G. Worth in Buffalo Springs, North Carolina. The latter ad offered "five sacks of coffee, which we will sell cheap for cash." The last page advertised for the Pine Forest Academy, where Harrington both studied and taught. "The second session of the institution commenced on the second Monday in January," the advertisement read. "It is beautifully situated in Harnett County near Harrington P.O.,[15] in a society second to none in the state." The final advertisements of the first issue were a help wanted notice for "a first-rate hand to work at turpentine" and another notice for J. & D.G. Worth.

The remaining issues of *The Young American* each ended with four pages of display advertisements similar to those in the first issue. In April, Harrington published a full-page display advertisement for a Philadelphia-based retailer promoting "silk shawls and fancy bonnets" along with riding hats, Panama hats, and others "in great variety." Harrington published advertisements for vendors of naval stores, which sold turpentine and related products. While turpentine had a variety of uses in the rural South through the 1940s, many families used it as a healing fluid for minor cuts. The oddest advertisement found in *The Young American* was printed on page twenty-nine of the first issue with the headline "Look out." It went on to say: "A Scoundrel named Elkins Jones has left our work but was in debt, [sic] the public are warned to keep a look out for the scoundrel as he will be apt to try some bad deals [sic] If he thinks he can get in debt to them." In a more litigious age, Harrington could have been charged with defamation unless he could prove the charges were true; however, the advertisement appeared only once and no other mention of Jones occurred in the 1858 issues of either *The Young American* or *The Nation*.

At eighteen years of age, Harrington lacked both literary and journalistic experience. Even his decision to publish such a potentially libelous advertisement could be excused. Nevertheless, Harrington did well with what he knew. Even as the dilettante journalist of Harnett County, Harrington was able to combine foreign news and locally grown "literature" that likely resonated with the cultural sensibilities of area readers. Even his more literary tales about human nature and the human condition were cast in terms of the moral values of those living in the region where he grew up, studied, and planted his newspapers. In effect, his literary publication served a similar function to news of the day by helping readers locate themselves semantically in the culture of their own time and place.

6

The News, Advertisements, and the Silent Partner of "The Nation"

During 1858, readers in Raleigh and Fayetteville enjoyed active printed newspapers, while John McLean Harrington worked in the rolling hills between these two North Carolina cities. To the north was the *Raleigh Register.* Founded in 1799, this paper was started as a voice for Jeffersonian Republicans by Joseph Gales. It became a Whig party organ in the 1830s. Another Raleigh newspaper, the *Raleigh Star,* began in 1808 but was suspended in 1852.[1] To the south was the *Fayetteville Observer. Semi-Weekly.* This newspaper, with the unusual use of punctuation marks in its name—a period between *Observer* and *Semi-Weekly* and one at the end of the name—carried articles similar to those that Harrington ran in his handwritten newspapers.

In the midst of these machine-press newspapers, Harrington handwrote his periodicals. He published *The Nation* on Saturdays, but switched to Wednesdays in the June 23 issue, noting that readers wanted to get their news earlier in the week. The first issue of *The Nation* (Volume 1, Number 1, April 17, 1858), included a nameplate with the tagline "The majority must rule, the minority must submit," the publication's location (Buffalo Springs), and the editor's and proprietor's names. Harrington employed a rustic form of calligraphy for the words "The Nation," and used short line strokes extending from the letters for a bit of flourish. Despite the cursive letters, the handwriting is fairly uniform. The lines flowing off the name suggest movement and a hint of formality (See Appendix A).

The second issue of *The Nation* (Volume 1, Number 2, April 24, 1858) appears to be penned with more care than the first and includes a revised nameplate with wavy rules to separate the elements. The feathery quality of the type drawn on the first issue is replaced with bold sweeping lines for the name, creating a shadow-like effect. The font looks like three wavy lines fanning out from the large letter N in the newspaper name, and a quarter-inch circle similar to a target.[2] These additions appear to be artistic flourishes, attempts at visual elements.

By the seventh issue (Volume 1, Number 7, May 29, 1858), the nameplate included wavy lines that suggest heat rather than movement, but the detail from the earlier editions is missing. Harrington employed this style until Volume 1, Number 9, when he used outlines for the letters of the name and a double-rule line under it with the date in brackets in the upper left-hand corner, but resumed the name with the wavy lines on the inside of the newspaper. Among the consistencies of *The Nation* was the prominent placement of the advance subscription rate of two dollars and slogans such as "The majority must rule; the minority must submit." This two-dollar subscription would be considered nearly $50 in 2010.[3]

All in all, the name with the various embellishments was a way for Harrington to transcend the criticism to be expected when a news product was handwritten rather than produced by a press. The name design may have been Harrington's way of suggesting that the newspaper, while handwritten, was nonetheless classy.

In keeping with the tradition of his day, Harrington did not make any of the letters bigger than the others, as is common in modern journalism where headline size varies with the importance of the topic. However, Harrington assisted the reader by using a single line to separate the articles. This convention still survives in twenty-first century print newspapers.

The Nation was approximately eight inches wide and about twelve inches deep—about the size of a standard legal tablet today. Each of Harrington's columns typically contained about thirty lines of script. Pages were not numbered and the sheets contained writing on both sides. Harrington corrected some spelling and grammar right on the page.

NEWS CONTENT OF *THE NATION*

Both *The Young American* and *The Nation* appear to have been inspired by the machine-printed *Fayetteville Observer. Semi-Weekly*. The Fayetteville periodical, a four-page broadsheet paper, featured paid advertisements on the front page with news and opinion on the inside pages. The newspaper circulated Wednesdays and Saturdays. Like *The Nation,* it featured political opinion side by side with discussions of medical remedies. In "Letter from Washington, Correspondences of the *Baltimore Patriot,*" on page two of the May 20, 1858, edition, the writer predicted, "Democracy is doomed to a most signal overthrow." The paper condemned the idea of Southern secession. On the same page was an unattributed note that kerosene oil caused an explosion in Augusta, Georgia, throwing a barrel into the chest of a "Negro girl" and killing her. On May 14, 1858, a brief article, listed on page three and marked "A Nuisance," called for railroad companies to charge double for passengers who chew tobacco because those who practiced it were involved in "abominations."

On June 10, 1858, the Fayetteville periodical included a news item on page two marked "A sharp sailor," which repeated an account from the *Louisville Journal* describing a sailor who asked a "Negro" to drink liquor in a nearby shop. The sailor heard that the liquor was poisonous and wanted to test the warning. Once he discovered the liquor was not poisonous, the sailor ordered his own alcoholic beverage. The account provides insight into the way some Southern editors regarded the life of an African American. This racial group was believed expendable—in this case valuable enough to work only as an assayer, a food-tester.

In *The Nation,* Harrington expressed the prevailing political opinion of the South along with a commitment to majority rule. Each copy of the newspaper included a slogan behind the nameplate on the front page. On April 17, April 24, and May 1, the tagline appeared as "The majority must rule, the minority must submit." By May 29, the tagline read "The voice of the people must be heard, The voice of the people is law," which appeared in three more issues (June 5, 12, 23). In eight subsequent issues (July 7, 14, 21; August 4, 11, 18, 25; September 1), Harrington's tagline read, "With pleasure or displeasures to friends or foes [sic] we sketch the world as it goes." This final tagline emphasized editorial independence as well as broadly cultural rather than just political content. On the one hand, it seemed contrary to Harrington's earliest stated mission to be a voice for Democrats. On the other hand, since the new tagline came late in the publication's serialization it might simply have reflected Harrington's shift from political editorializing toward cultural content that would appeal to readers across the political spectrum.

In Harrington's first article in *The Nation* (April 17, Volume 1), he offered

"A word to our democratic Friends" and urged like-minded readers to participate in the primary elections. Harrington repeatedly called for "organization of the party" to ensure democracy[4] and sought representatives who would work for state aid for Cumberland and Harnett counties. In addition, he called for completion of the rail route to the coal fields and beyond. But most of all, Harrington wanted his readers to defeat the party of Lincoln by conducting district meetings and electing strong Democrats. He included an aphorism on page two of the April 17, Number 2, issue to make his point: "The early bird catches the worm."

The third and fourth pages of the April 17 edition mentioned Democratic meetings, and the April 24 issue mentioned nominating candidates for the next general assembly. Harrington used the fourth, last page to joke about a guest at a New York boarding house who could tell when a new cook was on duty by the color of the hair in the biscuits. Next he fired a political salvo, warning his readers that a "Yankee is proposing to print a paper called the *Gridiron*" and that "Politicians had better be on the alert or they may be 'done up Brown.'"

The April 24, Number 2, issue included front-page content lifted from the Raleigh *Standard* and criticizing Horace Greeley's *New York Tribune*— a newspaper that was started in 1841 and supported abolition. Over and over on the front page, Harrington disparaged Black Republicans, a derogatory term for the newly organized Republican Party or for anyone who supported rights for slaves. At the bottom right corner of the paper was an odd news brief, "A Glad Bottle and Cork factory has been started in California and the cork grows in Los Angeles County in that state." As with the item on the *Gridiron* newspaper announcement, his line about a cork factory comes at the end of political commentary and may be Harrington's way of offering some lighthearted content to offset the seriousness of his political pronouncements.

On page three of the April 24 issue, Harrington called for the election of Judge John W. Ellis of Rowan County for governor. As stated earlier, Ellis was elected and re-elected but died in office in 1861. On page three, Harrington wrote that Ellis was the best candidate, and he urged his readers to go to the polls and do their duty "like men." In his May 1 issue, on page three, column two, Harrington provided a list of days when Ellis would be in the area campaigning for the seat of governor. The controversial news in this edition was the heated exchange between John Ellis and Duncan K. McRae, another candidate for governor. On page three, first column of the June 12 issue, Harrington reported a story that Ellis and his opponent criticized each other publicly in New Bern. The article reported Ellis's observation that a win for his opponent would be a victory for the Black Republicans. According to the story, this comment led to name-calling, particularly the term "liar," and the men fought a war of words. At the top of the second column on page three, Harrington wrote that after Ellis and McRae were physically separated they continued with their campaigning "as if nothing had happened."

The first issue of *The Nation* included a front-page article reprinted from the Raleigh *Standard* that said the *New York Tribune* published the names of House and Senate members who voted for the proslavery Lecompton Constitution.[5] Harrington praised Southerners who voted for the measure, and apparently expected his readers to know the background of this proposal, as he did not provide much in the way of explanation or impact to his readers. In his May 1, Number 3, issue, Harrington repeated a news report from the *Easton Standard* about the slavery question in Kansas. On the front page, left column, Harrington reported that the Lecompton Constitution, while in trouble, would have to pass in order for Kansas to be accepted as a new state. On page two of the June 12, Number 9, issue, Harrington wrote, "Kansas has already cost the government, the lowest estimate, fifty million dollars," but offered no further explanation.

In the June 5, Number 8, issue of *The Nation,* Harrington criticized McRae's campaign for governor in part because of his support from the Whigs. Harrington challenged McRae's identity as a Democrat. "His tongue may be slick enough talking about building railroads through this county, when this state gets her portion of the public lands, but there is no more chance of it than building a railroad to the moon. . . ." On page four of the June 12, Number 9, issue, Harrington declared that a McRae victory would be a triumph for the Black Republican party.

On page three of the August 4, Number 16, issue, Harrington published a note in the second column about John C. Williams's intention to run for office. Harrington wrote that Williams "unequivocally, unmistakably and [sic] realy [sic] he announced himself in beaming capitals [sic] 'To the Freeman of Cumberland and Harnett.' We haven't got room for his card, Ed."[6] Harrington underlined the sentence "We haven't got room for his card," and, in the same column, he wrote that Williams's defeat was sure and the candidate was duped into thinking he could win a political race. Clearly Harrington then opposed freeing slaves and opposed candidates who might lobby for any kind of emancipation.

One of the novelties of *The Nation* was an extra edition Harrington published on Saturday, August 7, 1858. It was a six-inch column apparently issued at noon, reporting election results from Fayetteville for the state House of Commons[7] and identifying the winning candidate, William M. McKay, with 1,817 votes. Harrington promised that other results would be published in the next issue.

GENERAL CONTENT IN *THE NATION*

At times, Harrington scolded his readers. At other times, he treated them as equals. On page three, bottom left-hand column of the June 23, 1858, issue of *The Nation,* Harrington reported that *Stedman's Magazine* was going out of business because of a lack of patrons. At the end of that item, Harrington scolded: "Shame to you North Carolina!!! [sic]" Yet at other times the editor, in his role as publisher, showed that he considered the wishes of his readers. On page two, in the right-hand column of *The Nation's* June 23, 1858 issue, Harrington demonstrated his public sensitivity and business savvy when he told his readers he would be changing the publication day from Saturday to Wednesday due to the popular request of his subscribers, noting that readers would get their newspaper sooner. Nonetheless, on August 18, 1858, Harrington published a four-line brief announcement on the bottom, right-hand corner of *The Nation,* saying, "The 'Nation' office for sale by advertisement in todays [sic] paper it will be seen that we offer this office for sale." But on September 8, 1858, Harrington suspended *The Nation,* publishing on that day only one double-sided sheet.

After the first issue of *The Nation* was circulated, Harrington began to include some of the more typical content found in community newspapers. In the April 24, Number 2, issue he included an announcement of a wedding on page two in the first column and a market report in the second column. Coffee, for instance, was available at fifteen cents per pound in Buffalo Springs. On page three of the April 24 issue, Harrington praised other publications, including magazines in Boston and North Carolina. And in the second column of page three, Harrington offered a poetic weather report that metaphorically noted that *The Nation,* as well as the weather, has "burst into bloom."

Harrington republished content from the April 27, 1858, issue of *Easton Standard* for his May 1, Number 3, issue. He reported the weather from the *Easton Standard* area and said that a snow squall in the Buffalo Springs community left between two and three inches of snow on the ground. In the first column of page three of the May 1 issue, Harrington reported that the oldest inhabitant of his area, a person he did not identify, said the last time it snowed so hard was in 1847. In the second column on page three, Harrington reported that the snow and frost had killed the fruit.

In the June 5, Number 8, issue on page two, first column, Harrington reported that a grizzly bear weighing two thousand pounds would be on exhibit in Raleigh. In the same column, Harrington reported on a Union County baby who was eleven months old and weighed sixty pounds.

The July 7, Number 12, issue of *The Nation* reviewed the July Fourth festivities. Harrington wrote on the first column of page two, "The Birthday of American Freedom, 82 years ago, old England trembled at the idea that the Rebel Colonies would be the powerful nation which it now is." He continued, "We hope we will not live to see the day when it [the date of July 4th] will be otherwise, than one of reverence and praise." The line suggests that Harrington suspected the tension between the North and South was aggravating the Union.

In international news, Harrington frequently referred to the Atlantic Telegraph project. The Atlantic Telegraph Company was formed in 1856 to lay a commercial telegraph cable across the Atlantic Ocean. On the first and second columns of page three of the July 14, Number 13, issue, Harrington reported that the *Wilmington Journal* found the telegraphic fleet hadn't been seen. Harrington was not optimistic about the project and predicted it would end in failure. But despite Harrington's gloomy prediction, history records that the project succeeded.

ROLE OF ADVERTISING IN *THE NATION*

On page three of *The Nation's* June 12, Number 9, issue, Harrington explained his advertising rates. He charged four cents per line for the first line and two cents for each subsequent line insertion. He also sought agents to help him sell advertisements.

From the first to the last issue, Harrington always included paid advertising. The April 17, 1858, issue included the advertising rates on the second column of page four. This issue included advertising for a Buffalo Springs dry goods store, a commission merchant in Fayetteville, and an advertisement for *The Nation* which claimed that the periodical will be a "first class [sic] journal," printed weekly and containing "as much reading matter as most any of the papers of present-day." Also, it would be "strictly Democratic." This notice was repeated every issue.

In *The Nation's* May 1, Number 3, issue, in the first column of page four, Harrington included a paid advertisement that told readers a dry goods store could no longer extend credit. "All those indebted to the firm of J. Worth," said the paper, "are earnestly requested to come and close their accounts."

By the May 29, Number 7, issue, Harrington was publishing paid advertising on the left and right columns of his front pages. He continued this format for most of the remaining issues. A reprinted article from the *Fayetteville Observer* invited readers to come see a good, long piece of the Atlantic cable. Four-inch pieces sold for fifty cents at Tiffany's in New York. Harrington announced that he bought out the interest of the other parties in the paper and he would soon discontinue publication of *The Nation*. He offered to substitute it with *The New American* if subscribers wanted to replace their paper; however, no record of this later publication's existence could be found. He may have meant to replace *The Nation* with *The Young American,* not having decided on the final name of his other publication.

The front page of the August 25, Number 19, issue of *The Nation* featured only display advertising with all of the news moved to the inside. In the next issue, news returned to the front page, but half the page was still filled with advertisements. And in the September 8 issue, the all-advertising front page returned.

CESSATION OF *THE NATION*

Harrington indicated that publishing was a very difficult avocation. On page two of the May 1, Number 3, issue, he reported that times were difficult for editors, and he repeated the story of a Pennsylvania editor who appealed to his readers for pork, tallow candles, whiskey, linen, beeswax, wool, and anything he might eat. On page three of the July 21, Number 14, issue, Harrington published a brief under the heading: "*Wilmington Herald.*" He wrote, "Cheer up [sic] friends of the Herald [sic] don't give up to it yet—'Never say die while there is a shot in the locker [sic]' We will agree things look rather blue but always look on the bright side of things. We cant [sic] see why it is that it cant [sic] succeed. [Word unclear] this it is decided [sic] we hope to hear of its proving entirely successful—Ed."

On page two of the August 18, Number 18, issue, Harrington wrote that *The Nation* was for sale. He repeated the message on page two of the August 25, Number 19, issue. Therein Harrington splashed the sale across the first of two columns and wrote, "One of the parties desiring a change in business [sic] we offer the office of the Nation for sale with all its fixtures at a moderate price—To any person desiring such a situation [sic] we would respectfully request him to call and see our office books."

Harrington repeated the notice of the sale on page two of the September 1, Number 20, issue with a modest change. He said he bought out the "other parties" and "I will discontinue the issue of the Nation but will send in its place, [sic] the Young American for the balance of the year."

Although September 1 was to be the last issue, one more issue appeared. As stated earlier, on page two of the September 8, Number 21, issue, the last issue of *The Nation,* Harrington penned, "Now we state emphatically that this indeed will be the last [sic] our connections with the press will hereafter cease and friends of the Nation hope that they will be satisfied in the exchange as I know the senior partner [sic] Mr. Harrington [sic] will do all in his power to make the Young American what it ought to be. Hoping long life and pleasant associations to all [sic] I bid you adieu!! [sic] Editor Nation."

Harrington oddly listed advertising rates as if the newspaper would simply accept new advertisers for the old publication while commencing a new one. The dilettante journalist-publisher was nonplussed over the trifles of suspending a publication, and did so with little fanfare and apparently without a lot of forethought.

THE SILENT PARTNER

It is unknown if anyone assisted Harrington in copying the newspaper repeatedly for his circulation of up to one hundred. Harrington talked of a partner, but a careful reading of all the extant copies of *The Nation* suggests that he published alone. On page three of his first issue of *The Nation* (April 17, 1858), Harrington told his readers that he had enlisted the service of a "little Democrat to edit the paper" with the goal of keeping the content "straight forward."

In the June 30, 1858, issue of *The Nation,* Harrington referred again to the availability of *The Young American,* on the bottom left column of the front page. At the top of column two on the right side of the page, Harrington said he would edit this publication. He also said *The Young American* was previously published by another person who became ill and turned it over to him. Harrington ended this explanation by writing, "In the meantime [sic] we would inform the subscribers of the Young American that we will attend to them as before." Harrington assured these readers they would not be neglected even though the previous editor was leaving. The identity of the previous editor remains unclear—if there ever was one.

On page 234 of the September 1858 issue of *The Young American,* Harrington told his readers that *The Nation* would be discontinued. Harrington penned that he as editor "will do his utmost to please all" readers. His third-person voice and the reference to the end of *The Nation* suggest that Harrington worked alone, even though in the same September issue of *The Young American* he suggested that another editor was also involved in the publication. Moreover, Sion A. Harrington, John's younger brother, printed at least one known copy of a handwritten newspaper called the *Weekly News* on February 2, 1869, and two issues of *The Leasure Hour.,* a monthly publication, in May and June 1869.[8] Since he was younger, presumably shorter than John McLean, Sion Harrington may be the "little Democrat" whom Harrington referred to as his helper and partner.

Perhaps Harrington had no partner and this editorial sleight of hand was his way of avoiding criticism should a reader become upset. By suggesting an unidentified partner, Harrington would be able to deflect criticism and blame the "other" editor for the offensive content or for causing *The Nation* to suspend its publication. However, Harrington *did* advertise for an editor in his last issue of *The Nation,* a fact that further clouds the mystery.

In his September 1, 1858, issue of *The Nation,* page two, top left column, Harrington told patrons of *The Nation* that he bought out his unidentified partner. He told readers that he planned to discontinue the publication and give his *Nation* subscribers *The Young American* instead. He wrote that patrons who would prefer a refund instead of *The Young American* subscription might still get the remaining subscription to *The Nation.* Harrington hoped to revive *The Nation* as a way to satisfy their subscriptions. The remainder of his September article told *The Nation* patrons that he would regretfully retire: "And if we have said anything that will maim the feelings of any man [sic] we will cheerfully make amends. We bow to our audience and retire for the present. Former Editor Nation."

In the last issue of *The Nation,* published September 8, 1858, Harrington wrote: "We only printed half sheet this time thinking that a half loaf is better than no bread at all-Ed." After the nameplate in the first column on the left side of the newspaper, he penned, "Closing scenes. In the last no. of The Nation we stated that that number would be the closing no. Such was not the fact [sic] however [sic] as this number will show [sic] but now we state emphatically that this indeed will be the last [sic] our connection with the press will hereafter cease and to my old patrons and friends of The Nation [sic] I hope that they will be satisfied in the exchange as I know the senior partner Mr. Harrington will do all in his power to make *The Young American* what it ought to be, hoping long life and pleasant associations to all I bid you adieu!! [sic] Editor Nation." As stated earlier, while *The Nation* ceased publication, *The Young American* continued. In all, twenty-one issues of *The Nation* were published from April 17, 1858 to September 8, 1858.

7

Harrington's Other Newspapers

J ohn McLean Harrington started and stopped seven publications in his eleven years as the dilettante journalist of Harnett County. By the end of 1858, he had suspended both *The Nation* and *The Young American,* at about the same time Daniel Emmett's "I Wish I Was in Dixie's Land" swept the nation and was adopted as the South's unofficial anthem.[1]

THE WEEKLY EAGLE

Harrington did not publish in 1859, but he resumed his handwritten work with *The Weekly Eagle,* published only once, on April 20, 1860. With turmoil simmering across the nation, Harrington included news from other areas. On the front page, he told the story of a death from tainted, canned strawberries. Harrington referred to the victim as a military man. "A United States soldier named Herzon died a short time since at Steilacoom, near Pudgets [sic] Sound [Washington] through eating strawberries which had been preserved in a tin can. It was found that this poison had formed through the acidity of the fruit coming in contact with the metal of which the can was composed, the effects when eaten being to ulcerate the stomach and finally to cause death."

THE SEMI-WEEKLY NEWS AND THE WEEKLY NEWS

Harrington published two other newspapers in 1860, including *The Semi-Weekly News,* which ran from July 24, 1860, to August 17, 1860, and the *Weekly News,* which ran from June 7, 1860, to March 2, 1864. The newspapers included references to politics, poetry, local election results, and other general content.

The first issue of the *Weekly News* was published on June 7, 1860, and included a front-page appeal addressed to the "Democratic Union" and pleading for it not to secede. A few weeks later, on page three of the August 17, 1860, issue, Harrington told patrons of *The Semi-Weekly News* about political victories by Gov. John Ellis and other Democrats who had won office. Harrington also informed readers that *The Semi-Weekly News* would stop publication because subscription support was scant; however, Harrington went on to say that he would continue the *Weekly News*.

By the December 25, 1860, issue of the *Weekly News*, Harrington apologized for the hit-and-miss circulation. In an article titled "To our old family and Friends," he wrote, "We again make our appearance to our old friends after a long absence and we hope they may recognize their old friend again. Several changes have taken place since you have last seen a copy of the 'News' [sic] a Black Republican president has been elected in these United States [sic] which threatens to demolish this firm republic of the Constitution of Washington. Several states say they will not suffer or be ruled by a Black Republican man elected who is openly opposed to slavery. South Carolina has already seceded and it is expected that the Gulf States will soon follow. Secession is moving in NC [sic] but to what extent I am not able to say." President Abraham Lincoln was considered a radical abolitionist, referred to derisively as a Black Republican, and Southern Democrats especially opposed his inauguration.[2]

On January 1, 1861, the *Weekly News* reported on page two, "Another year has fled." Harrington predicted that 1860 would be "remembered with the things that we passed and will only be remembered as a matter of history and maybe only with regret as the Union has been dissolved. South Carolina has spoken [word unclear] for herself, but let us hope for the best and when 1861 closes [sic] may peace and tranquility rest on this fair republic of ours. We will close this by wishing our readers a happy new year."

South Carolina seceded from the Union just days before these words from Harrington, on December 20, 1860. According to a Harnett County historian, "The event that precipitated the War Between the States was the success of the abolitionists in electing their candidate on the Republican ticket as President of the United States."[3] He writes, "Lincoln did not receive a single vote in Harnett County."[4] The reason: Lincoln was not on the ballot in North Carolina. "Despite their disappointment at the outcome of the election, most North Carolinians did not feel that it was cause to leave the Union."[5] In May of 1861, the state's stance would change due to the calling up of Union troops to "crush secessionists in South Carolina and other Southern states."[6]

On page two of the January 1, 1861, issue, Harrington reported that South Carolina's Fort Moultrie was abandoned by U.S. troops who retreated to Fort Sumter. In the article titled "Fort Moultrie," Harrington wrote that the Palmetto flag, the state flag of South Carolina, waved at Fort Moultrie and at other buildings throughout the area. "We do not know what the result of this rash proceeding will be. We fear bad times are at hand," Harrington opined, adding on page three the news that Fort Moultrie was in trouble. Reprinting a report from Charleston from December 27, 1860, Harrington informed readers that "the building in which the soldiers of Fort Moultrie were quartered was burned last night and the guns of the Fort spiked."

In a later dispatch in the January 1, 1861, issue, Harrington reported more war news: "Major [Robert] Anderson stated that he evacuated Fort Moultrie in order to allay all discussions about that post, and at the same time strengthen his own position at Fort Sumter. Capt. [John L.] Foster with a small force remains at Fort Moultrie. Also [word unclear] several military companies have been ordered out and a collision is not improbable. The military of Charleston are ordered out to protect the magazines and arsenals in that vicinity [word unclear]. It is reported that several military corps are in route to Charleston from the interior. No further news from Charleston [sic] it has been believed that restrictions are placed on the telegraph."

In 1861, Harrington wrote the following on page two of the *Weekly News*: "Today being Christmas we were almost tempted not to issue any paper but fearing our friends might be disappointed we make our appearance and wish you a Merry Christmas and Happy New Year. We hope by next Christmas that all the political troubles may be over and our infant confederacy [sic] moving on as smooth as life." Harrington also reported that he was resigned to the existence of the Confederacy.

THE WEEKLY NEWS' ADVERTISING SHEET. MONTHLY. AND THE WEEKLY NEWS

In 1861, Harrington also published *The Weekly News' Advertising Sheet. Monthly.*,[7] of which only three issues survive.[8] This very odd publication included a grand boast on page one of the February 1861 issue that it would be "sent to 20,000 merchants in the South [sic] the way we wish to make it pay is by advertisements. Any person advertising can name any persons he may wish it sent to to [sic] the no. of 100 or less." No record of thousands of copies of this handwritten, four-page publication can be found.

In the January 1, 1862, issue of the *Weekly News,* Harrington led the front page with Civil War coverage of Port Royal reprinted from the *Charleston Mercury.* He wrote this report across two columns and continued it on page four at the top of the left of two columns:

> The Charleston Mercury has the following account of a recent brush with the enemy in which a North Carolina battery was engaged. Gardner's Corner via Peastaligo Dec. 19. "About ½ past 1 o'clock yesterday afternoon one of the enemies [sic] gun boats passed by Port Royal Ferry. Our batteries opened fire upon her, striking her, three times. Upon meeting with this rather hot reception, she steamed rapidly past, and ran aground about three miles on the other side of the ferry. As soon as our troops became aware of the fix in which the yankees had got themselves, Sgt. M. Henry [name unclear] of Capt. Moon's field battery (from Wilmington, NC) was dispatched with a section of the battery to a point just opposite to the shoal on which the gun boat ran aground. In the meantime, three flats crowded with the enemy's troops had moved from the opposite shore, under a sharp fire from one of their batteries directed against our troops on the main. At that point, our forces consisted of Capt. M. Henry [name unclear] [sic] Battery arrived just as the flats had come out about midway of the stream. He immediately opened fire upon them with tremendous effect. One of the flats was soon gaining and our fire created terrible havoc among the soldiers on the other two flats put back, [sic] night came on and ended the commotion [word unclear]. The enemy's lost among the men with flats must have been very heavy."

Although Harrington reprinted war reports in the *Weekly News* from another newspaper, the 1862 account agrees with other historic accounts. By the end of 1862, Harrington reported on the front page the Battle of Fredericksburg, Virginia. The battle, fought December 11–15, was considered a decisive victory for the Confederate Army. Harrington ran the following account on the front page with the headline "Fight at Fredericksburg." Using the dateline "Richmond, Dec. 13," he reported, "On Thursday night the enemy under cover of artillery firing crossed the river and occupied the city. At daylight Friday morning the artillery opened with firing [and] reached as high as 10 per minute and continued all day [sic] under its cover the pontoon bridges were thrown across. The force landed said to be 50,000." Harrington continued, "Many of the enemy were killed or wounded. The opposition to the passage could not have been determined since only [William] Barksdale's brigade opposed the enemy and no artillery on our part was used. Highlighting yesterday over in Burunds [word unclear] woods about 2 ½ miles this side of the town and was very heavy a [word unclear] against is expected to come off soon. *Enquirer.*"

Harrington continued his war news with the following: "There was desperate fighting in the streets of Fredericksburg on Thursday in which both sides suffered severely. The shelling commenced on Thursday morning and not fifty buildings of any value are standing. An Episcopal church and several other handsome public buildings were destroyed—no fighting on yesterday. *Examiner.*"

These war accounts suggest that Harrington took seriously his role as a war-time editor who was duty-bound to provide news to his community, even if he had to borrow it from other publications and handwrite it over and over for his readers. Harrington began the January 1863 issue with an update on Fredericksburg. The *Weekly News* was brutally honest about the Confederate losses at Fredericksburg. On the front page of the January 6 issue Harrington wrote: "From the army intelligence office we learn that the Confederate 'casualties' in the battle of Fredericksburg amount to 4,000, that of these 500 were taken prisoners, and 500 received mere bruises or scratches [sic] leaving the number of killed and wounded in reality at 3,000. The number of deceased is not more than 400, Rich Whig [short for *Richmond Whig*]."

History suggests that the figure of Confederate casualties was closer to 5,000 in this battle between Gen. Robert E. Lee of the Confederacy and Maj. Gen. Ambrose E. Burnside of the Union that took place on December 11–15 in Fredericksburg, Virginia. Burnside entered battle with 120,000 troops while Lee commanded 78,000 troops. The Union may have lost up to 12,500 soldiers, and the battle was considered a victory for Lee.

At the end of 1863, Harrington once again left his readers with a hopeful wish for the future. In his December 23 issue, page two, under a column marked "Christmas," Harrington wrote, "Old Santa Claus will hardly be around [word unclear] to see the young people this year. Wish [word unclear] readers in tradition the compliments of the season, and hope by next year that peace will be restored to our once happy nation."

By February 3, 1864, the front page of the *Weekly News* reported that "the enemy" was on the move toward Fredericksburg and had retreated from the Cumberland Gap. Harrington noted that the governor of North Carolina was supplying clothing to the soldiers. In the last available issue of the *Weekly News* (March 2, 1864), he wrote on the front page that his newspaper was temporarily suspended. On page two, Harrington addressed his "patrons and friends": "We are again compelled to suspend the publication of the 'News' for the present. We hope [sic] however [sic] that it will not be long before we are again to the breeze. We expect to issue a number occasionally." Apparently the suspension was permanent, because no subsequent issues exist.

THE TIMES.

The next publication Harrington released was *The Times.*, on October 17, 1867, and he published one of his short stories on the front page. Under the label "Choice Literature," Harrington published dark fiction suggestive of the work of Edgar Allen Poe in the 1830s. Harrington called the story "The Highland Herdsman." The story is reprinted below using Harrington's own line breaks. In this literary piece, Harrington explored the bad blood between the English and the Scots in the same fashion as Scottish writer Walter Scott's 1827 short story, "The Two Drovers." In his account, Harrington pits an Englishman against a Scotsman, but this approach may merely be a veiled reference to a people who speak the same language and share much in common yet who insist on fighting to the death—as was the case during the Civil War. The piece was initially presented over two columns.

THE HIGHLAND HERDSMAN

The summer dawn's reflected hue
To purple changed Lock Kathrine blue;
Mildly and softly the western breeze
Just kissed the lake, just stirred the trees
And the pleased lake, like maiden coy
Trembled, but dimpled not for joy.
Lady of the Lake.

It was summer when
We reached the Highlands.
Three hours riding from Stir-
Ling brought us to the bor-
ders of that Sylvan lake of
Which the Scottish band has
Given such irresistible des-
criptions. Having spent an
Hour on its calm sunny
Waters, our party landed
And proceded [sic] to Lock Lo-
mond; some in Carriages
While others preferred to walk
Through the country which was
Once the abode of those proud
Mountaineers, the Macgregors.

Along the pastoral slopes and,
Mountainous ridges of Bevenue
I discovered (word unclear) the wild goats crop-
ping the fresh herbage, while
Here and there, along the base
Of the oak and the birch, stood
The hamlets of the Highland Shep-
Herds. From the lips of these
Simple herdsmen the
Stranger may gather, if he choose, many
Incidents of local and tra-
itionary [sic] interest, and which
Serve to throw light on the eth-
nographical history of the people.

The following narrative shows
The truth of the remark applied
By a German author to the Scotch
Man: "He is as brave as a

Spaniard, as shy as a fox, and
As slippery as an eel."

    Several years ago a brave,
Hardy Highlander, whom we
Will call Duncan, left his
Home among the glens and
Hills of Argylshire [sic] with a large
Herd of cattle destined for
The summer fields and more
Fertile meadows of Yorkshire.

    With his uniform success,
He soon disposed of his
Stock to the English grazers,
And with a well settled
Pace, he started on his re-
turn. He had nearly rea-
ched the confines of Scot-
land, when, quietly walking
Along the highway, accompa-
nied by his faithful dog, he
Was overtaken by an Englishman,
Well dressed, and of pleasing
Appearance. He drew near
Duncan, and familiarly ac-
costed him, "Well, my good
Fellow, whither are you bound?
You are a herdsman, I see."
"Yes, from Argylshire, sir."
"And do you not fear to travel
Alone with your wallet well
Filled, I doubt not, with Eng-
lish gold."

    "Not quite alone," the brave Highlander

Replied, drawing
His dirk, for there's a real
Scottish blade that never failed
Me yet; and here too, is as
Fine a day as ever roamed
Highlands or Lowlands.

   "A noble fellow indeed, but
Is that really a true Scotch
Blade?" inquired the gentle-
Man, as he approached still
Nearer to examine it.

   "Sure, man, it is; take it
In your hand," and the un-
Suspecting drover, as he
Walked along examined its
curious workmanship with
Apparently great interest.
Watching his opportunity, the
Gentlemanly highwayman
Plunged the dagger into the
Neck of the dog beside him
And at the same instant
Sprung upon the astonished
Duncan, threw him on the
Ground, and planting his
Knees upon his breast, held
Him firmly by his throat.

   "Now," cried the robber,
"Give up your money or I'll
Take both your money and
Your life," adding cruel
Sarcasm, "you see how even
A Highlander may be outwitted."

> Poor fellow, he was in a fix. His
> Faithful dog had expired without
> A groan; and his trusty stul [sic] was now
> In assassin's hand. To be continued.

In the October 24, 1867, edition, Harrington finished the final installment of his poetic short story in a single column on the front page. He wrote:

> It was all the work of a moment.
> Seeing no possible alternative,
> He very reluctantly gave up his gold,
> And was surprised to rise,
> The highwayman still holding fast.
> "Who'll believe," said the crestfallen Scotchman,
> "That such a man as I, with such a dog,
> Could have been robbed by an Englishman?"
> "Don't give yourself any uneasiness on that score,
> Old fellow," retorted the other,
> "For you are not the first of your
> Countryman that made my acquaintance.
> Besides, I always give them a mark to remember me by."
> At the same time he drew out his sword
> And leading him to the stump of a decayed old oak near by,
> Bade him lay his hand there.

> Now the idea of losing this useful and
> Important member and especially by such
> An unnecessary and inscrutable amputation,
> Was particularly disagreeable to the worthy Scotchman.

> A bright thought just then suggested itself to his mind.
> Without saying a word, he did as he was ordered,
> And very meekly placed his hand on the stump,
> Calmly awaiting the blow.

The robber drew himself up to his full length,
And lifting his sword high in the air,
Brought it down with a thundering stroke.
But the cunning Highlander, at that very instant,
Had slipped aside his hand,
And while the enraged Englishman was vainly
Trying to withdraw the sword from the wood
Into which it had deeply penetrated,
He rushed upon him with as fierce a grip
As Roderick held Fitz James at Corilantogle Ford.

"Now gallant Saxon, hold thine own!
No maiden's hand is round thee thrown!
That desperate grasp thy frame might feel
Through hands of brash and trifle steel."

The brave Duncan soon had his foe completely
In his power; but he would not take his life.
He, however, securely bound him,
Took his purse again in spite of the important threats
And curses of the robber,
And hastened back to the house of the nearest magistrate.

Then he informed the police where they might find
"A rogue that richly deserved the gallows."
It is unnecessary to add that the Scotchman
Received ample justice, and highwayman
Soon after incurred the punishment due his crime.

Harrington may have considered the Englishman to be a figure of the Union and the Scotsman to be a dignified, Southern gentleman minding his own business. A victim of an unprovoked attack, the Scotsman had to act as he did or he would have lost his hand, which was his means to work. Harrington knew the importance of a hand for doing one's work, as he used his own hands to produce his publications. He may have considered a hand to be a metaphor for a laborer, suggesting that the loss of a hand cuts off a vital part of one's ability to earn a living. The North's attempts to cut off the laborers—the slaves—led to economic hardships in the South.

Harrington's divided loyalties in the Civil War may be questionable in the light of his early claims about being a Democrat, but the short story provides some insight into Harrington's understanding of justice. Following the war, Harrington held that he was never a Confederate sympathizer, an assertion making this short story all the more intriguing.

On December 19, 1867, Harrington penned another short story on the front page of *The Times.* titled "An Affecting Scene." Harrington retold the tale of a romantic gesture by Richard Bennett, a man who died in battle. Harrington wrote, "Richard Bennett, when mortally wounded in one of Nelson's great battles, had requested that a miniature [a small portrait], and a lock of his hair should be given to his sweetheart by Lt. P. [for Parsons] to his sweetheart Lusette in Scotland." Harrington described the woman as beautiful but frail, and once she felt the lock of hair, "she pressed it to her lips and heart, and fell back. Her mother and I [the lieutenant] thought she had fainted; but the pure and innocent soul had returned to God—the God who gave it." This short story likely reveals the sentimental side of Harrington, who mourned the losses of war.

By the beginning of 1868, Harrington once again offered optimistic sentiments for the coming year. On Thursday, January 2, 1868, Harrington reported in *The Times.* that "the New Year has just dawned upon us and the year 1867 is numbered with the things that are passed and gone forever. Go old year with your joys [sic] your lairs and your sorrows [sic] let this be buried in the unforgotten past. And let us turn with joy to your successor, who may have much joy for us and whose Sorrows [sic] are at least, hidden from our view, only to be brought to light by the ceaseless revolutions [words unclear] of old Father Time."

In the same issue, Harrington noted the dying words of notable people on the front page, and regularly recalled Sir Walter Scott's dying words from September 21, 1832: "I feel as if I were myself again." Apparently Harrington was thinking about the restoration of the Union and the hope that with impending peace would come a return to normalcy.

Harrington went on to report light news on page two with an article about a steamboat. "Maj. R. M. [Orrell] has just completed his new steamboat the 'Halcyon' and has already very successfully made one or two trips between this place and Wilmington. The Halcyon is a very trim and pretty passenger and freight streamer. She is tastefully and elegantly fitted up with every comfort and convenience. Her length is 112 feet, beam 19 feet, hold up 4½ [word unclear] feet and tonnage between 600 and 700 barrels. She runs easily and with good speed. Fay. [Fayetteville] News."

On Friday, December 25, 1868, Harrington jubilantly wrote a page-two column labeled "Christmas": "Christmas is upon us again with all the fun and jollity of former times. We hope all will enjoy it and especially the young people who have looked forward to its approach with so much anxiety and we hope to be excused ourself [sic] from writing long articles on account of Christmas. We're [word unclear] hoping all may enjoy it to the ultimate [word unclear] of their desires and second to their wish."

Harrington ends his handwritten publications in 1869 with the last issues of *The Times*. In his January 1, 1869, issue, Harrington offered a New Year's greeting, his customary short story, a joke, and hard news. He reported on page three a murder: "A most distressing homicide occurred in Moore County [a county adjacent to Harnett County] at Mrs. Elizabeth Wickens on Wednesday night last. It seems that Dennis Thomas (colored) had a wife who cooked for Mrs. Wickens. On the night in question he came into the kitchen where his wife was and asked for supper; [sic] which was prepared for him [sic] immediately after he sat to the table [sic] he was shot in the head by an unknown assassin and instantly expired. Dennis was a very peaceable and good negro [sic]."

Harrington offered no commentary on this incident, but, taken in context, the news account hints at the uneasiness of the new social order in the South, where an African American could be summarily executed as he ate dinner. Nevertheless, since Harrington frequently reprinted crime reports from other periodicals, we do not know if this murder was reported to him by an unidentified local person or if it was a story that Harrington simply lifted from another periodical.

Harrington's last issue of *The Times.*, dated Friday, April 2, 1869, included a telling front-page account about slavery in another country. In "Abolition of Slavery in Cuba," Harrington wrote, "The insurgents in Cuba have abolished slavery. This action will tend greatly to strengthen the Cuban cause at home and abroad. The substance of the abolition proclamation is as follows: Slavery brought to Cuba by Spanish domination ought to be extinguished with it. The Central Assembly there for decree first, the abolition of slavery; second, opportunities in-disunifications [sic]; third, freedom to bear arms; fourth, freedom to have the rights and privileges of white men; fifth, all hatred of whatever color, are under the same obligations to the cause." The article, compelling because of the United States' recent brush with conflict over slavery, is of interest for the interrelated nature of slavery in Cuba and the United States.

In 1868, Cuban slaves produced 720,520 metric tons of sugar, which was more than forty percent of all the cane sugar in the world.[9] Steps toward the emancipation of slavery on the island began in 1868, however, it took almost two decades to completely dissolve the institution. The abolition of slavery in the United States affected the slave trade in Cuba because the former was the island's main trading partner. Before the War, some planters in the United States wanted Cuba to be annexed as a slave state. Others feared that the abolition of slavery in the United States might lead to a "disruption of the internal order of the Cuban slavery."[10] The delay in permanent abolition in Cuba was due to doubts about political reform. Officials in Cuba believed that as long as slavery existed "there will be no government established here in which they [slaves] can have a voice, that the island will continue to be governed by a repressive, censorious system, under pretext of preserving order."[11]

The first attempt to abolish slavery in Cuba occurred in 1868, several months prior to Harrington's news article. Slave workers in Cuba sang, "Advance, Lincoln, advance. You are our hope."[12] This song illustrates the influence of the American example on the neighboring island, where the Cuban workers desired to enjoy the same freedom found in Harnett County and the rest of the United States. Whether Harrington was pro-Union or pro-Confederacy in the recent war, this particular article likely illustrates a liberalization of his views, whereby the abolition of slavery in Cuba would "strengthen the Cuban cause at home and abroad."[13]

Harrington's last publication in his output of 302 issues of newspaper and journals comes full circle in establishing the editor's written legacy. His eventual recognition that slavery was a corrupting institution provides more evidence that Harrington was a thoughtful journalist who could change his convictions. Some critics may consider Harrington to be an opportunist. Other may others will see him as a product of his time and culture, a man who gradually changed his position on one of the greater issues in U.S. history, the role of slavery in American life. When Harrington started writing in 1858, the content of *The Young American* and *The Nation* revealed a journalist with a lyrical heartbeat and a quiver full of writing topics and techniques. The dilettante journalist of Harnett County, Harrington wrote passionately throughout his publishing career, and he continued until he penned his last paragraph in 1869.[14]

8

Why and How Harrington Handwrote Newspapers

Even the thought of handwriting 302 newspapers with multiple copies over an eleven-year period is staggering. Yet John McLean Harrington met that challenge, starting when he was age eighteen in 1858 and continuing until he turned thirty in 1869. His work provides a peek into an area that has been seldom researched,[1] namely, the handwritten press. Questions about the staying power of handwriting constitute a part of the history of this intriguing phenomenon. Johannes Trithemius argued in his *de Laude Scriptorium* (1492) that the printed word was inferior to written words on parchment because the written words would endure longer than the printed words.[2] Working at the time of the earliest use of the printing press in Europe, Trithemius, who served as the Abbot of Sponheim and St. James at Wurzburg, may have undercut his argument by using a commercial printing shop to publish his frequent works, including *de Laude Scriptorium*. In the person of Harrington, history has an example of a writer who not only admired the art of handwritten publication, but who committed eleven years to its practice, likely the greatest single output of handwritten newspapers in the United States by anyone.

When someone attempts and accomplishes this rare publishing feat, at least three questions come to mind:

1. Why did Harrington handwrite his periodicals, some up to one hundred times each?
2. How did he manage to handwrite so many?

89

3. Finally, why did John McLean Harrington handwrite seven distinct publications over an eleven-year period, including the Civil War years?[3]

Probably at least four reasons for Harrington's work are at play:

- Harrington wanted to do something noteworthy, and his volume of handwritten newspapers provides ample proof that he accomplished this feat.

- Harrington wanted to make a literary contribution, and his handwritten newspapers supported the literary tradition of the region.

- Harrington wanted to personally amuse himself, and his handwritten newspapers became his own form of entertainment.

- Harrington possessed a psychologically acute storytelling need, and handwritten newspapers fulfilled his need.

HARRINGTON'S WORK AS PROOF OF HIS ACCOMPLISHMENTS

Harrington's reasons for stopping and starting a series of seven periodicals are just as unclear as his reasons for opting to handwrite instead of using a movable-type press. However, if a writer wants the world to know with certainty that he authors a publication, the best evidence is the personal touch of handwriting. Handwriting is among the most personal communication activities available, and the autograph is the most concise example. An autograph can refer to a document completely handwritten by its author or to the author's signature alone. The key is that the document is not typeset or transcribed by another person. The value in the document is that the autograph can be compared to other handwritten documents by the same person to prove authenticity. Included in this notion of authenticity is the idea of the holograph, a term often used to refer to a handwritten last will and testament; however, the term also applies to a document written by the person whose signature it bears. To this day, signing a document is required to establish authenticity and verifiable provenance or origin of the document.

Each time Harrington penned a newspaper, he included his autograph as proprietor, thus establishing a holograph of his work. The signature and handwriting allow for comparisons, and each of Harrington's handwritten newspapers provides more proof that John McLean Harrington was the author. Harrington may have had the weight of authenticity in mind with his holographs, or he may have yearned to leave behind a handwritten legacy.

The economic benefit of publishing without a press may have transcended Harrington's need to sign his work. Harrington may have opted not to use the movable-type press because of the added expense. Because he handwrote each copy, he controlled the waste and produced only enough copies for his subscription list. In the impoverished and somewhat backward South of the antebellum period, Harrington beat the system and left what may be the greatest collection of holographic newspapers in the United States.

HARRINGTON'S WORK AS PART OF THE LITERARY TRADITION OF THE REGION

Harrington's news manuscripts generally were what one historian calls "a primary means for many amateur journalists to stimulate public discourse in communities without printed newspapers or printing businesses"[4] This was the case with Harrington, the amateur journalist of Harnett County. He started and stopped publications as any dabbler would do, yet his handwritten work is the best example of a literal fingerprint any writer can leave as a personal legacy.

He was an active participant in an intellectual wave that passed through North Carolina between 1840 and 1860 and led to the establishment of many literary journals.[5] Most were associated with literary societies of the University of North Carolina at Chapel Hill, but Harrington single-handedly created his own literary journal and newspaper without the benefit of a printing press.

Although a publisher of handwritten newspapers, John McLean Harrington anticipated the popular content of *The Saturday Evening Post* by developing both a literary publication and a political publication.[6] Cyrus Curtis began the modern *Saturday Evening Post* in 1897 by purchasing a nearly defunct magazine. He soon discovered that middle-class men and women both enjoyed the general-interest content.[7] Harrington tried to make his reputation by publishing the same kind of general-interest content as *The Saturday Evening Post* in the years immediately before the Civil War, but not everyone considered his effort a success—at least in terms of "print" quality. An administrator at one historical collection of his works called them "crudely printed." In 1958, a librarian suggested that the "sheets look as if they may be drafts prepared for publication, but no published copies have been found."[8] Indeed, no machine-printed copies have been found even though many handwritten copies exist.

HARRINGTON'S WORK AS PERSONAL AMUSEMENT
AND FOLK ART

Harrington wrote to entertain himself as much as others—at least that's what he said in print. In the Wednesday, May 14, 1862, issue of the *Weekly News,* Harrington noted on page two, "This will probably be the last paper issued for the present. If the document should happen to fall in the hands of anyone [sic] they [sic] must look on them in no other light than an idle pastime." Although Harrington handwrote his work as personal amusement, he also apparently wanted to contribute to public discourse and to be remembered for it. His desire to contribute to society outweighed his need to resort to a printing press.

Harrington the self-conscious writer may have been understating his role. He wanted a stage on which to project his blend of political passion and worldly observations, and he wrote for a community that he hoped would respect him. Harrington's work can be seen as a cross between a private letter he knew others would read and a public performance that showcased his writing talents. This written performance, free of any intermediary such as typesetter, printer, or delivery person, established Harrington's credibility. As a native of western Harnett County, Harrington possessed the best credential: his lifelong connection to the community. His credibility in print depended on his personal reputation with his neighbors.[9]

In his inaugural issue of *The Times.,* Thursday, October 17, 1867, Harrington told readers that he wrote to entertain and inform others and to entertain himself. This straightforward declaration helped solidify his credibility. On page two of the October 17, 1867, issue, Harrington wrote, "We can promise nothing in the beginning of our enterprise, but will spare no pains to please. Our paper is intended for a repository of Pure Literature, Poetry and general news information and as a past time for myself to jot down my thoughts as they may come to the surface." Again, Harrington, the personal editor, appears to be writing largely for his own amusement. His impulse to share his thoughts is the same spirit that drives bloggers of the twenty-first century. He wrote his newspapers as a letter for others, a letter for himself, and a letter for posterity, if for no other reason than to leave his scrawl mark as evidence of his existence.

In a bit of droll from the August issue of *The Young American,* Harrington self-consciously brought his role as the editor to the forefront while amusing himself at the same time. He joked on page two, "An editor in Iowa has become so hollow from depending on the printing business alone for bread that he proposes to sell himself for a stove pipe, at three cents a foot." Harrington may not have savored the life of a poor publisher, yet it likely amused him to share the identity of the overworked publisher with his fellow journalists and readers across the country.

The handwritten copies, all one-of-a-kind works, are a type of art in which the text itself is aesthetically notable. For Harrington, the shape of the lines and the flow of the handwritten letters provided a sense of satisfaction in the visual work that he created. While no framed copies of Harrington's work are available, the pages are artistic enough to be the kind of work that calligraphy collectors sometimes display as art.

HARRINGTON'S WORK AS FULFILLMENT OF HIS STORYTELLING NEED

Harrington also fulfilled the aesthetic function of the press partly through storytelling.[10] He printed election results and other factual news, the "truth values of news," but mostly he published enjoyable content with "consummatory value" that readers enjoyed and used to interpret their own lives.[11] This content helped readers relate to their community through stories chosen to highlight what was important and valued in that community. In his emphasis on storytelling, Harrington anticipated the work of Joseph Pulitzer and the New York *World's* entertainment content.

Harrington went against the tide of his time by refusing to use a printing press, missing out on the benefits that accrue from commercial printing. Unlike Benjamin H. Day, who pioneered his New York *Sun* newspaper in 1833 with one goal in mind—to show how well he could print using his printing press—Harrington had no use for a press. Day emphasized "plenty of advertising"[12] and Harrington filled his publications with advertising, too. But unlike Day, Harrington did not engage in the commercial production of letterhead and calling cards.[13]

In 1833, about 1,200 newspapers were published using a press in the United States and most were, by the standard of the time, quite expensive.[14] By 1850, paper and printing expenses had declined significantly and more than 2,000 newspapers were published in the United States, all printed by a press,[15] with the exception of those of Harrington and possibly a few others.

Harrington worked during the Penny Press era, between 1833 and 1861. The period gets its name from inexpensive newspapers that emphasized news, mass appeal, and political autonomy.[16] The development of high-speed printing presses helped produce cheap newspapers. Day's New York *Sun* was considered the first successful penny daily in 1833[17] because it took advantage of technological advances such as the printing press and the creation of inexpensive paper from wood pulp instead of cloth rags. The popularity of the Penny Press was part of the burgeoning middle class's interest in engaging in society by reading a newspaper at home.[18]

During the pre-Civil War period, with technological changes making publishing less expensive, newspapers became less and less dependent on partisan support. However, the shift from a Party Press, where political parties financed newspapers from 1783 to 1833, to a more politically independent press was probably more the result of changes in society and culture.[19] Harrington's work provides a case study of a small community where a journalist rejected the advances that were common decades earlier and used handwriting over a high-speed press to satisfy reader interest in politics, business, and literature.

Harrington began handwriting newspapers in 1858, near the end of the Penny Press era. He continued publishing off and on during the Civil War (1861–1865). And he ended his handwritten newspapers in 1869 at the beginning of the Industrial Press period (1865–1883). The Industrial Press was marked by independence in the political identities of newspapers, emphasis on the human interest story, and sensationalism.[20] By the end of the Civil War, the "stunning success" of such papers as the *Sun*, Horace Greeley's *New York Tribune*, James Gordon Bennett's *New York Herald*, and Henry Raymond's *New York Times* led many people to think of such newspapers in the Northeastern metropolises as the proper sort of journalism and of the old partisan newspapers as aberrations."[21]

Whether "proper" newspapers or not, Harrington's pre-war papers in 1858 covered a tumultuous period in which he reported the grim news of events from a Southern perspective while giving his readers hope for the future. Following the war, however, he wrote to President Andrew Johnson (1808–1875) insisting that he was a loyal Unionist throughout the conflict. Harrington also switched his political allegiance from the Democrats to Republicans. This dramatic outward change of partisan affiliation complicated the picture of the man who served his rural community as a postmaster, farmer, teacher, and writer. His handwritten publications remain holographs that establish his authenticity as the author, but the papers also raise questions about the true identity of John McLean Harrington and his genuine opinions.

THE SPENCERIAN STYLE OF HANDWRITING

Handwriting, available since the fourth millennium BC, can be viewed "as one index of the history of thought."[22] In addition, when a writer pens a work based on a standard model of handwriting such as the Spencerian model used by Harrington, the work can demonstrate the author's individuality outside the harness of conformity.[23] With these ideas in mind, Harrington's work can be explored partly by examining the handwriting method that he employed, the one that was most common during his day. Harrington's longhand suggests the style of penmanship developed by Platt Rogers Spencer (1800–1864), a New York public official who is credited with originating a style of cursive handwriting that is called "Spencerian."[24] The most enduring visible influence of Spencer's script may be the Coca-Cola logo.[25] The Spencerian writing style can still be found in the widely available Spencerian calligraphy kit as well.

The story of Platt Rogers Spencer possesses a mythical quality. One historian notes that even at an early age Spencer was "was crazy about handwriting but, in a family too poor to provide him with paper, he was forced to practice on leaves and bark, in the snow, and on the sandy beach of Lake Erie, where sometimes his obsessive script would stretch for a half a mile."[26] By 1857, he met President James Garfield when Garfield served in the U.S. Congress, and both hit it off because they opposed slavery.[27] Garfield praised Spencer for both his opposition to slavery and his script, which he called "the pride of our country and the model of our schools."[28] To say Spencer was obsessive about his handwriting doesn't quite capture the utter devotion of his approach; he couldn't look at a leaf or stone without thinking how to turn it into a letter of the alphabet.[29] He wanted his script to be rhythmic and comfortable, a reaction against the tedium of the copperplate style that dominated handwriting at the time. Spencer encouraged his adherents to practice six to twelve hours per day.[30]

First published in 1848, the *Spencerian Key to Practical Penmanship* moved longhand writing from the simple goal of legibility to rapid movements of the hand and arm using an economy of motion that resulted in graceful letters and bold ovals of capital letters.[31] For the half century "from before the Civil War to the end of the Victorian ear, the hegemony of Spencerian was a testament to an appreciation for beauty that lurked in the souls of Americans—an appreciation that was closely tied to upward striving: such an extravagant, impressive, high-class script, such an obvious love of the noble and beautiful—these were surely the mark of a gentleman or lady."[32]

Spencer noticed even as a ten-year-old boy that the most common forms in nature were the oval of the beach pebble and the angle of the waves, and both inspired him to create a form of handwriting.[33] He taught whole-arm movement so that a penman could write for hours and not tire.[34] The use of fifty-two-degree slant and seven basic strokes helped writers achieve the greatest speed in handwriting.[35] Spencer admired the signature of John Hancock on the U.S. Declaration of Independence and used it to develop a system of writing that dominated the public school system for almost one hundred years and influenced his five sons to continue the work after his death. A workbook on mastering the Spencerian method declares that writing is "a secondary power of speech, and they who cannot write are in part dumb."[36] The workbook adds, "Scrawls that cannot be read may be compared to talking that cannot be understood; and writing difficult to decipher, to stammering speech."[37]

Spencer apparently revolutionized handwriting education partly by linking handwriting with high morals and intelligence.[38] No standardized way of writing script existed in the eighteenth century and styles were associated with specific occupations, a gender, or a social class. Spencer considered his approach to handwriting to be an art. His descendant Henry Cable Spencer noted the importance of well-formed handwriting: "He who loves nature and admires all that is truly beautiful, will find in the prosecution and study of this art, something to enlarge and develop the highest faculties of the mind—something to make him more interested in that which pertains to the welfare of those around him. Let, then, every one seek to gain a practical knowledge of this art, and as long as he lives will it be to him a source of pleasure, profit, and improvement."[39]

Spencer followed a long tradition that had begun as early as the seventeenth century, when penmanship self-instruction manuals could be purchased.[40] The practice of penmanship often branched from mere instruction into study at a university or training for a life of commerce.[41] Handwriting was varied and included such diversities as roman style for females and an italic style for affluent men.[42] The styles provided an added benefit by alerting the reader to the gender and status of the writer, which told him or her "the appropriate degree of authority to grant the handwritten word."[43] Women who used the printing press exposed themselves to "every buyer," which was unseemly, "culturally tantamount to prostitution."[44] However, with time the idea of publication in print "was conceptualized as the way public discussion usually and ideally takes place and the mechanism whereby the public itself is constituted."[45]

Before Spencer, handwriting leaders included Benjamin Franklin, whose *The American Instructor* (1748) offered instruction known as copperplate, the style used to etch copper plates for engraving.[46] Franklin founded the Academy of Philadelphia, later the University of Pennsylvania, with the stipulation that if a young man wished to be admitted, he must write a legible hand.[47] By 1803, the metal nib pen supplanted the quill pen, making handwriting much more efficient. This innovation arrived just in time for the Spencerian revolution.[48] Not until 1897 did the first successful fountain pen appear.[49]

In the twentieth century, however, Austen N. Palmer took over dominance in the handwriting field. Spencer's loops and curls, which took time, waned in favor of Palmer's more rapid and plain method.[50] Palmer noticed that the lifted arm movement of the Spencerian method required too much time and too much pain.[51] He eliminated the "wifty [sic] meanderings about flowers and sunbeams. . . ." Palmer declared that his little red book on handwriting "would help American writers be 'good, practical business writers.'"[52] Palmer agreed with Calvin Coolidge that the business of America was business.[53] Yet his approach gained wide support and appealed to Roman Catholic as well as public schools.[54]

Efforts to promote good handwriting continue in the United States. Zaner-Bloser of Columbus, Ohio, offers a program that "delivers developmentally appropriate instruction for students in PreK through Middle School and helps increase overall student achievement."[55] Charles Paxton Zaner and Elmer Ward Bloser have had a lasting impact on American penmanship.[56] Today speed remains a crucial component to handwriting. One scholar reported that a student who "can write quickly and legibly is likely to have more cognitive capacity available for the compositional aspects of writing."[57] Researchers have found that when writers are under pressure, as in a deadline situation, people who excel in handwriting fluency (fast handwriting that is legible) tend to outperform others.[58] Researchers have also found that writers who use handwriting that is rapid and efficient score better on examinations, reportedly because the automated transcription process allows the writer more time for higher-order thinking.[59] Harrington, the dilettante journalist, needed to write fast in order to produce timely copies of his publications for a subscription list that numbered up to one hundred. The output that Harrington achieved suggests that he was a bright, energetic and relatively efficient person. He was also committed to using these talents to publish numerous papers on behalf of the community in which he was raised, without the world stage of the Internet or the easy duplication of modern printers.

9

Harrington as Writer, Businessman, and Politico

John McLean Harrington was a journalist who bridged the oral and literary traditions.[1] He was among the last in a line of American journalists who crossed the gulf between these traditions, but he accomplished this feat without resorting to the use of a printing press. A pioneer media ecologist, he was aware of the current technologies of the day, the modes of information, and the codes of communication, but he chose to use handwriting to delight, inform, and persuade his audience, mainly because handwriting was readily available and, perhaps, because a costly printing press was not at hand.[2] Harrington probably appreciated the personal approach of handwriting newspapers as a means to comfort his audience in an uncomfortable time. His handwriting was partly like a personal letter, communicating insider knowledge that drew on the shared experiences only a small community can enjoy. While his experiments in holding off the printing press and the anti-slavery movement were doomed, Harrington succeeded in creating a rural enclave where the new and old coexisted uneasily. His handwritten work symbolized the disappearing older and to some extent deeply Southern ways of life. The raft that he and his community inhabited eventually capsized in the face of the bigger, faster, and more powerful industrial currents that overcame Harrington and the South.

As Neil Postman argues, "Technology giveth and technology taketh away." Every "new technology sometimes creates more than it destroys. Sometimes, it destroys more than it creates. But it is never one-sided."[3] Postman contends that new technologies can alter the symbolic environment in which the world is socially constructed, particularly through the sensory world of meanings. If that is the case, the opposite could also be true. Harrington's readers experienced the world through the medium of the handwritten text, and their perceptions were shaped by it. While Harrington, the writer, could be geographically separated from his readers, he maintained a residual sense of being one with his audience. Perhaps Harrington's letter-writing style was an intermediate step between Marshall McLuhan's Tribal Age, where the acoustic dominated, and the Age of Literacy, where the visual dominated.[4] McLuhan argued that when oppressed people learned to read, they became independent thinkers. In addition, one may surmise that when oppressed people read *handwritten* newspapers they experience the added bonus of feeling like they have received a personal message; the handwritten words read like a letter meant just for the reader and they work along the lines of a motivational message. Readers feel a kinship with the writer and are inspired to actively participate in their shared life. The handwritten message helps build solidarity in a geographical community that defines itself by what it shares in common—perhaps similar to the ways that online social networks do so today for people across geographic areas.

The content of *The Young American* and *The Nation* of 1858 reveals a lyrical writer. Even at eighteen years of age, Harrington was a creative and ambitious eccentric who used all the resources at his disposal to express himself. In *The Young American,* he borrowed from his literary background to craft a tragic but unsentimental poem of a groom struggling to achieve genuine love. At the same time, as with much other partisan journalism even today (One cable TV network claims to be "fair and balanced," without spin.), his attempt at sloganeering on his nameplate may sound a bit amateurish if not silly, but it also suggests a writer of conviction who was trying to define for his audience who he was and what he aimed to accomplish. Harrington believed in allowing the weaker voices of his community to be heard, but he also firmly believed in democracy's principle of majority rule. Perhaps that is even why he ultimately opposed slavery. In both cases, he labored to be a medium through which the community expressed itself.

As a literary journalist, he addressed in *The Young American* topics that showed that actions have consequences. His short story from January, "An incident of the French Revolution," examined unbridled and unrequited love. "The Bridal Feast," published from May to October of 1858, emphasized the deadly results of duplicitous love and betrayal. The January 1858 issue of *The Young American* included "Rearing Boys," a narrative that scolded parents who did not restrain their children. The love poems throughout the year celebrated the romantic and idealized version of amorous love—a characteristic of the Victorian period. This kind of storytelling revealed both a romantic and a moralistic editor committed to maintaining the social order. Harrington the young bachelor valued the abstract and very Victorian ideals of noble love and heroic living. His later years, when he lived alone and struggled with alcoholism, are a tragic end to a writer of such early promise.

As a reporter, Harrington in *The Young American* was a passive journalist who included news from other periodicals and over-the-transom reports such as local obituaries, weddings, and news of political conventions. However, his editorials rarely concerned politics and focused instead on the hot weather in August or the benefits of reading his publication. This lack of overt ideology became a standard for publications that want to appeal to the greatest number of potential subscribers.

Harrington the thinker loved words, and he wrote as much to entertain himself as he did to supplement his income as a postmaster and a teacher. He was a bit of a show-off who used his publications as a kind of one-man play to establish himself as an authority on all things cultural and moral. No one knows if he succeeded in winning the approval of his readers or his community at large. Nonetheless, as the only local journalist Harrington doubtless impacted his rather isolated but beloved rural area.

Aside from the amazing and enormous achievement of Harrington in handwriting multiple copies of each of his newspapers, his content becomes the next most notable feature of the editor's work. Moreover, the Spencerian method of handwriting, which allows writers to work for long periods without tiring, explains Harrington's ability to make so many copies by hand. But Harrington's papers showcased a writer, thinker, and shrewd businessman who weighed in judiciously on secession and other controversial issues of his day. He seems pro-Confederate at the beginning of the Civil War, but claimed to be pro-Union following that conflict.[5] It took resolve to maintain external clarity in the face of inner dissonance. Harrington displayed the fortitude of a well-educated man living in an isolated rural Southern community, successfully publishing some of the most unusual newspapers in North Carolina's history.

Harrington's handwritten press also emphasized the personal nature of his quest. His words were penned by sinew and muscle over and over again. He developed a strong conviction of the correctness of his own ideas when he absorbed them through constant repetition. Some writers might second-guess themselves, but Harrington was steadfast and wrote his personal messages as if he were producing repetitive letters to a circle of friends.

Harrington's work also reflects the internal struggle that existed in his community, where some confronted cognitive dissonance over slavery. The area in which Harrington lived was the part of Harnett County least suited for slavery. On what side did local people's true allegiance lie in the war? What about Harrington's innermost loyalties? Harrington's true convictions regarding secession remain unknown. His later work suggests that he considered slavery wrong. But records show that Harrington and his family owned slaves. His clearest support for abolition was penned after the Civil War, when the slaves had already been freed. On the front page of *The Times* for April 2, 1869 he wrote that freedom for slaves in Cuba would strengthen both the island and the United States. Was Harrington parroting the prevailing White House policy, or was he revealing his innermost conviction? His amnesty request—which argued that he served as a sub-postmaster to evade Confederate military service—does little to mark him as an heroic figure. Publicizing one position and personally believing a different one is at best expedient and at worst hypocritical, and it casts a shadow on Harrington's role as the inspirational cheerleader for a community battered by need and hungry for hope.

A WRITER WHO KNEW HIS AUDIENCE

Aware of his rural roots, Harrington kept his prose accessible. According to the Flesch-Kincaid readability scale, *The Nation* newspaper was written on the 3.2 grade level while *The Young American* was written on the 8.7 grade level. This readability scale tests reading comprehension. The differences in reading level reflected the wide audiences he hoped to attract—the higher level for the most well-read audience of *The Young American* and the lower level for the politically-active readers of *The Nation*. The Flesch-Kincaid scale also indicates that *The Nation* was easier to read at 77.9 on a scale of 100 while *The Young American* was 66.6 on the same scale. In both cases, an educated teenage reader would have been capable of understanding Harrington's prose. However, Harrington did not use punctuation as it is used today, with commas separating dependent clauses, for instance. Yet, the use of a kind of "p" or "f" for an "s," common in this period, can still be read and understood today. The occasional scratched-out word and odd spelling also does not reduce the readability of his work. In short, Harrington's work was very accessible then as now, although the handwriting is a reading hurdle for some.

The ease of readability coincided with the kinds of topics Harrington covered, whether it was a farm market report, the cost of coffee, the types of merchandise area businesses advertised, news of Europe's royalty, international conflict, or the fate of the *Leviathan* ship. These topics and his local news, humor, fiction, and poetry all reveal a writer who was sensitive to his own community of people who did not travel far from home and who struggled for survival during the last grinding days of slavery. The stories and humor, tame by today's standards, reveal not only the self-deprecating humor Southerners enjoyed, but also that life could always be worse. For example, Harrington's quip about the coffin that could be rented as a room offered a touch of humor to the reader. The joke, however, takes a darker turn when the coffin becomes a frequent sight in a community that began the war impoverished and ended it in financial ruin.

Harrington's written legacy extends beyond the run of *The Young American* and *The Nation* in 1858 and provides insight into his approach to journalism and writing. Harrington's journalism exhibited a European model of modern news reporting where readers expected to get the editor's viewpoint along with news. Harrington feigned impartiality in his first issue of *The Young American,* but his opinions crept in. His editorial voice was unashamedly partisan in *The Nation;* both of his 1858 publications prepared him to be a decisive voice in the years ahead. For instance, by 1860 Harrington adopted a columnist's posture as he wrote about events leading to the Civil War. In the *Weekly News,* published in December of 1860, Harrington described South Carolina's secession from the Union as a "sad day" and said his state of North Carolina should stand strong, regardless of South Carolina's act. Later, in the April 9, 1861, issue of the *Weekly News,* Harrington offered an article from the Raleigh *Standard* about a letter from a man he calls "Gen. Jackson" to a parson in Georgia in 1833. Harrington described Jackson's letter as saying the "disunionists like those in 1833 would seize upon the Negro or slavery issue as the pretext for dissolving the union." These instances, among others, show that Harrington provided timely news and analysis. In general, Harrington produced such content for at least four reasons.

- He was a businessman who worked as a bookkeeper and in a retail business. He understood the idea of consumption and the costs of production versus the profit to be made. For him, the publications were a cost-effective enterprise. Mail deliveries were not as regular as they are today. Harrington, the U.S. postmaster at the community post office, probably had ample time to work on his publications as a kind of part-time job. Without the expense of a printing press or the need to travel outside his office to have his work printed by a movable press, Harrington kept his expenses low. He needed pen and paper and the stamina and dexterity to copy his work over and over. He seemed to understand that handwriting could offer an inexpensive solution to publishing while also serving as a novelty that would impress readers.

- The son of an elected official, Harrington understood the power of politics to influence a person's life. He also understood the need to garner favor. Deliberate personal obfuscation allowed him to keep his friends close and his enemies closer. His work in *The Nation* demonstrated that he cared about the social order, and he worked with missionary zeal to galvanize his readers to vote and work for Democrats. At age eighteen, he was too young to vote, yet he sensed the importance of politics—along with family and religion—in the life of the community. On page two of the June 12 issue of *The Nation,* Harrington reported on a revival in Maine that he said was "progressing with beneficial results." Apparently he respected religion and its role in improving and maintaining the community. His political ambition may have found an outlet when Harrington became sheriff of Harnett County in 1865.[6]

- A well-educated person, Harrington used his periodicals, particularly *The Young American,* as a literary outlet for aspirations likely cultivated through his classical education. Surrounded by farmers, Harrington helped bring a non-elitist sense of culture to his rural area. His readers, while few, were likely the best-educated in the county, perhaps the opinion leaders. By producing two publications in a rural area where education was admired, Harrington elevated himself to the top of the literati. He established himself as the gatekeeper for the area's locally-produced insights. Readers in Harnett County as elsewhere usually would value a local rather than outside voice.

⚜ Harrington lived in a community in denial. A new way of life was coming with its railroads, telegraphs, textiles, and industries dependent on the meshing of mechanical gears. Heavy manual labor represented by unfettered slavery, a staple in the South, would soon be a memory. But the community of 1858 still valued the old ways. By handwriting his newspapers, Harrington provided a visible symbol that the community could participate in the news of the day without having to acknowledge that mechanical industries would dominate the nation of the future. By using a method of production that dated to ancient times, Harrington demonstrated, at least momentarily, that the tide of modernity was not fully inevitable. Creative men and women could compete by using the methods that had served their ancestors. Like today's Amish, the community in which Harrington lived valued the rhythms of traditional agricultural life without engines and mechanical presses. The fact that these farmers could not afford machines did not seem to matter. It was important to defend the preferred old ways known and trusted. Harrington's handwritten papers reinforced the idea that he was personally in control and had authority over their content. His community probably yearned to have some control over their lives and their future in a day when outsiders, an unwelcomed authority, were threatening their way of life.

These four reasons behind Harrington's work suggest four portraits of his journalistic endeavors.

⚜ *The artist-journalist.* In a black-and-white world where the color of one's skin largely determined one's fate, Harrington worked primarily in dark ink and white paper. He was as interested in the look of his dark letters on white paper as he was in what those letters said.

⚜ *Amateur journalist.* Harrington copied more news than he discovered. He offered little original reporting and was satisfied to repeat others' reports. He may be the nation's first type of blogger who couldn't resist the impulse to weigh in, even if he was not a bona fide member of the proper journalistic establishment.

🐦 *Literary journalist.* Harrington was more interested in original literary work than news. Readers may have bought his handwritten newspapers for the news, but they also found original fiction and verse. Harrington wanted to impress his readers with his literary flair more than with his newsgathering prowess.

🐦 *Self-absorbed journalist.* Harrington tried to use his periodicals to establish himself as part of the intelligentsia, but the plan apparently backfired when he had to renounce his role as a firey pre-war Democrat and plead for an identity as a post-war Republican.

Overall, Harrington's hand-penned press was a kind of three-act performance. His first act was to establish himself as a committed Democrat who challenged the dominant approach used by the mainstream printed press. In the second act, he revealed a more literary voice and became less committed to his chosen political party. The final act ended in a reversal; Harrington renounced his years as a Democrat and angled for patronage from the dominant, Republican party. Through the entire play, Harrington maintained his unique approach. His ambivalent politics aside, Harrington never gave up his status as an amateur journalist or a blossoming literary force in the region. He remains one of North Carolina's most underrated artist-journalists.

Harrington's publications did much to reinforce the values of hard work and thrift in a day when farming life was a dirty, back-bruising, and demanding occupation.[7] Harrington portrayed a partisan world and encouraged political participation, but he gave the reader more. His short stories and poetry presented a fantasy world of words far removed from the mundane experiences of everyday life. Harrington used symbols, handwritten marks on a page, to transport his readers to New York, France, England, and beyond. Most readers could not afford a new bonnet and other luxuries, but they likely realized that this other world of consumption existed. Through Harrington's publications, the reader could participate vicariously in the ever-expanding world of consumption, even though that reader may have had mixed feelings about the modern world.

Above all, Harrington successfully addressed life in his rustic community and in a manner that matched the values of his day. The handwritten periodicals were a metaphor for the "can-do," independent nature of a community that did not have enough wealth to machine print a work, as did other communities. The desire to share, belong, and participate in community was probably so strong that handwriting a newspaper—the means of last resort—nevertheless established a sense of shared identity for the community. Harrington contributed to the shared values of his community and left a remarkable legacy of ingenuity, imagination, and commitment. He was part literary-journalist and part news-journalist, presumably as comfortable at writing fiction as he was at publishing news. Whether producing his poetry or prose, Harrington was—and is—an inscrutable figure deserving of attention.

Harrington challenged the publishing conventions of his day, but his archaic approach did not usher in a new era. His work symbolizes the last flicker of the Southern flame of opposition to modernity. The bold protest of rebellion against the change represented by the North failed. Northern armies, backed up by modern capitalistic production, crushed the institution of slavery just as the better printing technologies crushed Harrington's handwritten press. However, the uniformity of printed newspapers could never compete aesthetically with the singular works of art that Harrington handcrafted with their irregular letters and typographical novelties. Harrington produced individualized works during a day when standardization triumphed in everything from printed newspapers to mass-produced military uniforms. Like independent artists today, Harrington took on the newspaper establishment of his era and found himself marginalized. Although Harrington's efforts were doomed, he, like Shakespeare's Hotspur, mounted a valiant struggle. His was a "lost cause" of another type.

UNANSWERED QUESTIONS

Harrington's work is more than an account of the way culture impacted periodicals. Harrington the artist produced unique pieces of art, painted with English letters in a one-of-a-kind "art work." A scholar who studies the typography of the journalist's work may discover newer insights in each reading. What does the canvas of Harrington's periodicals reveal about the writer and the world in which he wrote? Should his one-of-a-kind newspapers be displayed in an art collection as fine or folk art rather than in a collection reserved for old documents?

What about Harrington's helper? Was his helper his younger brother, Sion? Did the younger Harrington handwrite at least three issues of his own newspapers because he yearned to follow the business model of a handwritten paper, because he wanted to perform a service to the community, because of sibling rivalry, or for some other reason? The mystery of Harrington's helper and the mystery of the full year of *The Young American* and the partial year of *The Nation* are baffling. Why did Harrington publish *The Nation* for only a few issues but *The Young American* for the entire year? Harrington used his December 1858 issue of *The Young American* to predict a good 1859, yet he soon suspended publication of both periodicals, only to print one known copy of the *Weekly Eagle* on April 20, 1860, and then begin the *Semi-Weekly News* on June 7, 1860. He produced 182 issues of the *Semi-Weekly News*, which ran until March 2, 1864, only to stop it and begin *The Times.*, which ran from October 17, 1867, until April 2, 1869.

Another unanswered question concerns why Harrington early on gave the appearance that he supported the Confederacy, particularly with respect to slavery. Did he suffer a genuine crisis of conscience, perhaps over time coming to the conclusion that the South was wrong and that the slaves deserved justice? Or did he admit his true feelings only after his career was threatened? Perhaps he discontinued his publishing because the community rejected his reversal of support or his appearance of subterfuge. If that is the case, did he abandon his calling as an editor to faithfully report the war and provide his personal perspective? By apparently feigning support for the Confederacy, did he unduly confuse, even hurt his readers? As the voice of the community, was Harrington a fraud? And does this issue of allegiance even matter, given that much of his content included entertainment such as his original short stories and poetry?

Despite these fascinating questions, John McLean Harrington was a champion of the free press. He left a handwritten legacy for generations to come, but his complicated life and work need deeper exploration. No one could ask a journalist to take a more basic approach to getting the news circulated. He may be one of the nation's greatest example of the independent journalist, publishing the news despite his lack of the typical news-printing apparatus. With only a pen in hand, Harrington ultimately made his mark, not primarily as an editor-reporter, but as a unique and eccentric literary figure who foreshadowed the similarly far-reaching, compulsive, and sometimes baffling world of online blogging.

APPENDIX A

*Photographs and
Transcription of
"The Nation", first issue*

The Nation

The majority must rule; the minority must submit,

Vol 1   Buffalo Springs April 17th 1858,   no 1

J. ML Harrington Ho. $2 Per Year
Editor and Proprietor   in advance.

A word to our democratic friends, the time fast approaching when the nominations should be made by the democracy of this and other counties of suitable persons a person by the party for both branches of the legislature, occupying the position that we do it becomes our duty to urge upon the members of the party in each captain's district, the importance of holding primary meetings in order to appoint delegates to the county conventions so that satisfactory nominations may be made and that the party be thoroughly organized.

Our friends in Cumberland Harnett should remember that the work of May superior court for this county is drawing near and they should commence holding their district meetings at once, and send delegates to reflect their respective wishes.

It is not for us to dictate to the good people of this or any other county, who is the most suitable person or persons to represent their our province is to call their attention to the importance of thorough organizations of the party so as to insure specific. We care not what names you use so that they are good and true democrats, and men who will exert themselves in behalf of this section using their best endeavors to obtain state aid to enable Fayetteville, not only to continue the rail Road to the Coal

The Nation

The Majority must rule; the Minority must Submit,

Vol 1 —— Buffalo Springs April 17th 1858, —No—1—

J. W. Harrington &c.
   Editors & Proprietors

$2 Per Year
in advance.

A Word to our democratic Friends. The time is fast approaching when nominations should be made by the democracy of this and other Counties of suitable persons to run by the party, for both branches of the Legislature, Occupying the position that we do it becomes our duty to urge upon the members of the party in each Captain's district, the importance of holding primary meetings in order to appoint delegates to the County Convention, so that satisfactory nominations may be made and that the party may be thoroughly organized,

Our friends in Cumberland and Garrett should remember that the south of May Superior Court for this County, is drawing near

and they should commence holding their district meetings at once, and send delegates to reflect their respective wishes

It is not for us to dictate to the good people going to any other County, who is the most suitable person or persons to represent them

Our province is to call their attention to the importance of thorough organization of the party so as to insure success, We care not what names you run so that they are good and true democrats, and men who will exert themselves in behalf of this section using their best endeavors to obtain State aid to enable Fayetteville, not only to complete the rail Road to the Coal

The Nation

Fields, but also extend
it 100 miles beyond if necessary. We have men in the
party who can and will
carry out this project if
they are elected. Let
our friends in this and Harnett County see to it that
such men are nominated.

The Democracy of
Moore, Robeson, Sampson and
Bladen ought also to busy
themselves and have county
conventions for the purpose
of making suitable nomi-
nations. Remember that it
is by organizing in time that
you will be most likely to succeed.

Delay is dangerous and
will probably bring about
defeat. We hope the party
in these counties will
commence at once to hold
Their district meetings.

North Carolinian
well done Carolinians. You
have took up the notion
rightly if we can get a
convention in this county,
we will be prepared to defeat
the opposite party. There
will be a convention held in
all the districts in this county.

Mr. McRae at
Salisbury
we learn from the Carolinian that this gentleman
delivered his district plea-
d at Salisbury on the
26th. The "Watchman"
appears to have been highly
delighted with it.
The "Banner" speaks of it as
A very ordinary affair in
point of forcible argument,
But says it was quite flowery
& c. From what we can
gather, the oratory was
similar to those delivered
["this" scratched out]
by Mr. McRae in Fayetteville and
other Places

A search for legislators,
an old member of the Pennsylvania Legislature, who
maintained his seat [scratched out word]
and popularity for several
years, always voted "no" said
he, when asked his reason
when a good law passes,
no one looks for the yeas
and nays on it. When a
bad one does, they alw-
ays do.

The early bird catches the worm.

The Nation

fields, but also extend it 100 miles beyond if necessary, we have men in the party who can and will carry out this project if they are elected, let our friends in this and adjoining Counties see to it that such men are nominated. The Democracy of Moore, Robeson, Sampson and Bladen ought also to better themselves and have county conventions for the purpose of making suitable nominations. Remember that it is by organizing in time that you will be most likely to succeed.

Delay is dangerous and will probably bring about defeat, we hope the party in these Counties will commence at once to hold their district meetings.

North Carolinian Well done Carolinian you have took up the notion rightly if we can get a convention in this county we will be sure to defeat the opposite party, there will be a convention held in all the districts in this county.

Mr McRae at Salisbury

We learn from the Carolinian that this gentleman delivered his distribution speech at Salisbury on the 25th ult, the "Watchman" appears to have been highly delighted with it. The "Banner" speaks of it as a very ordinary affair in point of forcible arguments, but says it was quite flowery &c. From what we could gather the address was similar to those delivered by Mr McRae in this and other Places.

A secret for legislators, An old member of the Pennsylvania Legislature, who maintained his seat and popularity for several years, always voted "no" said he, when asked his reason. When a good Law Pfs, no one looks for the yeas and Nays on it. When a bad one does they always do.

The early bird catches the worm

The Nation

The Nation

Buffalo Springs,
Saturday April 17th, 1858

Salutory
In commencing the labors
of an editor, we would like
to say to those who are
always find flaws
with what an Editor says,
what we will not pretend
to have everything in accor-
dances with "theory," [word unclear] but
to all such we would say
"view us not with a critic's eye,
but pay [word unclear] affections by,"
with this first kind
friends we hope you will
understand. But as
we were saying, we have
got the voice of a
little democrat to Edit
this paper whose name we
will suppress for a while.
But allow him to say
that he will endeavor to
do the best he can to promote the cause of the dem-
cratic party. We intend
to keep that thought forward.
let it please whom it may.

Or displease whom it may.
we will stop for the present.

We refrain from going
to press early in the day
to give the particulars
of the meeting of the democracy of this district.
The following delegates were
appointed to meet there
in Fayetteville in the
second Monday in
May next John Harr-
ington and J. Cameron
George McGaegon on mo-
tion of David McCormick and seconded
by J. ML Harrington the Chairm-
an was Jno W. Cameron was
added to the list of del-
agation on motion this
meeting adjourned. We will
give full particulars as
soon as received.
A democratic meeting will
be held at the store of
J. M. Monary on Saturday the
22th of April to send delegates
to the county convention
to nominate candidates for the
general assembly.
Many Citizens
April 22, 1858

The Nation

The Nation
Buffalo Springs,
Saturday April 17th 1858

Salutory
In commencing the Labors
of an editor we would like
to say to those who are
always trying to pick flaws
with what an Editor says
That we will not pretend
to have everything in acc-
-ordance with "Reagle" but
to all such we would say
view us not with a critics Eye,
But pass our imperfections by "
with this hint kind
friends we hope you will
understand, But as
we were saying we have
got the Divorce of a
little democrat, to Edit
this paper whose name we
will represent for a while
But allow him to Say
that he will indeavor to
do the best he can to pro-
-mote the cause of the democratic Party, we intend
to keep I right forward.
let it please whom it may

or displease whom it may
we will stop for the present.

we refrain from going
to press early in the day,
to give the particulars
of the meeting of the dem-
-ocracy of this dashrick
the following delegates were
appointed to met those
in Fayetteville on the
second monday in
may, next John Har-
-ington, J. Cameron
Gorry McGregor, on mo-
-tion of Daul McCormick & seconded
by J McHunington the Chairm
-an was Jno W. Cameron was
added to the list of del-
egation on motion the
meeting adjourned, we will
give full particulars as
soon as received

A democratic meeting will
be held at the Store of
Jim ____ on Saturday the
17th of April to send delegates
to the County Convention
to nominate Candidates for the
general Opembly.
Many Citizens
April 2nd 1858

The Nation

A Democratic Meeting
will be held at the store
of J & D. G. Worth's on Saturday the 17th of April for
The purpose of sending delegates to the county convention to nominate cand-
idates to represent us in
The next general assembly-
April 2nd 1858   Many Citizens

Wit and Humor,
"A little nonsense now and then
is needed by the best of men."

"The victory is not always with
the strong as the boy said,
When he killed the Skunk
with a brickbat."
  Domestically speaking of
new jobs, Boarding houses,
signs, you can tell when
they get a new cook by
the color of the hairs in
the Briscuit, doesticks (unclear)
has been 'round some.
      A Yankee proposes to
Print a paper called the
"Gridiron." Politicians
had better be on the alert,
or they may be "done
up Brown."

Rates of Advertising
4 cts. per line for the first and
2 cents per line for each subsequent
insertion, double column adver-
tisement-8 cts for first and 4 cts.

J. & D. G. Worth
      Owners [word unclear] to
J. Worth and Sons
      Dealers in
Dry Goods Hats and [word unclear]
      Book and Shoes
And Ready Made Clothing
Groceries etc.   Buffalo Springs, N.C.
April 1. # 1 t

      Worth and Willey
      General
   Commission Merchants
      Fayetteville
J. A. Worth #1t N.C. Jod [word unclear] Atty
      The Nation
This first-class Journal
will be printed hereafter
weekly. It contains as
much reading matter as
most any of the papers of
the present day.
      It will be strictly
Democratic-
Terms $2 per year,
Clubs of this and upwards
J. ML. Harrington, Ed.
      Buffalo Springs, N.C

The Nation

A Democratic meeting
will be held at the store
of J & D.G. Worth on Saturday the 17th of April for
the purpose of sending delegates to the County convention to nominate candi-
dates to represent us in
the next general assembly.
April ——   Many Citizens

First rate Humor,
"a little nonsense now and then
is relished by the best of men"

The victory is not always with
the strong, as the boy said,
when he killed the skunk
with a brickbat.

Doesticks speaking of
New York Boarding houses,
says you can tell when
they get a new cook by
the color of the hairs in
the Biscuits, doesticks
has been round some.

A yankee proposes to
print a paper called the
"Gridiron." Politicians
had better be on the alert,
or they may be "done
up Brown."

Rates of Advertising
11 cts per line for the first
1 cent per line for each subsequent insertion. double column advertisement — 8 cts for first and 4 cts

E. & D.G. Worth
One door to
D. Worth & Son,
Dealers in
Dry Goods Hats caps
Boots and Shoes
and Ready Made Clothing,
Groceries &c
Buffalo Spring N C
April 1, $1 — 1t

Worth & Utley
General
Commission Merchants
Fayetteville
J. A. Worth $1—1t N.C. Jos Utley

The Nation
this first class Journal
will be printed hereafter
weekly. It contains as
much reading matter as
most any of the Papers of
the present day.
It will be strictly
Democratic.
Terms $2 Per Year,
Clubs of ten and upwards $1.50 ea
J. M. L. Harrington & Co
Buffalo City N.C

APPENDIX B

Photographs and Transcription of "The Young American", first issue

The

Young   American

<table>
<tr><td>Volume 1</td><td>No. 1</td></tr>
</table>

January 1858

Price 20 Cents

John M.L. Harrington

Editor & Proprietor

Published By

John M.L. Harrington

Buffalo Springs

NC

cover

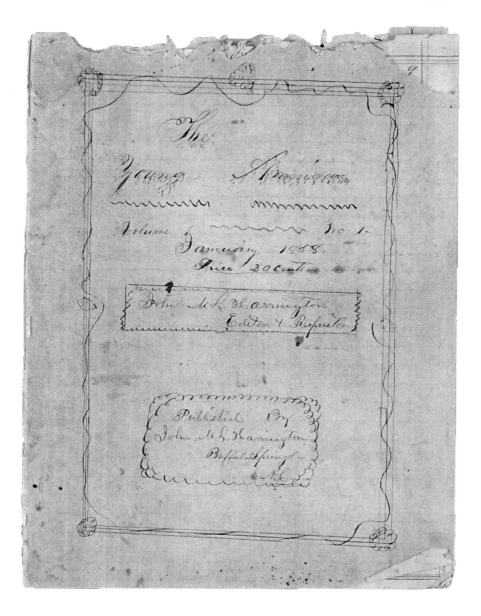

No. 1 Contents Vol.1

January 1858

Title Page		1
An incident of the French Revo		
Lution, Founded on Fact		2
Odds and ends		12
Foreign News		13
Ourselves	Editorial	14
North Carolina		15
Editorial		16
Reader		16
The Leviathan		17
Death of an Editor		18
How Long		18
Oh! Sing again	(Poetry)	19
Littles on Nothings		20
Epigram		20
Spittin on the Floor	(Poetry)	21
Thanatos	(Poetry)	22
Humorous		23
Hard Times	(Poetry)	24
Riddle		25
Literary Notices		26
Advertisements		27

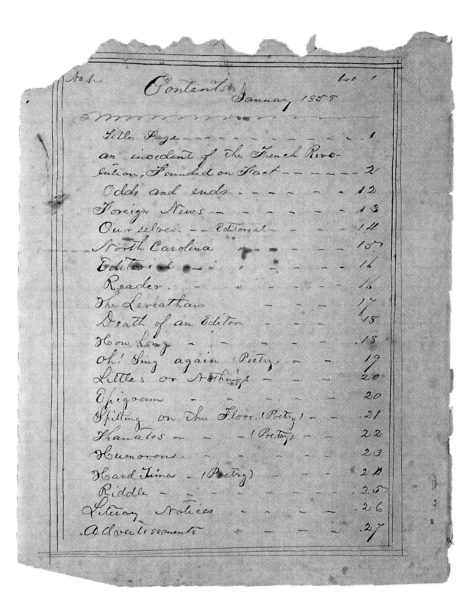

No 1   Contents   Vol. 1
                        January 1858

Title Page - - - - - - - - - - - 1
An incident of the French Revo-
lution, Founded on Fact - - - - - - 2
Odds and ends - - - - - - 12
Foreign News - - - - - - 13
Ourselves - - Editorial - - - 14
North Carolina - - - - - 15
Editorial - - - - - - 16
Reader - - - - - 16
The Leviathan - - - 17
Death of an Editor - - - 18
How Long - - - - - 18
Oh! Sing again (Poetry) - - 19
Littles or Nothings - - - 20
Epigram - - - - - 20
Spitting on the Floor (Poetry) - - 21
Thanatos - - - (Poetry) - - 22
Humorous - - - - - 23
Hard Time (Poetry) - - - 24
Riddle - - - - - - 25
Literary Notices - - - - 26
Advertisements - - - - 27

The Young American

"No pent up ethic contracts our powers,
For the whole boundless Continent is ours"

Devoted to the News of the day poetry prose, Original and
selected pieces comical says of various persons & c-

Neutral in politics and Religion-

John M L Harrington

     Editor and Proprietor

Terms. Two dollars in

advance. three at the end of the year

Vol 1   Buffalo Springs N.C.   January 1st 1858   No 1

Terms

$2 dollars	in	advance		The club money
4 copies for $5 "	"			must invariably be paid
10 " " 10 "	"			in advance—Ed.

Rates of advertising

One Dollar per square of twelve lines

for the 1st and twenty five cents for each subsequent

insertion. Business & professional

of five lines & for one year longer ones in proportion.

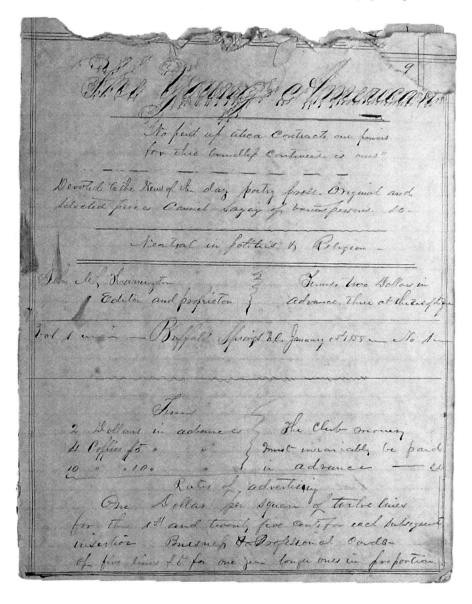

The Young American

Miscellaneous

"Unless some sweetness at the bottom lie

who cares for the crumbling of the pie."

An incident of the French Revolution

Founded on Fact

The Countess Villeneuve de La Floret was

one of the most beautiful and accomplished women in

France and the Count her husband, was the very followers

of the old nobles. Before her marriage she had the

misfortune to become acquainted with a young officer named

Pierre Duhem, who at once conceived for her violent attach

ment. Her heart, however, had long since been bestowed

upon the young Count de La Floret, and even had not that been the

case, it is scarcely probable that Duhem's heart would have

met with a more favorable reaction for there was nothing

in either his appearance or attitude to win the regard of a

young girl whose very thought had been from earliest youth associated

with intellect and refinement for his manners were brusque

and almost rude, and to would not have required a very

shrewd psychomonical to read indelibly stamped upon his

hard featured face unmistakable evidence of a cruel disposition

and how true an index his countenance was of his heart

the legend with will abundantly show.

His attractions were of course

discouraged by the lady, but nevertheless he insisted

The Young American

Miscellaneous —

"Unless some ———— dwell of at the bottom lie
Who cares for the crumbling of the tie."

An incident of the French Revolution.

Founded on fact ————

The Countess de Villeneuve de La Fleret was
one of the most beautiful and accomplished women in
France, and the Count her husband, was the very flower
of the old noblesse. Before her marriage she had the
misfortune to become acquainted with a young officer named
Pierre Duhem, who at once conceived for her a violent attach-
ment. Her heart however, had long since been bestowed
upon the young Count de La Fleret, and even had not that been the
case, it is scarcely probable that Duhem's suit would have
met with a more favorable reception, for there was nothing
in either his appearance or address to win the regard of a
young girl whose every thought from earliest youth associated
with intellect and refinement, for his manners were brusque
and almost rude, and it would not have required a very
shrewd physiognomist to read indelibly stamped upon his
hard featured face unmistakable evidence of a cruel disposition
and how true an index his countenance was of his heart
The sequel will abundantly show.

His attentions were of course
discouraged by the Lady, but nevertheless he insisted

The Young American
upon making her a tender of his hand, which she declined
with firmness, but at the same time with great kindness and consideration
assuring him that she felt deeply grateful for his earnestly expressed
admiration and hoped he would yet find one more worthy than
her self to become his bride.

Duhem listened with apparent
calmness to her words, but a keen observer would have compre-
hended by the deadly pallor that over spread his brow and the
nervous twitching of his thin bloodless lips for the fearful
out break that followed.

"Is this your final irrevocable determination," he asked in a low,
hissing tone at the sometime seizing her arm roughly.

"It is," she answered, and would have proceeded further
in her attempt to conciliate him, but he interrupted her fiercely.

"Listen to me," he cried and she shrank back trembling
from his cold flashing grey eyes. "Listen to me, you triumph now,
but mark me, my day will yet come. I curse you from the
bottom of my heart and my own hand and brain will
work out the fulfillment of that curse. If you ever wed,
I will gloat over the dying agony of your husband.
If you are ever the mother of a child these hands shall
crush its young life before your eyes."

"Leave me; Leave me," was all she had strength to say.

He only held her white arms together in his
iron grasp and hissed closer in her ear;

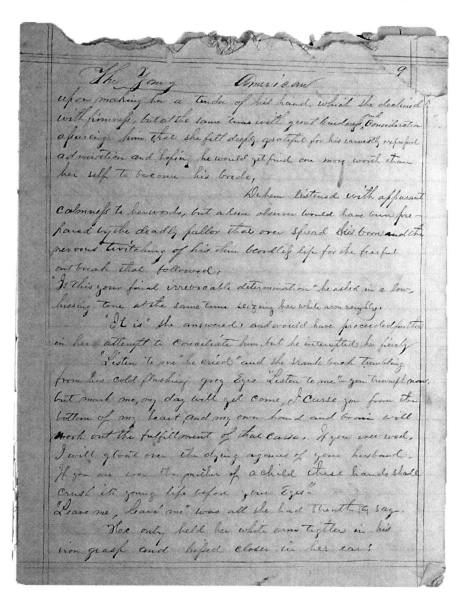

The Young American

"You think that those are vile threats: but so sure as the
sun is in the Heaven, will I make them a terrible truth.
Woman you have made a demon of me. Tremble, tremble
at the fiend you have yourself raised up." So saying she
dashed her from him and rushed from the house.

Time passed on, and as the happy wife
of the Count De La Floret. The terrible scene that
so shortly preceded her marriage was almost erased
from her memory, and nothing occurred to mar the
serenity of her every day life until the out break of the
Revolution that fearful saturnalia of blood that spread
terror and desolation over all Europe.

In common with others the young Count and his
lovely wife were forced to fly before the exasperation populace.
Assisted by a devoted friend who though warm Republican
remained true to them and succeeded in effecting their
escape from Paris. And aided by the papers he had
procured reached unharmed the little village of Collure.
After spending a night in this place, they once more set out
on their journey towards the coast was suddenly, at
the outskirts of the town the carriage was stopped by a
platoon of soldiers drawn up before the horses' heads.

Count De La Floret spoke a word of
encouragement to his terrified wife and was about to spring
out to enquire why they were stopped when they carried papers.

page 4, left side

The Young American

"You think these are idle threats; but so sure as the Sun is in the Heaven, will I make them a terrible truth. Woman you have made a demon of me—tremble, tremble at the fiend you have yourself raised up." So saying, he dashed her from him and rushed from the house,

Time passed on, and as the happy wife of the count de La Fleur, the terrible scene that so shortly preceded her marriage was almost erased from her memory, and nothing occured to mar the serenity of her every day life, until the out break of the Revolution—that fearful saturnalia of Blood that spread terror and desolation over all Europe.

In common with others the young Count and his lovely wife were forced to fly before the exasperated populace. Assisted by a devoted friend who though a warm Republican remained true to them they succeeded in effecting their escape from Paris, and aided by the Passes he had procured reached unharmed the little village of Coline.

After passing a knight in this place, they once more set out on their Journey towards the Coast when suddenly, at the outskirts of the town the Carriage was stopped by a platoon of soldiers drawn up before the horses' heads.

Count de La Fleur spoke a word of encouragement to his terrified wife, and was about to spring out to enquire why they were stopped when they carried papers—

The Young American
from The National assembly when suddenly that carriage
door was torn open a harsh voice commanding them
both to alight.

Perceiving that resistance was worse than useless, the
Count stepped out and assisted his wife follow. Almost
instantly he was rudely seized by two soldiers, while
he who had conducted the outrage approached close
to the unhappy couple threw aside his plumed hat brushed
the tangled mess of hair back from his dark brow
and standing full in the light of the rising sun
demanded of her if she had any reflections of ever meeting
him before? She looked up earnestly in his face for
one instant and then with a cry of anguish fell on her
knees before him "Yes, yes we have met before. Spare us!
Spare us! Oh, spare us"!
The wretch answered with a brutal laugh. "So the
beautiful and proud Countess De La Floret kneels, kneels to me!
It was I who knelt when we last met.

She only replied through her tears "Do be generous. Forget the
past and save us."
"My name is Pierre Duhem, once a poor captain in the
King's Army, now General under the glorious republic.
I swore an oath that if you ever married mortal man,
except me, I would revel in his dying agonies. The
time for the fulfillment has arrived."

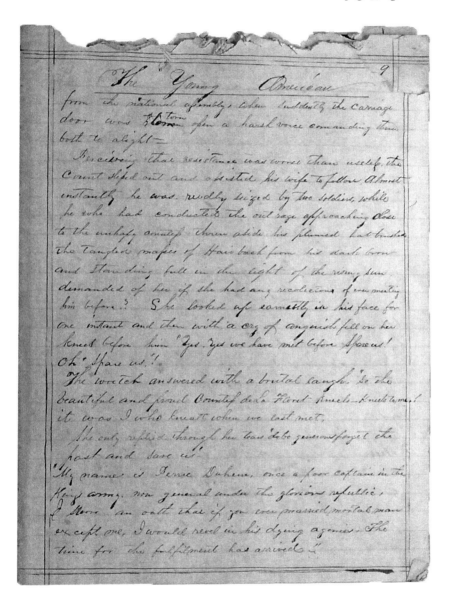

The Young American

from the national assembly, when suddenly the carriage door was thrown open a harsh voice commanding them both to alight—

Perceiving that resistance was worse than useless, the Count slipped out and assisted his wife to follow. Almost instantly he was rudely seized by two soldiers, while he who had conducted the outrage approaching close to the unhappy couple threw aside his plumed hat brushed the tangled masses of Hair back from his dark brow and standing full in the light of the rising sun demanded of her if she had any recollections of ever meeting him before? She looked up earnestly in his face for one instant and then with a cry of anguish fell on her knees before him "Yes. yes we have met before Spare us! Oh Spare us."

The wretch answered with a brutal laugh "So the beautiful and proud Countess de La Florit kneels—kneels to me! it was I who knelt when we last met.

She only replied through her tears "Oh be generous forget the past and save us"

"My name is Pierre Duhene, once a poor captain in the King's army. now general under the glorious republic, I swore an oath that if you ever married mortal man except me, I would revel in his dying agonies. The time for the fulfilment has arrived."

The Young American

"Oh, unsay those terrible words, have mercy! In heaven's
name, have mercy!" shrieked the countess clasping his knees
and turning her streaming eyes up to him.

"Rise love, do not debase yourself by saying
to such a wretch" the count said struggling in vain
to free himself as he spoke we are protected by letters
from The National assembly let him violate them
at his peril.
Duhem looked around at the speaker with at
fierce stare. "That for yourself" he cried snapping
his fingers. "Soldiers away with the aristocrat, obey
the orders that I gave you an hour ago."

At the word the wretches who panted for the
blood of a noble dragged the count a short distance
toward a frame barn and having torn his clothing
from his body, they actually in broad daylight
and before the face of his agonized wife, nailed or
rather crucified him to the wall of a barn, and
a company of soldier-citizens amused themselves by
firing at him eight hours before death made
them insensible to their atrocities. For by their
commander's stern orders they aimed only at the
count's leg thighs feet neck and right side of
the breast and to make the agony more lingering
ten men only were to fire during each hour, and
at the distance of eighty steps.

The Young American

Oh unsay those cruel words, Oh have mercy, in heavens name, have mercy! shrieked the countess clasping his knees and turning her streaming eyes up to him.

"Rise love, do not debase yourself by suing to such a wretch" the count said, struggling in vain to free himself, as he spoke "we are protected by letters from the national Assembly let him violate them at his peril.

Duhem looked around at the speaker with a fierce sneer, "That for your pass" he cried snapping his fingers. "Soldiers away with the aristocrat, obey the orders that I gave you an hour ago."

At the word the wretches who panted for the blood of a noble, dragged the count a short distance toward a frame barn, and having torn his clothing from his body, they actually, in broad daylight, and before the face of his agonized wife, nailed or rather crucified him on the wall of a barn; and a company of soldier-citizens amused themselves by firing at him for eight hours before death made him insensible to their atrocities. For by their commander's orders they took aim only at the counts legs thighs feet neck and right side of the breast and to make the agony more lingering ten men only were to fire during each hour, and at the distance of eighty steps.—

137

The Young American

During all this time Duhem remained seated
on a pile of stones exulting in excruciating
tortures he caused to be inflicted upon his victim.

Now he would deliberately smoke his pipe and
anon drink his wine, or eat his food which he
caused to be brought out to him in order that
he might not loose one thread; and to add to
the horror, the wretch caused the agonized
wife to be forcefully detained in full view of fearful sight, until utterly prostrate both in mind and
body she was borne insensible from the scene
and placed in the care of her faithful waiting
woman who did everything in her power to mitigate
her cruel suffering.
Observing at last that the unhappy nobleman was dead
Duhem ordered that body to be taken down and
a large fire to be kindled in the market place
upon which the corpse was placed until it was completely
roasted. After this horrible to relate all the
young ladies of the place were assembled together
although it was now quite late at night and
under pain of instant death obliged by Duhem
who did the honors of the table to give their
opinions of the flavor of the flesh of a
roasted aristocrat.

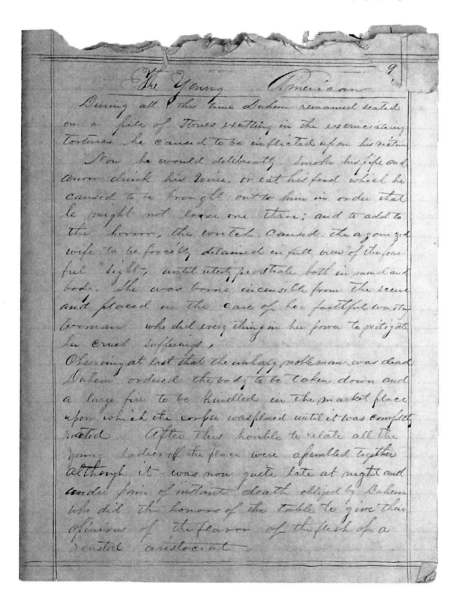

The Young American
No sooner was the fearful feast ended than
a fraternal dance began, and twenty young women who
from terror fell into fits, were only saved from becoming
victims to an another auto-da-fe by the liberality
of their friends who for furiously [phrase unclear] qualities of
twice to these monsters drowned them all at length
in devious sleep.
During the night that succeeded this terrible day
the countess gradually recovered her consciousness and
appeared total, oblivious to what had passed.
Taking advantage of her temporary calmness, her maid
having hired a faithful guide, conducted her
mistress to Dijon where she possessed a house.

    Nearly a week elapsed before the miserable
wife seemed to recall any manner the horrors
she had witnessed, but at length an awakening
from a sound sleep, she related minutely all that
had occurred saying that she had just dreamed in and thanked heaven that it was
but a vision of her disturbed fancy. She
then asked if any letters had arrived from
her husband, who she said had been dispatched on a foreign mission, of great importance.

    But her trials were not yet ended within
a month after her return to Dijon she was
with her maid arrested and shortly after in a convent,

The Young   American

...women was this fearful feast ended than a fraternal dance began, and twenty young women who from terror fell into fits, were only saved from becoming victims to another auto-da-fe - by the liberality of their friends who furnished immense quantities of wine to these monsters drowned them all at length in burnish sleep.

During the night that succeeded this terrible day the countess gradually recovered her consciousness and appeared totally oblivious of what had passed. Taking advantage of her temporary calmness, her maid having hired a faithful guide, conducted her mistress to Dijon where she found a house.

Nearly a week elapsed before the miserable wife seemed to recall in any manner the horrors she had witnessed, but at length on awaking from a sound sleep she related minutely all that had occurred saying that she had just dreamed it and thanked heaven that it was but a vision of her disturbed fancy; she then asked if any letters had arrived from her husband, who she said had been dispatched on a foreign mission, of great importance.

But her trials were not yet ended within a month after her return to Dijon she was with her maid arrested and shut up in a convent,

The Young American
transformed by the republicans into a prison.

During her confinement she was attacked by a
brain fever and by this disease her life was preserved
for during its continuance, the Committee of The Public
Safety sent orders to transport her with other suspect-
ted aristocrats to the Concierge at Paris and
thence to the guillotine. When however the members
of the committee arrived at the Dijon they found her raving
and yielding to the entreaties of her aid [unclear], contented for
the present not to remove her, and she was then overlooked
until the death of Robespierre took the national
seal [unclear] of her prison, and she was permitted to return
to her house.

The countess was in 1801 as collected as at any
period of her life, except when any question was
discussed concerning the Revolution and its horrors
which she considered but a fearful dream of her own.

She believed Louis XVI still reigning upon the
throne of his ancestors and her own husband, still
absent on his important mission from his King.

Bonaparte was in her opinion was a purely imaginary
being and all the changes she perceived around her
were supposed to be merely inventions or undertaking
to delude her. When she heard any one complaining
of her hopes of dear friends on the sequestration of estates

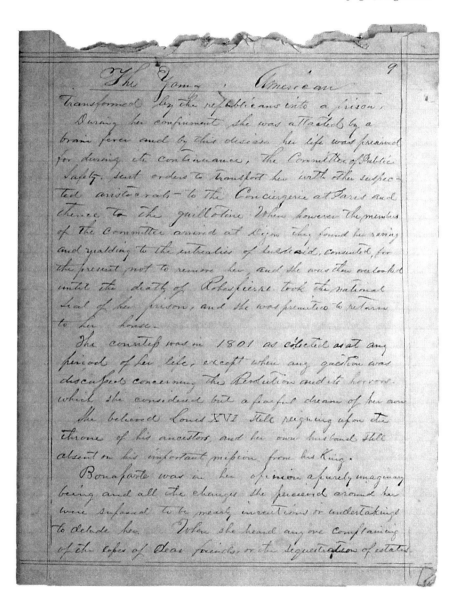

10   The Young American
by the Revolution she would exclaim "Mon dieu, I
would I had never told that terrible dream; how
many, many people it narration has made insane.

One day however she insisted upon visiting Paris,
in order that she might discover how much
longer the count would be detained abroad. Nothing
that could be urged by her friends could induce her
to forego this journey, so she set forth. It was a
glorious morning that on which the countess de la Floret
approached Paris, the sun shone bright and clear and
the verdure [words unclear] of early summer clothed the trees and meadows.

Before reaching the gates however the vehicle was
stopped by a long procession of soldiers followed by
crowds of excited people. The countess looked forth
in utter astonishment. Everything was new to her, the
uniform of the soldiers the tri color banners, the
soul stirring Marsaillaise; and from the varying emot-
ions depicted upon her still beautiful face, her friends
began to fear pleasing delusion she had so long cher-
ished was about to be dispelled. The carriage
has become so embargoed in the crowd that
either to advance or retire was impossible and there
fore no alternative presented itself but to remain
and watch their proceedings.
It soon became apparent that a military execution
was about to take place, and they were situated as

10 The Young — American

by the Revolution she would exclaim "Woe then I
would I had never told that terrible dream! how
many, many people its narration has made insane;"
One day however she insisted upon visiting Paris
in order that she might discover how much
longer the Count would be detained abroad; nothing
that could be urged by her friends could induce her
to forego this journey; so she set forth. It was a
glorious morning that on which the Countess de la Pluvt.
approached Paris, the sun shone bright and clear and
the verdure of early summer clothed the trees and meadow

Before reaching the gates however the vehicle was
stopped by a long procession of soldiers followed by
crowds of excited people; The countess looked forth
in utter astonishment — everything was new to her, the
uniforms of the soldiers, the tri color banners the
soul stirring Marsaillaise; and from the varying emot-
ions depicted upon her still beautiful face, her friends
began to fear the pleasing delusion she had so long cher-
ished was about to be dispelled. The Carriage
had become so embarrassed in the crowd that
either to advance or retire was impossible and therefore no alternative presented itself but to remain
and watch their proceedings;

It soon became apparent that a military execution
was about to take place, and they were so situated as-

145

The Young American

to obtain a full view of it. The soldiers were
formed into line the drums beat, and presently
a man with head bare and dressed only in pantaloons
and shirt was led by to the gen. de-arms into the field.
As he passed the coach the countess started, passed
her hand over her eyes and looked forth intently.

"Great Heaven!" she murmured, "What does
all this mean; that man; that I have seen that
man before, was it not a dream then not a dream.

With a wild heart rending shriek she
broke away from her friends and sprang from the
carriage, by this time the criminal had been forced to kneel down before the platoon of soldiers, and
a bandage was being placed over his eyes. Breaking like a
tiger through the barrier the countess darted forward
and tore away the handkerchief from the doomed
man's face! Then gazing at him for an instant with
a fixed look [unclear] absolutely appalling, she cried.

"Pierre Duhem is it thou? Heaven be praised we meet again!" Then without pausing she
rushed [unclear] quickly to the commanding officer and asked in
an excited voice, "Is he to die?"
"He is Spare yourself the trouble for no entreaties
can save him, thief and murderer that he is"

"Save him—Save him!" she shrieked hysterically.

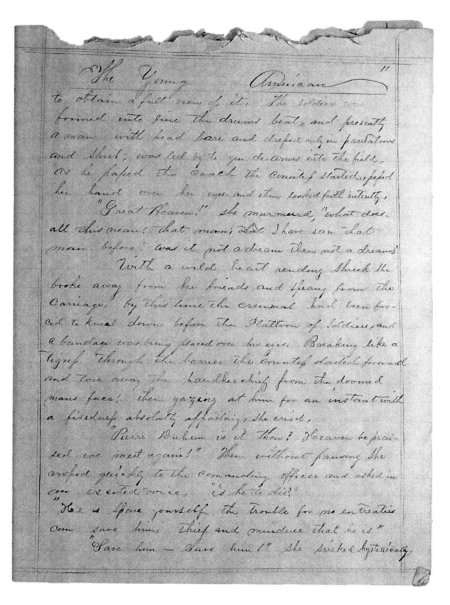

The Young American

to obtain a full view of it. The soldiers were formed into line the drums beat, and presently a man with head bare and dressed only in pantaloons and shirt; was led by the gen de-arms into the field. As he passed the Coach the Countess started, passed her hand over her eyes and then looked forth intently.

"Great Heaven!" she murmured, "what does all this mean? that man; But I have seen that man before! Was it not a dream then not a dream?

With a wild heart rending shriek she broke away from her friends and sprang from the Carriage, by this time the criminal had been forced to kneel down before the Platoon of Soldiers, and a bandage was being placed over his eyes. Breaking like a tigress through the barrier the countess darted forward and tore away the handkerchief from the doomed mans face! then gazing at him for an instant with a fixedness absolutely appalling, she cried,

"Pierre Duhem is it thou? Heaven be praised we meet again!" Then without pausing she crossed quickly to the commanding officer and asked in an excited voice, "is he to die?"

"He is spare yourself the trouble for no entreaties can save him, thief and murderer that he is."

"Save him — Save him!" She shrieked hysterically.

12   The Young American
"Oh leave him to my mercy and you will see
how I will save him!"
"Fire!" cried the commander.
       A volley of musketry echoed around the walls
of Paris, and over a dozen bullets riddled
the heart of Duhem.
       "Avenged, avenged!" the countess
murmured as she fell into the arms of her
friends, and there from her lips poured a
stream of crimson blood. Her dream and
her life was over.~ML

       Odds and Ends
"You have smart speeches of the four-year olds
in the drawer; what do you think of this?
       My little ones had been amused themselves
with a parcel of kittens. I did not suppose they
were particularly attached to them, and finding
them very much in the way. I had them drowned. John took on dreadfully about his kitten, Netty.
       "Why Johnny said I you make as much
fuss as if your father was dead."
       Oh boohoo! cried the chick I could get
a new father any time but I shall never get
another kitten like Netty."

                                    "Harpers Magazine"

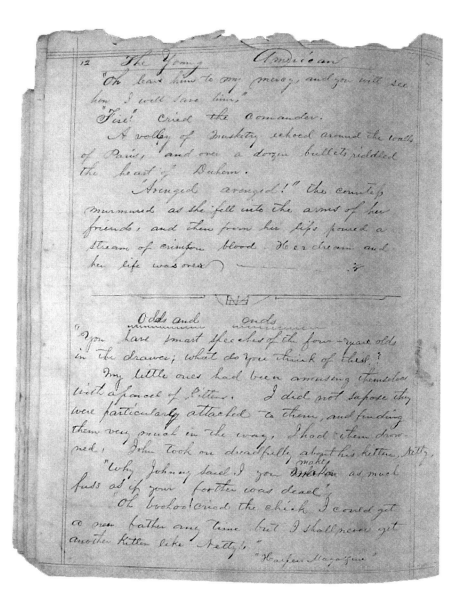

Young American

Foreign News- Steamship Atlantic
_____
"He comes, the herald of a noisy world--
"News from all nations lumbering at this back"
_____
The Colins steam ship Atlantic arrived at New York
on the 6th bringing Liverpool dates to the 23rd all [word unclear].

President Buchanan's message attracted great
attention in England. It was telegraphed entire from
Liverpool to some of the London Journals, being the
longest dispatched ever sent by telegraphed in England.

Further attempts to launch the Leviathan were postp
oned until the spring tides at the commencement of January.
The hydraulic power was to be more than doubled.
The ship remained even and fair on the ways, and
at high tide had nearly six feet of water under her.
The report of an intended alliance between the Prince of
Orange and the Princess Alice of England is without
foundation. Nothing from India has been received.

Three days later arrived of the Africa
she bring later dates from India Lucknow has been
relieved after much hard fighting the Insurgents had
been defeated at various points Sir Calvin Campbell was wounded.

The bank of Prussia has reduced the rate of [word scratched out]
discount to 6½ per cent.
Hamburg Dec. 23rd. The aspects of monetary affairs daily brightens.

13.

The Young American

Foreign News — Steam Ship Atlantic

"She comes, the herald of a noisy world —
News from all nations lumbering at his back"

The Colins Steam Ship Atlantic arrived at New York on the 6th bringing Liverpool dates to the 23rd ult —

President Buchanan's message attracted great attention in England, It was telegraphed entire from Liverpool to some of the London Journals, being the longest dispatch ever sent by telegraph in England

Further attempts to launch the Leviathan were postponed until the spring tides at the commencement of January. The hydraulic power was to be more than doubled, The ship remained even and fair on the ways, and at high tide had nearly six feet of water under her.

The report of an intended alliance between the Prince of Orange and the Princess Alice of England is without foundation. Nothing from India has been received.

Three days later arrival of the Africa She brings later dates from India Lucknow has been relieved after much hard fighting the Insurgents had been defeated at various points Sir Colin Campbell was slightly wounded

The Bank of Prussia has reduced the rate of discount discount to 6% per cent.

Hamburg Dec 23rd: The aspect of monetary affairs daily brightens

14

The Young American

"No pent up ethics contracts our power

For this bountiful continent is ours."

Buffalo Spring. N.C. January 1st 1858

John M.L Harrington- Editor

Fayetteville, NC—

Terms

The terms of the Young American are $2 in advance

or $3 if not paid in advance. The first years

subscription must be paid in advance.

Editorials

"our time to speak now."

Ourselves

We have got out the first number of the

Young American. We are rather late but as

the old time worthy [unclear] saying "Better late than never"

and to tell you the truth friends we feel

proud to look at our sheet, we think it

is the best published in the old "Rip Van

Winkle" state and you owe all this

to us. We intend to devote ourselves

to the advancement of pure and sound literature

from Frolie and amusement and we

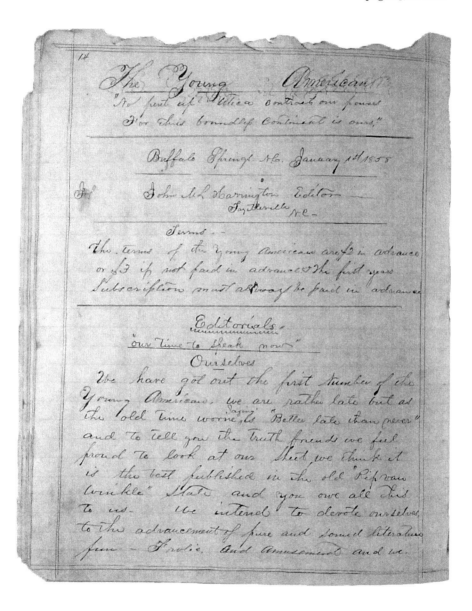

14

The Young American

"No bent up Utica contract our power
For this boundless Continent is ours,"

Buffalo Springs N.C. January 1st 1858

John McL Harrington Editor
Fayetteville N.C. —

Terms —

The terms of the Young American are $2 in advance
or $3 if not paid in advance & The first years
Subscription must always be paid in advance

Editorials

"Our time to speak now"

Ourselves

We have got out the first number of the
Young American, we are rather late but as
the old time worne, says "Better late than never"
and to tell you the truth friends we feel
proud to look at our Sheet, we think it
is the best published in the old "Rip van
winkle" State, and you owe all this
to us — We intend to devote ourselves
to the advancement of pure and sound literature
fun — Frolic, And amusement and we

A Free Press in Freehand

The Young American   15
do not intend to let any subject pass unnoticed
our paper will give a true and fair statement
of the policies of the day, but will not for the
present take sides with any particular party
but we expect to exercise the rights of a
Freeman and vote for whom we please, and
that is the way I hope every true friend to
American Freedom will do and also subscribe to the Young American.--(Editor)

North Carolina
North Carolina has long been termed the 'Rip
Van Winkle' state of the union but I think
she has waked up her interests. North Carolina
is advancing with rapid strides towards the
topmost rounds of the ladder of this great
Confederacy. We are independent of the other
state in almost everything. We have just as good
coal as any other state just as good from Copper
and in fact anything. Passing Mr. Hales book
store the other day I just stepped in and saw
a young man folding something which I thought
was the minutes of proselytizing [unclear] or something of that sort.
I asked him what it was and he told me that it was
the advance sheets of the North Carolina Justice. A large book as large
as the Revised code. He is going to get me all telegraphs so it will be days
with it [word unclear] of Fayetteville all of it.—Ed.

The Young American.   15

do not intend to let any subject pass unnoticed
our paper will give a true and fair statement
of the Politics of the day, but will not for the
present take sides with any particular party
but we expect to exercise the rights of a
Freeman and vote for whom we please, and
that is the way I hope every true friend to
American freedom will do and also subse-
ribe to the Young American, ——— Editor.

————— — —————

North Carolina —

North Carolina has long been termed the 'Rip
van winkle' State of the union, but I think
she has waked up to her interests, North Carolina
is advancing with rapid strides towards the
topmost round of the ladder of this great
Confederacy, we are Independant of the other
States in almost everything we have just as good
Coal as any other State just as good Iron Coffee
and in fact any thing: passing Mr Hales Book
Store the other day I just stepped in and saw
a young man folding something which I thought
was the minutes of Presbytery or something of that sort
I asked him what it was and he told me that It was
the advance Sheet of the North Carolina Justice. I have books as large as
the Young One. he is going to get me Templeton what I set it with to sign
with it kind of together. all of it ——

16   The Young American

Well kind reader! Of the Young American we
have put this number right through as we told you
we would do in our prospectus. We said that
it should be done "up Brown" if we think we
have done that thing "satin" well without joking
we think we have done pretty well considering
it was now the first piece in this new we
rather long longer than we thought it would
be but in our next issue we intend to
have that piece filled up with something funny
our next will have more pages better selections
and in fact it will be better if possible than
this our first number, and now kind friends
one and all you may look for us about the
first of February. Until then we bid you a kind adieu.—Ed

Reader—
One word in your ear—
All those of you who have sent in your names as
subscribers will do us a kind favor by remitting your
dues. $2 to this office and help your kind friend
with his enterprise addressed J.M.L Harrington Fayetteville
N. Carolina—and one and all we will tip our
thread bare Beaver¹ to you once more—Ed

16.

The Young American

Well Kind Readers of the Young American we have put this number right through as we told you we would do in our prospectus. We said that it should be done "as Brown" and we think we have done that thing "justine" well without joking we think we have done pretty well. considering it was as now the first piece in this was adds rather long longer than we thought it would be. but in our next issue we intend to have that place filled up with something funny one and we will have more pages better selections and in fact it will be better if possible than this our first number, and now kind friends one and all you may look for us about the first of February. until then we bid you a kind adieu

Ed

Reader —

One word in your Ear —
all those of you who have put in your names as subscribers will do us a kind favor by remitting your dues. of 2 to this office and help your kind friend with his enterprise adress J M Harrington Fayetteville N. Carolina — and one and all we will tip our thread bare Beaver tiper one more —

Ed

The Young American   17
The Leviathan

As the sixth trial to launch the 'Leave-her
high-and-dry-athan' has failed in England about
$75,000 having already been expended in vain.
Some gentleman of Philadelphia have taken
pity in John Bull's perplexity have sent out by
the Persia proposals for the launch in question.
The machinery which the design using in
their proposals, are excepted was patterned by Mr.
Dick of Pennsylvania. The sum stipulated for
is not to be paid unless the launch is brought
is a successful termination. x x x

    Though we are afraid that the thought
of American ingenuity doing that which the
greatest British Engineers have failed to do
will be an insurmountable obstacle it's the Exceptions
of the Pennsylvania proposition.

    The Book of Job asks ironicaly as our readers
remember "Canst thou draw out Leviathan with a hook?"
So far the answer seems to be as made by English science.

    "We canot even tame the artificial sea monsters
which our own hand have made'

    When it was first proposed to christen this
huge vessel Leviathan instead of the "Great Eastern"
certain religions Journals of Great Britain were
very much shocked seeing in it.

The Young American
17

The Leviathan

As the sixth trial to launch the "Leave-her high-and-dry-athan" has failed in England about £75,000 having already been expended in vain, Some gentlemen of Philadelphia have taken pitty on John Bulls perplexity, have sent out by the Persia, proposals for the launch in question;

The machinery which the design using if their proposals are excepted was pattened by Mr. Dick of Pennsylvania The sum stipulated for is not to be paid unless the launch is brought to a Successful termination, + × ×

Though we are afraid that the thought of American ingenuity, doing that which the greatest British Engineers have failed to do will be an unsurmountable obstacle to the Example of the Pennsylvania proposition

The Book of Job asks ironicaly as our readers remember "Canst thou draw out Leviathan with a hook? So far the answer seems to be as made by English science "We can't even tame the artificial sea-prowlers which our own hands have made"

When it was first proposed to christen this huge vessel Leviathan instead of the "Great Eastern" Certain religious journals of Great Britain were very much shocked seeing in it —

18   The Young American
(We do not exactly understand why "Something
savoring of irreverence, of course the Journals
in questions now are tempted to cry aloud
"We told you so"

Death of an Editor.
Talcloth Burr Jr. editor of the Wilmington Herald
died of typhoid fever at the residence of his
Father. In Wilmington on the Evening of the 5th
January aged 35 years and 3 months
    Mr. Burr was best loved but those who
knew him best and was respected by all, though
for seven years an Editor of a paper he died
without a personal enemy. He was born
he lived in North Carolina, and
was ever true to the interests of his native State.
    "Yet half I hear the farthing sign
    Tis a dread and awful thing to die"

How Long
With this present yearly income it will take the
Bible Societies more than 600 years to supply a copy of the Sacred Scriptures to each
of the seven hundred millions in the heathen
world. The same assembly spent in Great Britain
for intoxicating liquor would do it in one year
                                        N.C.A.

18 The Young American

(we do not exactly understand why) something
savouring of irreverance, of course the Journals
in question now are tempted to cry aloud
"We told you so"

Death Of An Editor.

Dalcott Burr Jr Editor of the Wilmington Herald
died of typhoid fever at the residence of his
Father. In Wilmington on the Evening of the 5th
January, aged 38 years and 3 months

Mr Burr was best loved by those who
knew him best; and was respected by all, though
for seven years an Editor of a paper he died
without a personal enemy. He was born
He lived he died in North Carolina, and
was ever true to the interest of his native State.
"Yet half I hear the parting sigh
Tis a dread and awful thing to die"

How Long

With the present yearly income it will take the
Bible Societies more than 600 years to supply a copy of the sacred scriptures to each
of the several hundred Millions in the heathen
World The sum annually spent in Great Britain
for intoxicating liquors would do it in one year

rea

The Young American   19

Poetry
"Ranged on the hills, harmonious daughters swell
the mingled tones of the home and harp and shell."

Oh Sing Again.

By Finley Johnson.

Oh sing again that melting strain

That love delights hear;

For still my heart those sounds retain

Which are to me so dear,

And as I listen to the times,

To distant years I fly

When every hour was filled with joy

Ere sorrows weakened a sigh

Ah, me! Ah, me! the happy past

Can never come again;

And thought I often wished it back

That wish, alas! is vain

Me sun is set, my hopes destroyed,

And garlands, pale and dead

Are wreathed around the blighted hopes

That are forever fled

North Carolinian Argus

One line to fill this page

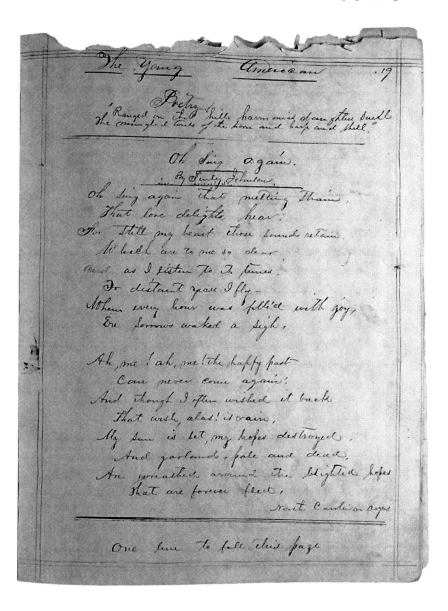

20   The Young American
     Littles on nothings

An Irish gentleman lately fought a duel
with his intimate friend, became he vocally
asserted that he was born without a shirt
on his back.

A young sprig went courting in California
lately and when he went to go to bed he
put his Buckskin pants in the crack of
the house during the night the calves pulled
them out and chewed about half of the
legs of it says the old man brought them in
the morning and he put them on and left—
we don't blame him

Epigram
What a treasure I have called from the garden
        today.
Exclaimed Jennie to me in a casual frank way.
And she placed in my hand such a charming
        bouquet.
That I thought it had borrowed its hue
        from her cheek.

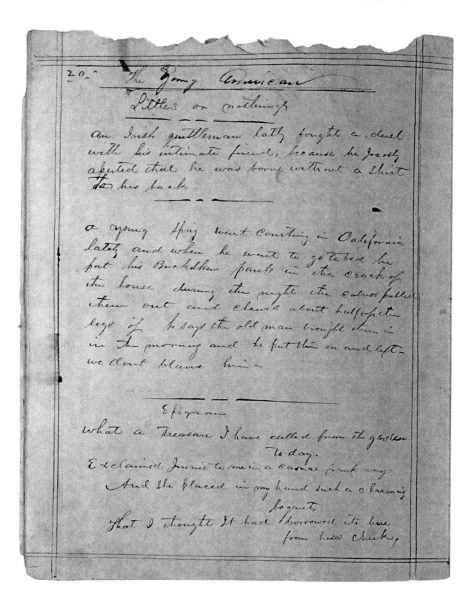

20. The Young American

Littles or nothings

An Irish gentleman latly fought a duel
with his intimate friend, because he greatly
asserted that he was born without a shirt
to his back —

A young Sprig went Courting in California
latly and when he went to go to bed he
put his Buckskin pants in the crack of
the house. during the night the calves pulled
them out and chew'd about half of the
legs of. he says the old man brought them in
in the morning and he put them on and left.
we don't blame him —

Epigram

What a treasure I have culled from the garden
to day.
Exclaimed Junie to me in a casual frank way.
And she placed in my hand such a charming
boquet,
That I thought It had borrowed its hue
from her cheek,

The Young American   21

Poetry
"Ranged on the hills, harmonious daughters swell
the mingled tones of the home and harp shell"
Spitting on the Floor–
The men they chew tobacco,
  While working out of door,
And then corner in on purpose,
  To spit upon the floor.

A spittoon in each corner,
  The hold not any more,
Than they do the filthy habit,
  Of spitting on the floor.

They ought to live alone,
  Far in some lovely moor,
Where the ladies could not see them,
  Spitting on the floor.

Women are obliged to scrub,
  Til scrubbing makes them sore,
Oh! Dear how I hate this
  This spitting on the floor

For What

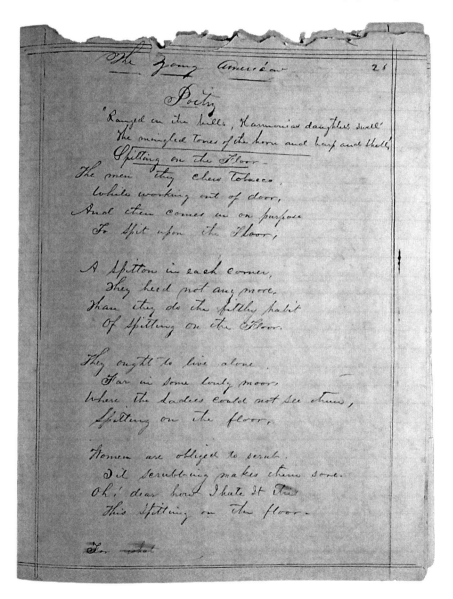

22   The Young American

For what is more repulsive,
  What can, be disgusted more,
Then to see the men forever, spitting on,
  Spitting on the floor.

If you wish to please the ladies
  Those being you adore,
Do avoid that dirty habit,
  Of spitting on the floor.

From the dollar news paper
  Thantos~ By James A. Bostly arn [word unclear]
Yes she has died—her balmy breath,
  That 'scaped her gentle breast,
Her young heart pulses's former play
  Has erased in endless rest.
Earth now receive her gentle form,
  A thing itself divine.
And fold in love the sweetest clay
  That ere may must with thine.

Heaven open thy golden gate again,
  And let her spirit pass.
To mingle in championship,
  With her own fittin clasp,
Unfold the gale of amethyst,
  And take to worthy home,
The gentlest soul that God ever gave,
  Brief days on earth to roam.
Halifax County, NC 1857

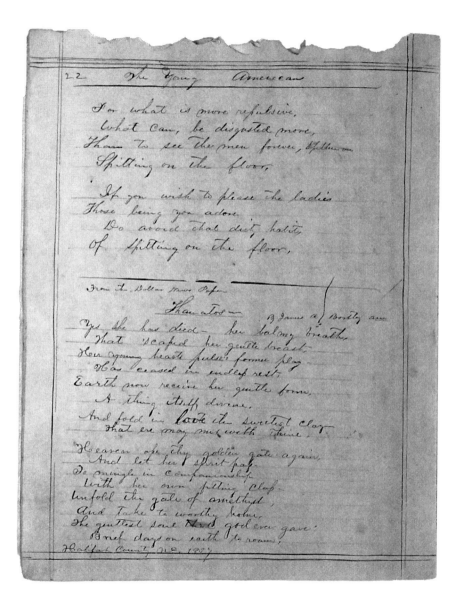

The Young American   23

Humorous—
"A little nonsense now and then
is relished by the wisest men."

"Did you attend church yesterday?" I was so confined
to my room was the reply. "Oh! You had the
room atism there said Dick–

We have a bachelor friend that we think
much if, who was cunningly entraped an evening
or two ago. He was industriously plying with his with attentions a young and very handsome widow, when some
one remarked that Miss Blank, a very lovely young
lady by the way, was without our attendant.
I can't leave said caleb [word unclear] I'm engaged
Oh! Exclaimed the widow, with a charming
naivete, I did not think we had gone as far as that.

On last Sunday Evening I was enjoying
myself at a neighbors house among some young
ladies where when who should step in but (Taylor) Shaw
who was sport enough for the girls– Some young
children were working with matches close by Shaw when
the Lady of the house ordered them a way. She said go away
with your matches you will burn Mr. Shaw. Oh! says one
of the girls, he is too green to burn.

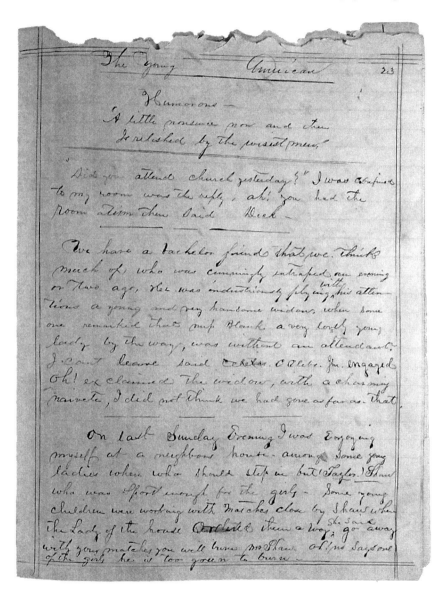

24   The Young American
      Poetry
      Hard Times

"Hard Times" is now on every lip,
     And breathed from every tongue,
The banks are cursed by one and all,
     The aged an the young,
The merchant has to close his doors,
     And throw his Ledger by,
Such times he vows were never seen,
     By any mortal eye,
The shopman quit the counter's side,
     For customers are so few.
The times are now so very "tight"
     It makes then all look "blue."
The citizens in vain essays,
     To make more than has bread!
A pound of which he now declares
     Won't weigh a pound of Bread!
There's not a day but someone fails,
     Some house that goes to smash,
And names that once stood high on change;
     Are out for want of cash,
Those whom we thot were millionaires,
     And rich in shares and stocks.
Their "Million Heirs" now disappoint,
     Fail and leave no "Rocks."

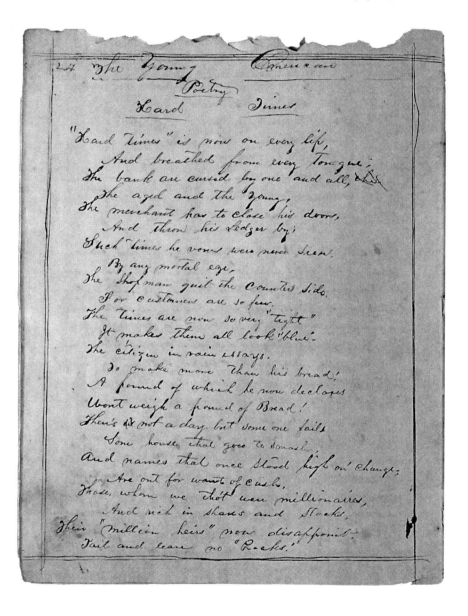

The Young American   25
"Hard Times! Hard Times! was ever seen
        Such hard times as hard as these?"
This is the cry from morn til night,
        In which each one agrees:
A remedy I think I've found–
        Say, how do you think "twill do"
"Pull of your coat Roll up your sleeves,
        and work these hard times through!".

        Riddle
I often murmurs, yet I never weep;
I always lie in bed, but, never sleep;
My mouth is wide and larger than my head,
And much disgorges though it ne'er is fed;
I have no legs or feet, yet swiftly run,
And the more full I get move further on,
(Answer in next paper)[2]

Conundrums-
What part of a ship is a man like who supports a
family? A—The main stay.
Sam? Why are de hogs de most intelligent
folks in the world? Because they nose everything.
Why is a ladies hair like the latest news?
Because in the morning, it is found in the papers.

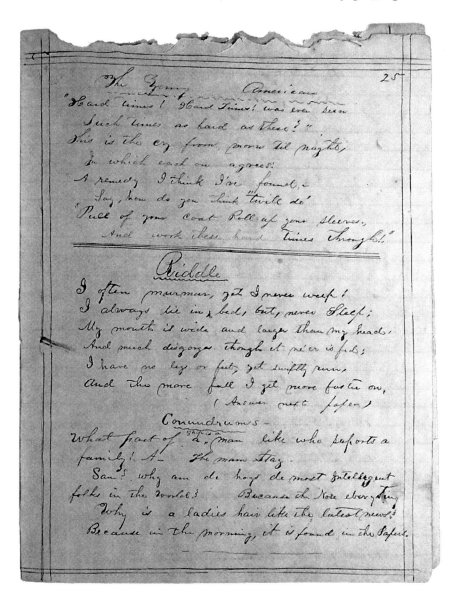

26   The Young American

Literary Notices

The dollar news paper is received it is
a very good journal. Send one dollar to
Wm. M. Swain Jr. [unclear] Phila—

The Saturday Evening Post is one of the
best papers we have had the pleasure of seeing in
a long time. Send $2 to Deacon [unclear] Fellison [unclear] Phila.

The Fayetteville Observer is better worth
the subscription price than either--
price 2 per [unclear] year. Semiweekly 3 EJ Hale and Son.
Fayetteville, NC—
We could go on and on enumerate more
but will want until next issue. Our thanks
are due to several of the Southern exchanges for
sending in their paper in advance of our publication.

Curiosities   Freshly Imported
I am epistle written with a Hog Pen.
A tooth from the mouth of a river.
A feather from the wing of hen [word unclear].
A pillow from the bed of a river.

K.M. Murchison
Commission Merchant
No 104 Wall Street
New York
Usual Advances on Consignment #1 3 mo.

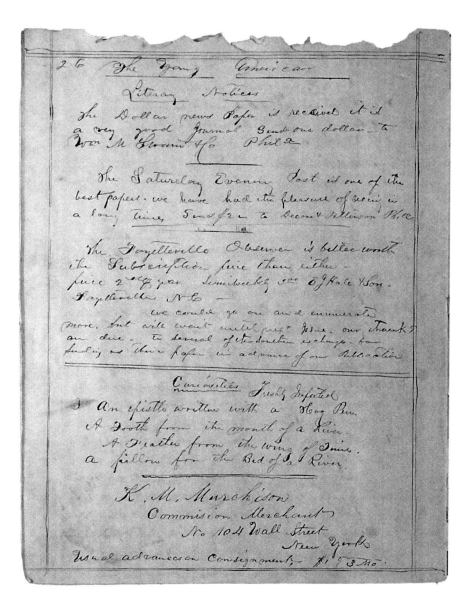

26 The Young American

Literary Notices

The Dollar news Paper is received it is a very good Journal. Send one dollar to Wm M Swain & Co Phila

The Saturday Evening Post is one of the best papers we have had the pleasure of seeing in a long time. Send $2 to Deacon & Peterson Phila

The Fayetteville Observer is better worth the Subscription price than either — price 2.oo per year Semiweekly oo E J Hale & Son. Fayetteville N C —

we could go on and enumerate more, but will wait until next Issue. our thanks are due — to several of our Southern exchanges for sending us their paper in advance of our Publication

Curiosities Freshly Imported

An epistle written with a Hog Pen
A Tooth from the mouth of a River.
A Feather from the wing of an Mire.
a pillow for the Bed of a River.

K. M. Murchison
Commission Merchant
No 104 Wall Street
New York
Usual advances on Consignments — $ 5 3 Mo.

The Young American 27

New Advertisements

Change of Firms

The business heretofore existing under the name
of J. Worth & Sons was disolved on the 1st day
of January 1858 with the view of settling
the interests of Jno McNeill died [unclear] a partner
in that firm.

The business will be conducted in
future under the name and style of J. & D.G. Worth

Persons having claims against
J. Worth & Sons are requested to present them for
payment. Those Indebted must come forward
immediately and settle as the business must be
closed up.

Buffalo Springs, Jan. 1th, 1858.   #1,-1 time

S.R Strand   G. P. Longhead

D F Stetson & Co. [word unclear]

Shipping and Commission Merchants

Philadelphia

D.F. Stetson   #1—6 mo   W.F Cushing

Wheedbee & Dickinson

Commission Merchants

In Naval Stoves Yellow Pine Lumber

Cotton & C.

Baltimore

#1-4 Ts

The Young American   27

New Advertisements–

Change of Firms

The business heretofore existing under the name
of J. Worth & Sons. was dissolved on the 1st day
of January 1858 with the view of settling
the Interest of Ino McNeill decd a partner
in that firm

          The business will be conducted in
future under the name and style of J.H.D. J. Worth
          Persons having claims against
J. Worth Sons. are requested to present them for
payment. those indebted. must. come forward
imediatly and settle as the business must be
Closed up
Buffalo Springs. Jany 11th 1858. $1– 1Time

S. R. Stroud   D. S. Stetson & Co   G. Longhead
     Shipping and Commission Merchants.
                    Philadelphia
A.S. Stetson $1– 6 ms.   W. F. Cushing

          Wheedber & Dickinson
          Commission Merchants,
          In Naval Stores Yellow Pine Lumber
               Cotton &C.
                    Baltimore. $1– 4 Ts

28   The Young American

Dibble & Bunce

Commission and Forwarding

Merchants

Calvin H. Dibble   New York City J.B Bunce

Late of Wilmington, NC   #1—2Ts   Late of Kingston, NC

Just Received this day

1 Hd [unclear] New Crop Molasses

5 Sacks. Coffee—we will

Sell cheap for cash J. & D. G. Worth

Buffalo Springs, NC Jan. 17, 1858.   #1—1t

J C & B. G Worth

Commission and Forwarding

Merchants

Wilmington,

Jan. 1th ,1858   NC

Worth and Utley

Commission & Forwarding

Merchants

Fayetteville

NC

J.A. Worth   #1--3ts   Jos Witey

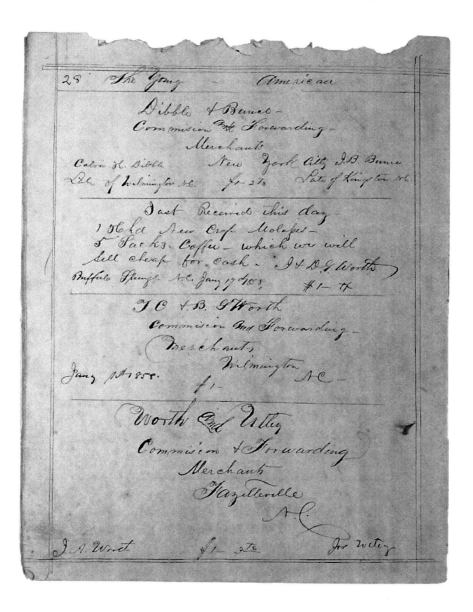

The Young American   29

Wanted! Wanted!

20,000 White Oak Staves

The undersigned will pay $15 per 1000
for Rough White Oak Staves
delivered at this Shop in Harnett
County Will pay cash or goods.
Buffalo Springs, NC January 28th 1858
#1—11   J. & D. G. Worth

    Look out
A Scoundrel named Elkins Jones has
left our work but was in debt, the public
are warned to keep a look out for the scoundrel as he will be apt to try some bad
deals If he thinks he can get in debt to them
Jan. 30th 1858   J. & D. G. Worth
                                     R. R. Contractors
              #1—11

    Wanted
2 likely mules.—apply to
              J & D G Worth

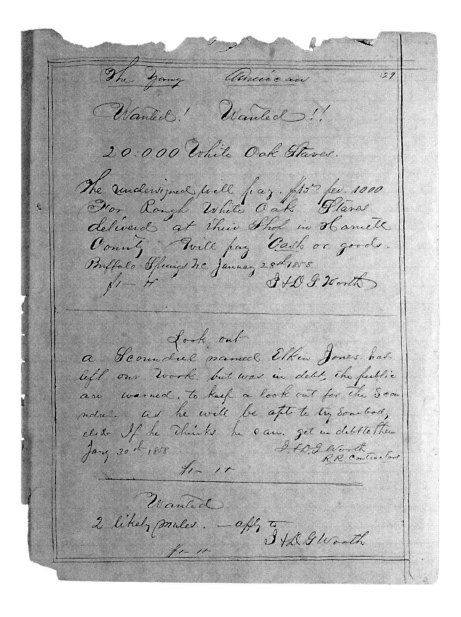

30   Pine Forest
     Academy

The Second Session of this Institution
Commences on the Second Monday
in January. It is beautifully situated
In Harnett County near Harrington P.O.
In a Society, Second to none in the State.
Persons sending children there can get them
Boarded for $6 per month within one
Mile of the Academy.
for further particulars address Jno Harrington
Jas L. Harrington Daniel M. McCormick
Or the principal.
Pine Forest, N.C. Jan. 1st , 1858   Duncan Sellers,
           # 1—#   Principal

     Wanted
A first rate hand to work at turpentine
Jan. 1st , 1858   # 1—#   James L. Harrington

     Randall Sheetings and Son
     For sale by   J. & D. G. Worth
Jan. 1st , 1858   # 1—#

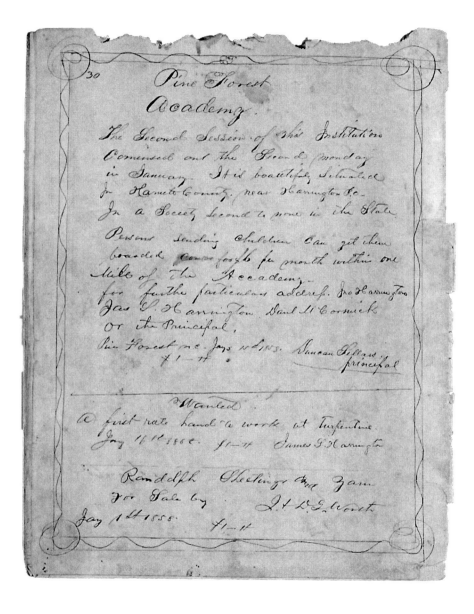

A Free Press in Freehand

APPENDIX C

U.S. Census Figures of the Harrington Household: 1850-1880

Year	Name	Age
1850	John's father, James Stephen	44
	John's mother, Margaret	35
	John McLean	10
	John's sister Ann	8
	John's brother Thomas	6
	John's brother James	2
	Slaves owned by James Stephen	
	a male	26
	a female	25
	a female	12
	a female	10
	a female	9
	a female	7
	a female	5
	a female	2
	a male	2

Year	Name	Age
1860	John's father, James Stephen	53
	John's mother, Margaret	45
	John McLean	20
	John's sister Ann	18
	John's brother, James Jr.	11
	John's brother, Sion	9
	John's brother, David	6
	John's brother Thomas was not listed	
	"J.S.H., adm." (this designation is unclear)	No age listed
	D. McLean (this designation is unclear)	No age listed
	Slaves owned by James Stephen	
	a female	38
	a female	22
	a female	20
	a male	19
	a female	18
	a female	17
	a female	15
	a female	11
	a female	7
	a male	3
	a male	1
	a female	1
	a female	1
	a female	1
	Slaves owned by John Harrington	
	Sarah	1
	a female	45
	a female	44
	a male	39
	a male	30
	a female	30

Year	Name	Age
	Slaves owned by John Harrington (continued)	
	a male	23
	a female	18
	a female	13
	a male	9
1870	John's father, James Stephen	63
	John's mother, Margaret	54
	John McLean	30
	John's brother, James Jr.	21
	John's sister Ann, not listed, perhaps married	
	John's brother, Sion	19
	John's brother, David	16
	Others	
	Louis, mulatto, no vocation listed	11
	Sarah, black, no vocation listed	11
	Batt McDougald, farm hand	22
	Charity McDougal, farm hand	21
	Leglaph Blue, domestic servant (unclear spelling)	27
	Will Blue, mulatto	1
	Lovey Brown, no vocation listed	19
1880	John's father, James Stephen	73
	John's sister-in-law, Eliza McLean Harrington	67
	John's mother, Margaret	65
	John McLean	40
	John's brother, James Jr.	31
	John's nephew, David Jr.	26
	William James Harrington, a servant	21
	John's sister-in-law, Nannie	20

A Free Press in Freehand

NOTES

EPIGRAPH

1. James D. Salinger, *Nine Stories* (New York: Random House, 1948), 273.

INTRODUCTION

1. Nikolai Gogol, "The Overcoat," in *Gateway to the Great Books,* ed. Robert M. Hutchins and Mortimer J. Adler (Chicago, IL: William Benton, 1963), 453–478.

2. *The Legislative Documents for Session 1858–59* lists James A. Harrington as sheriff. This document from 1859 refers to Harrington in a single, poster-like sheet, recorded as page one in the box of loose documents.

3 Harnett County is most notable for its native son, Paul Green (1894–1981), a Pulitzer Prize-winning playwright who is famous for his outdoor symphonic dramas, particularly *The Lost Colony*, a production from 1937 performed every summer in an outdoor theater at Fort Raleigh National Historic Site near Manteo, North Carolina.

4. The July and September 1858 issues of *The Young American* are not available through the North Carolina Department of Cultural Resources, however, the documents are considered to have existed at one time. On page 280 of the December 1858 issue of *The Young American*, Harrington wrote that the 1858 collection of *The Young American,* 321 pages, would be bound in cloth and ready for pick-up on January 1, 1859 for $2.50. This notice suggests that the collection existed at one time, but the author could not locate one.

5. Daniel Czitrom, *Media and the American Mind: From Morse to McLuhan* (Chapel Hill: University of North Carolina Press, 1982), 12.

6. Malcolm Fowler, "News of 'Boundless Continent' Mixed with Harnett Tidbits," *Sanford Herald* (Sanford, NC), May 22, 1963, 6.

7. Malcolm Fowler, *They Passed This Way: A Personal Narrative of Harnett County History* (Lillington, NC: Harnett County Centennial, 1955), 151.

8. Paul A. Pratte, "Origins of Mass Communication," in *The Media in America: A History,* 5th ed., William David Sloan (Northport, AL: Vision Press, 2002), 10–11.

9. Lloyd Chiasson, *Three Centuries of American Media* (Englewood, CO: Morton Publishing, 1999), 66.

10. Fowler, *They Passed This Way,* 94.

CHAPTER 1

1. William K. Boyd, *History of North Carolina, Vol. II, The Federal Period, 1783–1860* (Chicago: Lewis Publishing, 1919), 203.

2. Ibid., 208.

3. Ibid., 204.

4. Emma J. Lapsansky-Werner, *United States History* (Boston: Pearson, Prentice-Hall, 2009), 209.

5. Hinton Rowan Helper, *Impending Crisis of the South: How to Meet It* (Ann Arbor, MI: Scholarly Publishing Office, 2004). First published in 1857, Helper's book was circulated in a condensed version by the National Republican Party as a campaign document. A North Carolinian, Helper was well known; however, North Carolina, unlike its neighboring states of Virginia and South Carolina, produced no nationally recognized proslavery spokesman. See R. W. Faulkner, "Impending Crisis of the South," in *Encyclopedia of North Carolina,* ed. W.S. Powell (Chapel Hill: University of North Carolina Press, 2006), 605–606.

6. Kathleen Conway, *North Carolina: Land of Contrasts* (Atlanta, GA: Clairmont Press, 2009), 262.

7. Ibid., 263.

8. Boyd, *History of North Carolina,* 319.

9. Ibid., 319.

10. Ibid., 320.

11. Ibid., 322.

12. Conway, *North Carolina: Land of Contrasts,* 233.

13. Sion H. Harrington and John Hairr, *Eyewitnesses to Averasboro: The Confederates* (Erwin, NC: Averasboro Press, 2001).

14. John Hairr, *Harnett County: A History* (Charleston, SC: Arcadia Publishing, 2002), 61.

15. Ibid.

16. Ancestry.com, *1850 United States Federal Census* (database online).

17. Ancestry.com, *1870 United States Federal Census* (database online).

18. In addition to highlighting the presence of slaves, the census data provide another view of John McLean Harrington as a person who seeks political appointment and uses his pen to handwrite records. While the census data are only a list, they emphasize Harrington's role in the community as one who records information for the state.

19. Fowler, *They Passed This Way,* 150.

20. Ibid., 150.

21. Boyd, *History of North Carolina,* 377.

22. The title of the newspaper, *The Times.,* included a period.

23. Dick Brown, "To Roll the Presses," *Fayetteville Observer,* September 23, 1973, D1. According to Brown, Sion A. Harrington, John McLean Harrington's younger brother, printed another handwritten newspaper called the *Weekly News*

in 1869, and a photograph of the front page with a quotation from Henry Clay saying, "I would rather be right than to be President" appears beneath the name-plate on the February 2, 1869 issue, the year John McLean Harrington abandoned his handwritten newspapers. John McLean Harrington's last known handwritten newspaper was the Friday, April 2, 1869 issue of *The Times*, Vol. 3, No. 13. In that issue, Harrington gave no indication that it would be his last, but noted on page one a report on Congress would "be continued," which suggests that he had planned to keep publishing, but did not.

24. Geneva H. Cameron, "The James Stephens Harrington Family," in *The Heritage of Harnett County, North Carolina*, vol. I, ed. Mary Alice Hasty (Charlotte, NC: Delmar, 1993), 209.

25. *The Weekly News' Advertising Sheet. Monthly.* and *The Times.* used periods in their titles.

26. Zeb D. Harrington and Martha Harrington, *To Bear Arms, Civil War Information from Local "Folks," Chatham County and Adjacent Counties* (4780 Corinth Rd., Moncure, NC: Private printing, 1984).

27. Fowler, *They Passed This Way*, 104.

28. Ibid., 152; Cameron, "The James Stephens Harrington Family," in *The Heritage of Harnett County, North Carolina*, vol. I, 209.

29. Daisy Kelly Cox, *Sion Harrington Family History Book* (Unpublished history owned by John Burton Cameron III, Broadway, NC, 1960), 7.

30. Horace W. Raper, *The Papers of William Woods Holden*, vol. 1, (Raleigh: Division of Archives and History, North Carolina Department of Cultural Resources, 2000), 280.

31. Cox, *Sion Harrington Family History*, 7.

32. Ibid., 7.

33. Jane Cranford, "John McLean Harrington," second in radio series for WCKB, Dunn, NC (Script available in the genealogy room of the Harnett County Library, Lillington, NC, 1955), 1.

34. Fowler, *They Passed This Way*, 152.

35. Fowler, *They Passed This Way*, 113.

36. Dick Brown, "To Roll the Presses," D1; Cox, *Sion Harrington Family History*, 7; Fowler, *They Passed this Way*, 150.

37. Ibid., 150.

38. Ibid.

39. Cameron, *Sion Harrington Family History*, 209.

40. As indicated by the handwritten minutes of that organization which were recorded in a notebook that is now part of the Rare Book, Manuscript and Special Collections Library of Perkins Library, Duke University.

41. Fowler, *They Passed This Way*, 150.

42. A *naval store* sells products derived from pine trees, including the resin used to make turpentine and tar. Often the resin was used to seal and caulk sailing ships.

43. Malcolm Fowler, "News of 'Boundless Continent,'" *Herald* (Sanford, NC), May 22, 1963, 6.

44. Cranford, *John McLean Harrington*, 2.

45. Harrington's uncle, William D. Harrington, served as first postmaster. Others included James Harrington, John McLean's brother; Nannie McCormick Harrington, the wife of John McLean's brother James; and Sion Harrington, John McLean's brother. The post office remained in use until 1909, when Rural Free Delivery became available in Broadway, North Carolina. The last recorded owner of the building before it was razed was Rhett Denise Thomas, daughter of Ruby Harrington Denise, and a descendant of Nannie McCormick and James Harrington.

46. Fowler, *They Passed This Way*, 152.

47. "Handwritten Newspaper was Published in Western Harnett," *Harnett County News*, Feb. 2, 1944, 1, 6. According to the report on page one, "The title was stamped by hand from a wooden block carved for the purpose. The printing of the title bears the stamp of having been dabbed in printer's ink. All of the balance of the paper is written in pen-and-ink, including the borders around the pages, the little curlicues at the corners, and the column rules and dashes between the news articles." The article went on to report on page 6, "Inquiry among older people of the community fails to reveal any knowledge, even by hearsay, of the number of subscribers 'The Times' served. All of the copies at hand show unmistakably that they were copied by the same hand, thus showing that perhaps the publisher did all the work alone."

48. Sion Harrington, interview by Michael Ray Smith, June 22, 2008.

49. Kathleen Endres, "The Press and the Civil War, 1861-1865," in Sloan, *The Media in America*, 163.

50. Cranford, *John McLean Harrington*, 1.

51. Ibid.

52. Ibid.

53. Ibid., 10.

54. Ibid.

55. "Roster of Officers of the Militia of North Carolina," *Adjutant General's Records of North Carolina* (Printer unknown, 1861), 42. Information from the Special Collections Branch of the North Carolina Division of Historical Resources. In addition, Raper lists John McLean Harrington as a brigadier general of the Thirteenth Brigade, Harnett County, North Carolina Militia. (Horace W. Raper, William W. Holden, North Carolina's Political Enigma [Chapel Hill: University of North Carolina Press, 1985], 315.) In the 1870s, Holden's militia was decidedly sympathetic to the Republican party, which opposed the Ku Klux Klan. Harrington's association with Holden suggests that Harrington was an active Republican during that period. Like Harrington, Holden was a journalist with political ambition. Holden was the first governor of North Carolina to appoint African Americans to governmental positions. In addition, he gained a reputation as

supporting African-American political rights. When Holder died in 1892, his funeral procession in Raleigh included blacks and whites, a rare occurrence. Harrington's connection to Holden suggests that Harrington was a moderate on the race issue.

56. Raper, *The Papers of William Woods Holden,* 279.

57. Ibid., 280.

58. Petitions for Pardon, 1865–1868, Civil War Collection, Military Collection of the North Carolina Division of Historical Resources, Raleigh, NC.

59. Ibid.

60. Ibid.

61. Ibid.

62. Horace W. Raper, *William W. Holden, North Carolina's Political Enigma* (Chapel Hill: The University of North Carolina Press, 1985), 170, 315.

63. Sion Harrington, interview by Michael Ray Smith, June 22, 2008.

64. Cranford, *John McLean Harrington,* 10; Fowler, *They Passed this Way,* 152. Daniel L. Russell (1845-1908) of New Hanover County was a Republican Congressman who later served as governor of North Carolina in 1897-1901. See William McKee Evans, "Daniel Lindsay Russell," in *Dictionary of North Carolina Biography,* ed. William S. Powell (Chapel Hill: University of North Carolina Press, 1994), 5:271-273.

65. Brown, "To Roll the Presses," D6.

66. E. T. Mahone, Jr., "Earliest Printed County Newspaper Found," *The Harnett County News,* June 25, 1981, 2.

67. Ibid.

68. Ibid.

69. Ibid.

70. Ibid.

71. Ibid.

72. The Lois Byrd Local History Collection of Harnett County Public Library System includes a list of Harnett County newspapers compiled by James Vann Comer, no date listed.

73. Patricia Callahan, "Practically Everybody in Dunn, NC, Reads the Daily Newspaper." *Wall Street Journal,* August 10, 2001, A1, A4.

CHAPTER 2

1. Boyd, *The History of North Carolina,* 377.

2. Daniel Miles McFarland, "North Carolina Newspapers. Editors and Journalistic Politics, 1815–1835," *North Carolina Historical Review* 30, no. 3 (1953): 376.

3. Ibid., 377.

4. Ibid.

5. Ibid.

6. Ibid., 376.

7. Ibid.

8. Ibid., 379.

9. Ibid., 386.

10. Ibid., 400.

11. Margaret J. Boeringer, "Joseph Gales, North Carolina Printer", (master's thesis, University of North Carolina at Chapel Hill, 1989), 1.

12 Ibid., 49–50.

13. Ibid., 52.

14. Ibid.

15. Ibid., 28.

16. Ibid., 26.

17. Ibid., 27.

18. McFarland, "North Carolina Newspapers," 400.

19. Lorman A. Ratner and Dwight Teeter, Jr., *Fanatics and Fire-Eaters: Newspapers and the Coming of the Civil War* (Urbana: University of Illinois Press, 2003).

20. Boyd, *History of North Carolina,* 377.

21. Clarence Clifford Norton, "Democratic Newspapers and Campaign Literature in North Carolina 1835–1861." *The North Carolina Historical Review* 5, no. 4 (1929): 345–363.

22. Ratner and Teeter, *Fanatics and Fire-Eaters,* 8.

23. Boyd, *History of North Carolina,* 375.

24. Norton, "Democratic Newspapers," 345.

25. Ibid., 346.

26. Ibid. The Raleigh newspaper was known as the *Weekly North Carolina Standard* from October 30, 1850 to November 10, 1858, and the *Weekly Standard* from November 17, 1858 through 1865.

27. Horace W. Raper, *The Papers of William Woods Holden,* 33.

28. McFarland, "North Carolina Newspapers," 404.

29. Norton, "Democratic Newspapers," 348.

30. Ibid., 350.

31. Edgar E. Folk, "W. W. Holden and the North Carolina Standard, 1843–1848," *North Carolina Historical Review* 19, (January 1942): 22.

32. Boyd, *History of North Carolina,* 275.

33. Ibid., 350.

34. Ibid., 352.

35. Folk, "W. W. Holden," 47.

36. Norton, "Democratic Newspapers," 355.

37. Ibid., 356.

38. Ibid., 357.

39. Ibid., 359.

40. Ibid., 360.

41. John C. Ellen, Jr., "Newspaper Finance in North Carolina's Piedmont and Mountain Section During the 1850s," *North Carolina Historical Review* 37 (1960): 488.

42. Ibid.

43. Ibid., 489.

44. Ibid., 490.

45. Ibid., 493.

46. Ibid., 496.

47. Ibid., 499.

48. Ibid., 502.

49. Ibid.

50. John C. Ellen, Jr., "Political Newspapers of the Piedmont Carolinas in the 1850s" (Master's thesis, University of South Carolina, 1958), 184.

51. Ibid., 195.

52. Ibid., 203.

53. Folk, "W. W. Holden," 22.

54. Raper, *The Papers of William Woods Holden,* 36.

55. Ellen, "Political Newspapers of the Piedmont Carolinas," 217–218.

56. Ibid., 218.

57. Ibid., 293.

58. Ibid., 305. The decision upheld the idea that slaves could not be citizens and Congress had no authority to prohibit slavery in federal territories.

59. Ellen, "Political Newspapers of the Piedmont Carolinas," 310.

60. Ibid.

61. Hodding Carter, "Their Words Were Bullets: The Southern Press in War, Reconstruction and Peace," *Mercer University Lamar Memorial Lectures No. 12* (Athens: University of Georgia Press, 1969), 30.

62. William C. Harris, *William Woods Holden, Firebrand of North Carolina Politics* (Baton Rogue: Louisiana State University Press, 1987), 1.

63. Debra Reddin van Tuyll, interview by Michael Ray Smith, October 19, 2008.

64. Harris, *William Woods Holden,* 3.

65. Ibid., 2.

66. Boyd, *History of North Carolina,* 8–10.

67. Ibid., 13–16.

68. Ibid., 10.

69. Ibid., 2.

70. Ibid., 32.

71. Ratner and Teeter, *Fanatics and Fire-Eaters,* 75.

72. Ellen, "Political Newspapers of the Piedmont Carolinas," 321.

73. Ford Risley, *The Civil War: Primary Documents on Events from 1860 to 1865: Debating Historical Issues in the Media of the Time* (Westport, CT: Greenwood Press, 2004), 4.

74. Raper, *The Papers of William Woods Holden,* 34.

75. Ellen, "Political Newspapers of the Piedmont Carolinas," 323.

76. Carmen Cummings, *Devil's Game: The Civil War Intrigues of Charles A. Dunham* (Urbana: University of Illinois Press, 1994).

77. Henry J. Maihafer, *The General and the Journalists: Ulysses S. Grant, Horace Greeley, and Charles Dana* (Washington, DC: Brassey's Inc., 1998), 20.

78. Ibid., 44.

79. John F. Marszalek, *Sherman's Other War: The General and the Civil War Press* (Kent, OH: Kent State University Press), 1999, 3.

80. Ibid.

81. Ibid., 324.

82. Ibid.

83. Ibid., 325.

84. Michael Burlingame, *Lincoln's Journalist: John Hay's Anonymous Writings for the Press, 1860–1864* (Carbondale: Southern Illinois University Press, 1990).

85. Burlingame, *Lincoln's Journalist,* 164.

86. Sloan, *The Media in America.*

87. J. Cutler Andrews, *The South Reports the Civil War* (Pittsburgh: University of Pittsburgh Press, 1979), 42. Also see Debra Reddin van Tuyll, *The Southern Press in the Civil War* (Westport, CT: Greenwood Press, 2005); and Carl R. Osthaus, *Partisans of the Southern Press: Editorial Spokesmen of the Nineteenth Century* (Lexington: University Press of Kentucky, 1994).

88. Ibid., 42.

89. Ibid.

90. Fowler, *They Passed This Way,* 115.

91. Carter, *Their Words Were Bullets,* 26.

92. Andrews, *The South Reports the Civil War,* 43.

CHAPTER 3

1. Walter Ong, *Orality and Literacy: The Technologizing of the Word* (New York: Routledge, 2003). In 1796, Johann Alois Senefelder invented lithography to print handwritten books, and the process endures. A press is employed, and the published work looks like handwriting.

2. Merrie Spaeth, "Words Matter: Handwritten," *UPI,* July 1, 2004.

3. James W. Carey, *Communication as Culture: Essays on Media and Society* (Boston: Unwin Hyman, 1989).

4. Roy Alden Atwood, "Captive Audiences: Handwritten Prisoner-of-War Newspapers of the Texan Santa Fe Expedition and the War Between the States" (presentation, annual convention of the American Journalism Historians Association, Salt Lake City, UT, October 9, 1993). Atwood notes that journalism historians sometimes impose their stipulative definition on the word *newspaper* without

asking "to what degree their definition may or may not have been applicable in the period they are studying." Atwood says that the definition can best be understood in terms of how readers actually used and understood the term in a specific historical moment. "The question of whether the 19th century lexical definition is consistent with 20th century usage or not is simply, historically irrelevant."

5. Ibid., 2.

6. Ibid.

7. Ibid., 2–3.

8. Ibid., 1–26.

9. Roy Alden Atwood. "Shipboard News: Nineteenth Century Handwritten Periodicals at Sea" (presentation, annual convention of the Association for Education in Journalism and Mass Communication, Chicago, IL, August 1, 1997).

10. Newspapers [The University of Chicago, Theories of Media, Keywords Glossary, database online], (Chicago, University of Chicago); available from http://csmt.uchicago.edu/glossary2004/newspaper.htm (accessed January 31, 2009).

11. Stephen Perry, *A Consolidated History of Media,* 4th ed. (Bloomington, IL: Epistelogic, 2004), 9.

12. Roy Alden Atwood, "Handwritten Newspapers," in *History of the Mass Media in the United States: An Encyclopedia,* ed. Margaret A. Blanchard (Chicago: Fitzroy Dearborn, 1998).

13. Ibid., 249.

14. Roy Alden Atwood, "Handwritten Newspapers of the Canadian-America West, 1842–1910" (presentation, annual convention of the Association for Education in Journalism and Mass Communication, History Division, Kansas City, MO, August 11–14, 1993), 1.

15. Robert F. Karolevitz, "Pen and Ink Newspapers of the Old West," *Frontier Times* 44, no. 2 (February-March, 1970): 31.

16. Mitchell Stephens, *A History of News: From the Drum to the Satellite* (New York: Penguin Books, 2004), 330–331.

17. Ibid., 149–164.

18. Atwood, "Handwritten Newspapers of the Canadian-America West," 9–19. Atwood cited a Civil War-era handwritten newspaper, *The Right Flanker,* 1863–1864. This Civil War effort originated at the Fort La Fayette prison in New York. Other handwritten newspapers abounded after the Civil War, including The *Eagle City Tribune,* Alaska, 1898; *The Granite Times,* Nevada, 1908; *The Snowbound,* Nevada, 1890; *The Soldier Weekly-News,* Idaho, 1893; The *Bum Hill Gazette,* California, 1906; *The Old Flag,* Texas, 1864; the *Halaquah Times,* Oklahoma, 1871–1875; the *Alaska Forum,* Alaska, 1900–1906; *The Esquimeaux,* Alaska-Siberia, 1866–1867; *Lake Peak News,* Nevada, 1907; *The Payson Advocate,* Utah, 1865; the *Intelligencer,* Utah, 1865; *The Sanpitcher,* Utah, 1867; the *Bugle,* Nevada, 1880; the *Alaska Forum,* Alaska, 1900–1906; *The Little Chief,* Oklahoma, 1899, a Cheyenne and Arapahoe Christian mission newspaper; the *Camp Ford News,* Texas, 1865; *The Old Flag,* Texas, 1864; *The Philomathean Gazette,* Utah, 1873;

the *Smithfield Sunday School Gazette,* Utah, 1869; *The Magnolia,* Oregon, 1867; *The Cactus,* Utah, 1878–1884; and *The Illustrated Arctic News,* Alaska, 1850–185.

19. Scott Carney, "A Handwritten Daily Paper in India Faces the Digital Future," *Wired,* July 6, 2007, http://www.wired.com/culture/lifestyle/news/2007/07/last_calligraphers/ (accessed July 23, 2010).

20. Roy Alden Atwood, "Handwritten Newspapers," in Blanchard, *History of the Mass Media in the United States,* 249–250.

21. Atwood, "Handwritten Newspapers of the Canadian-American West," 27.

22. Roy Alden Atwood, "Handwritten Newspapers on the Iowa Frontier, 1844–1854," *Journalism History* 7, no. 2 (Summer 1980): 56–66.

23. "Pine Grove Lyceum Papers," *Nevada Historical Society Quarterly* 29, no. 3 (Fall 1985): 221–222; Phillip Earl and Eric Moody, "Type, Tripe and the Granite Times," *Nevada Magazine,* May-June 1982, 17–18.

24. Bernard Rogan Ross, "Fur Trade Gossip Sheet," *The Beaver: Magazine of the North,* Spring 1955, Robert Karolevitz, "Pen and Ink Newspapers of the Old West," *Frontier Times* 44, no. 2 (Feb-March 1970): 31; and Donald W. Whisenhunt, "The Frontier Newspaper: A Guide to Society and Culture," *Journalism Quarterly* 45, no. 4 (Winter 1968): 726–727.

25. Atwood, "Handwritten Newspapers of the Canadian-American West," 4.

26. Ibid., 8.

27. Roy Alden Atwood, "Handwritten Prisoner-of-War Newspapers of the Texan Santa Fe Expedition and the War Between the States," 1.

28. Atwood, "Shipboard News: Nineteenth Century Handwritten Periodicals at Sea," 5. Atwood found that the *Barometer, The Emigrant, Flying Fish, The Petrel* and *The Shark* were written onboard ships. He also found that passengers and crew onboard the H.M.S. Resolute off Alaska's Barrow Strait published *The Illustrated Arctic News* handwritten newspaper between 1850 and 1851. In addition, the stranded crew of Sir William Edward Parry's voyage in search of a Northwest Passage through the Canadian arctic archipelago in 1819–1820 published *The North Georgia Gazette* handwritten newspaper.

29. Atwood, "Handwritten Newspapers of the Canadian-American West," 13.

30. Fowler, *They Passed This Way,* 151.

31. "The Geelong Advertiser," *The Geelong Advertiser,* (Ryrie Street, Geelong, Victoria, Australia 3220), 191–195. Also available online at http://www.geelongadvertiser.com.au/about.html (accessed January 17, 2009).

32. "Handwritten Macao newspapers on display in Nanjing, Xinhau," *Emerging Markets Datafile, Xinhau Lexis/Nexis Academic* [database online], December 22, 1999, (accessed November 9, 2009).

33. Brier, "The *Flumgudgeon Gazette and the Bumblebee Budget,*" *Journalism Quarterly* 36 (Summer 1959): 317–320.

34. Ibid., 318.

35. Ibid., 320.

36. Karolevitz, "Pen and Ink Newspapers," 31.

37. Ibid.
38. Atwood, "Handwritten Newspapers on the Iowa Frontier."
39. Atwood, "Handwritten Newspapers of the Canadian-American West," 10.
40. Karolevitz, "Pen and Ink Newspapers," 31.
41. D. W. Working, "Some Forgotten Pioneer Newspapers," *The Colorado Magazine, State Historical Society of Colorado* 4, no. 3 (May 1927): 93–94.
42. Atwood, "Handwritten Newspapers of the Canadian-American West," 7.
43. Ibid., 12.
44. Ibid., 58.
45. Ibid., 67.
46. Ibid., 20.
47. Ibid.
48. Ibid., 21.
49. Ibid.
50. Ibid., 23.
51. Ibid.
52. Ibid., 24.
53. Ibid.
54. Karolevitz, "Pen and Ink Newspapers," 63.
55. Ibid.
56. Ibid.
57. Czitrom, *Media and the American Mind,* 14.
58. Ibid., 15.
59. Mike Boone, "Constant Force in Changing Community: Sidewalk Socialism." *The Gazette* (Montreal, Canada), May 24, 2004, A2.
60. "Handwritten Newspaper 'Published' in Central Baghdad," *Financial Times Information, BBC,* June 17, 2004.
61. "Antique 1887 'Sing-Sing' Prison Handwritten Newspaper," *Ebay.com* [database online], accessed July 16, 2008. Internet listing no longer available.
62. "Anthony Talks about Unusual NC Editor," *Newsline, A publication of Campbell University Friends of the Library* (Buies Creek, NC) 11, no. 3 (November 2003): 1.

CHAPTER 4

1. Michael Ray Smith, *The Jesus Newspaper, The Christian Experiment of 1900 and Its Lessons for Today* (Lanham, MD: University Press of America, 2002), 21.
2. William David Sloan, *Perspectives on Mass Communication History* (Hillsdale, NJ: Lawrence Erlbaum Associates, 1991).
3. Ibid., 4.
4. Ibid.
5. Ibid., 5.

6. Ibid., 6.

7. James D. Startt and William D. Sloan, *Historical Methods in Mass Communication* (Hillsdale, NJ: Lawrence Erlbaum, 1989), 29.

8. Smith, *The Jesus Newspaper,* 21.

9. Ibid., 8.

10. Ibid., 9.

11. Robert Park, "The Natural History of the Newspaper," in *The City,* ed. Robert Park, Ernest W. Burgess and R. D. McKenzie (Chicago: University of Chicago Press, 1925), 88.

12. Starrt and Sloan, *Historical Methods,* 36.

13. David M. Ryfe, "News, Culture and Public Life: A Study of 19th-Century American Journalism," *Journalism Studies* 7, no. 1 (2006): 60.

14. Ibid., 61.

15. Ibid., 60.

16. Michael Schudson, *The Power of News* (Cambridge, MA: Harvard University Press, 1995), 53–71.

17. Gerald J. Baldasty and Jeffery Rutenbeck, "Money, Politics, and Newspapers: The Business Environment of Press Partisanship in the Late 19th Century," *Journalism History* 15, no.2-3 (Summer/Autumn 1988): 68; Ryfe, "News, Culture and Public Life," 64.

18. Ryfe, "News, Culture and Public Life," 65.

19. Ibid., 73.

20. Connery, *Literary Aspects,* 316.

21. Sven Birkerts, *The Gutenberg Elegies* (Boston: Faber & Faber, 1984).

22. Em Griffin, *A First Look at Communication Theory,* 3rd ed. (Boston: McGraw-Hill, 2009), 312.

23. Marshall McLuhan, *Understanding Media: The Extensions of Man* (New York: New American Library, 1964).

24. Stephen John Barry, "Nathaniel Macon: The Prophet of Pure Democratic Republicanism, 1758–1837" (PhD diss., State University of New York at Buffalo, 1996), 297.

CHAPTER 5

1. Fowler, *They Passed This Way,* 150.

2. This periodical in Fayetteville, North Carolina, used periods at the end of the names: *Fayetteville Observer. Semi-Weekly.* The font used for *"Fayetteville Observer"* was similar to a modified Rosewood Standard Regular font with shadows, and the font used for *"Semi-Weekly."* was similar to Times New Roman boldface; both used capital letters. In 1817, the *Fayetteville Observer,* the state's oldest continuous published newspaper, began, and Edward J. Hale edited it as a Whig party supporter from 1825 until 1865 (Boyd, *History of North Carolina,* 376).

Boyd lists the newspaper without the periods or the "*Semi-Weekly.*" in the name, and this practice is used in this research for simplicity in reading.

3. David L. Swain of Asheville, North Carolina, Whig party member and governor from 1832–1835, is reported to be the first person to compare North Carolina to Rip Van Winkle, a character from a Washington Irving short story. Winkle fell asleep for twenty years and awoke to find everything around him changed. Swain called for a fairer form of representation Conway, *North Carolina: Land of Contrasts,* 222.

4. John McLean Harrington, "'The Young American' Editorial Statement," *The Young American* (Buffalo Springs, NC), January 1858, 14–15.

5. Richard T. Stillson, *Golden Words: Communications and Information Dispersal in the California Gold Rush* (PhD diss., Johns Hopkins University, 2003), 44.

6. According to Cranford, Harrington wrote in *The Nation,* "The Saturday Evening Post is the best paper we have the pleasure of seeing" ("John McLean Harrington," 7). Duke collection does not include the May 8, May 15, May 22 and July 28 issues of *The Nation.* Cranford's reference to *The Saturday Evening Post* may be in one of those issues because this researcher could not find it in the surviving issues. However, on page 26 of the January 1858 issue of *The Young American,* Harrington wrote in the "Literary Notices," "The Saturday Evening Post is one of the best papers we have had the pleasure of seeing in a long time."

7. Fowler, *They Passed This Way,* 152; Geneva Harrington Cameron, interview by Michael Ray Smith, October 20, 2006. Cameron, of Broadway, North Carolina, is a descendant of Harrington.

8. Avery was acquitted of the murder of Samuel Flemming because a jury deemed Avery justified, in accordance with the Southern Code of Honor that allowed an individual to exact vengeance if publicly humiliated by a person of lower social background so as to be mentally anguished. See W. Conard Gass, "The Misfortune of a High Minded and Honorable Gentleman: W.W. Avery and the Southern Code of Honor," *North Carolina Historical Review* 56 (1978 July): 278–297.

9. This passage is from Volume II, page 13. The two-volume set, also known as *Carolina Carols: A Collection of North Carolina Poetry,* was published by Pomeroy publishers in Raleigh and included 182 poems by sixty authors and featured a story of ancient Palmyra and a poem about the Indian gallows. Harrington's work is not part of the collection.

10. Cranford, "John McLean Harrington."

11. Boyd, *History of North Carolina,* 387.

12. Boyd, *History of North Carolina,* 387–388.

13. Dr. Mitchell is most likely Dr. Elisha Mitchell (1793–1857), a professor at the University of North Carolina for whom Mount Mitchell is named. Mitchell was an educator, geologist, and Presbyterian clergyman. See Elgiva D. Watson,

"Elisha Mitchell," in *Dictionary of North Carolina Biography*, ed. William S. Powell (Chapel Hill: University of North Carolina Press, 1991), 4:281–282.

14. I am indebted to Courtney E. Willey, who presented original, unpublished research on Harrington's "The Bridal Feast" during Harnett County's Sesquicentennial Scholarly Presentation at Campbell University in 2005.

15. "P.O." is the abbreviation for post office.

CHAPTER 6

1. Boyd, *History of North Carolina*, 375.

2. The second issue of *The Nation* (Volume 1, Number 2, April 24, 1858) appears to be penned with more care than the first and includes a revised nameplate with wavy rules to separate the elements. The feathery quality of the type drawn on the first issue is missing but replaced with bold sweeping lines for the name, giving a shadowy effect. In an independent study project under the direction of the author at Campbell University in Buies Creek, North Carolina, during fall 2004, student Jay Berube described the font as three wavy lines fanning out from the large letter N in the newspaper name, and a quarter-inch circle similar to a target. These additions appear to be artistic flourishes.

3. Retrieved August 21, 2010 from http://www.measuringworth.com/calculators/compare.

4. During this period, the phrase "the democracy" was used interchangeably with "Democratic Party."

5. As background, a bit of American history may be necessary to understand the report that Harrington featured on the front page, first column, of the May 1, 1858, issue. During this period, the U.S. Congress agreed to allow residents of the Kansas territory to decide the question of slavery in this new state, and both the Free-Soil adherents and the proslavery supporters worked to win their side. On November 7, 1857, the proslavery party met and passed the Lecompton Constitution, guaranteeing the possession of all property with slaves; however, when the Lecompton Constitution was submitted to the voters in January 1858, the slaves-as-property idea was rejected, putting the Free-Soil Party in control of this territory. A compromise was proposed in August 1858, but it was defeated and slavery was finally defeated in a constitution adopted on July 27, 1858, and ratified in October 1858. Kansas was admitted to the union on January 29, 1861.

6. Harrington underlined the final sentence of these comments for emphasis.

7. John L. Cheney Jr., ed. *North Carolina Government 1585–1979: A Narrative and Statistical History* (Raleigh: North Carolina Department of Secretary of State, 1975), 326.

8. *The Leasure Hour.* included a punctuation mark in its name and the creative use of the word "leisure." It is part of the Southern Historical Collection at University of North Carolina at Chapel Hill.

CHAPTER 7

1. David Feldman, *Who Put the Butter in Butterfly?* (New York: Barnes & Noble, 2003), 147.

2. John F. Cleveland and Horace Greeley, *A Political Text-Book for 1860: Comprising a Brief View of Presidential Nominations and Elections* (Whitefish, MT: Kessinger Publishing, 2007), 172.

3. Hairr, *Harnett County,* 61.

4. Ibid.

5. Ibid.

6. Ibid.

7. Harrington included a period after the name on the nameplate.

8. The February, March, and April 1861 issues are part of the Rare Book, Manuscript and Special Collections Library of Perkins Library at Duke University in Durham, North Carolina.

9. Rebecca Scott, *Slave Emancipation in Cuba: The Transition to Free Labor, 1860–1899* (Pittsburgh: University of Pittsburgh Press, 2000), 3.

10. Scott, *Slave Emancipation in Cuba,* 38.

11. Ibid.

12. Ibid.

13. John McLean Harrington, "Abolition of Slavery in Cuba," *The Times,* April 2, 1869, 1.

14. As John McLean Harrington finished his 302-newspaper output, his younger brother, Sion A. Harrington, began a handwritten, four-page publication, *The Leisure Hour.* Two issues are known to exist, May and June, 1869. In the May issue, Harrington wrote, "With this number we commence the publication of a monthly journal with the above title to be devoted to Literature [sic] Poetry [sic] Anecdotes [sic] the important 'News' of the month [sic] Etc [sic] Ect [sic] any other comment will be unnecessary as the Leasure Hour [sic] will show for itself." By June, the third page was blank and the fourth page was half-filled.

CHAPTER 8

1. Elizabeth L. Eisenstein, "The Rise of the Reading Public," in *Communication in History, Technology, Culture, Society,* ed. David Crowley and Paul Heyer (Boston: Pearson, 2007), 97.

2. Ibid., 99; Elizabeth L. Eisenstein, *The Printing Revolution in Early Modern Europe* (Cambridge: Cambridge University Press, 1986), 11; Johannes Trithemius, *In Praise of Scribes (de Laude Scriptorium)*, ed. Klaus Arnold (Lawrence, KS: Coronado Press, 1974), 65.

3. Walter E. Williams, "Rebellion in Oklahoma," *The Daily Record* (Dunn, NC), July 16, 2008, 4A. A professor of economics at George Mason University, Williams said the war should be called the "War of 1861" because civil war, by

definition, is "a struggle where two or more parties try to take over the central government. Confederate President Jefferson Davis no more wanted to take over Washington, D.C., than George Washington wanted to take over London."

4. Roy Alden Atwood, "Handwritten Newspapers," in Blanchard, *History of the Mass Media in the United States*, 250.

5. William K. Boyd, *History of North Carolina, Vol. II, The Federal Period, 1783–1860* (Chicago: The Lewis Publishing Co., 1919), 387.

6. Harrington wrote in *The Nation*, "The Saturday Evening Post is the best paper we have the pleasure of seeing," according to Jane Cranford in her WCKB radio script about John McLean Harrington, which is available in the genealogy room of the Harnett County Library, Lillington, North Carolina. The Duke collection does not include the May 8, May 15, May 22, and July 28 issues of *The Nation*. Cranford's reference to *The Saturday Evening Post* may be in one of those issues because this researcher could not find it in the surviving issues.

7. George Rodman, *Mass Media in a Changing World* (New York: McGraw-Hill, 2006), 115.

8. "John McLean Harrington Papers," (Chapel Hill: University of North Carolina, February 1958), in the Southern Historical Collection, University of North Carolina, accession number 3341, five items.

9. Richard T. Stillson, "Golden Words: Communications and Information Dispersal in the California Gold Rush" (PhD diss., Johns Hopkins University, 2003), 275.

10. The idea that journalism is a form of storytelling goes back at least to the early nineteenth century work of one of America's first sociologists, George Herbert Mead. See Michael Schudson, *Discovering the News: A Social History of American Newspapers* (New York: Basic Books, 1978), 89.

11. Ibid.

12. Dane S. Claussen, "Economics, Business, and Financial Motivations," in *American Journalism, History, Principles, Practices,* ed. William David Sloan (Jefferson, NC: McFarland & Co., 2002), 109.

13. Michael Buchholz, "The Penny Press, 1833–1861," in Sloan, *The Media in America*, 128–129.

14. Ibid., 123.

15. Schudson, *Discovering the News*, 116.

16. Startt and Sloan, *Historical Methods in Mass Communication*, 26.

17. Buchholz, "The Penny Press," 123; Hazel Dickens-Garcia, "The Popular Press, 1833–1865," in *The Age of Mass Communication,* ed. William David Sloan (Northport, AL: Vision Press, 1998), 147.

18. Schudson, *Discovering the News*.

19. John C. Nerone, "The Mythology of the Penny Press," *Critical Studies in Mass Communication* 4 (1987): 376.

20. Ted Curtis Smythe and Pauline D. Kilmer, "The Press and Industrial America 1865–1883," in Sloan, *The Media in America*, 199–222.

21. James D. Startt and William David Sloan, *The Significance of the Media in American History: Media in America* (Northport, AL: Vision Press, 1994), 6.

22. Maryanne Wolf, *Proust and the Squid: The Story and Science of the Reading Brain* (New York: Harper, 2007), 17.

23. Tamara Plakins Thornton, *Handwriting in America: A Cultural History* (New Haven, CT: Yale University Press, 1996), xiv.

24. Janie Cravens, personal email with Michael Ray Smith, August 18, 2008. Cravens at the time was president of the International Association of Master Penmen, Engrossers and Teachers of Handwriting.

25. Kitty Burns Florey, *Script and Scribble: The Rise and Fall of Handwriting* (New York: Melville House Publishing, 2009), 75.

26. Ibid., 63.

27. Ibid., 64.

28. Ibid., 84.

29. Ibid., 65.

30. Ibid., 66–67.

31. Henry Cable Spencer, *Spencerian Key to Practical Penmanship* (New York: Ivision, Phinney, Blakeman & Co., 1866), 9–11.

32. Florey, *Script and Scribble,* 69.

33. Joan Donaldson, "Dipping into America's Penmanship Past," *Christian Science Monitor,* August 6, 1997, 16.

34. Ibid.

35. Platt Rogers Spencer, *Theory of Spencerian Penmanship for Schools and Private Learners* (Fenton, MI: Mott Media, 1985), i.

36. Ibid., iv.

37. Ibid.

38. Donaldson, "Dipping into America's Penmanship Past," 16.

39. Spencer, *Spencerian Key to Practical Penmanship,* 175–176. Spencer included an appendix, pages 158–176, on the "Origin and Progress of the Art of Writing, or Chirography." On page 165, he traced penmanship to Mount Sinai through history until the early 1800s when, he explained, penmanship manuals before the Spencerian Key were little more than "copy-books, but do not aspire to the character of systematized works." On page 13 of his manual, Spencer explained that to be successful in penmanship a writer must seek "a definite ideal."

40. Thornton, *Handwriting in America,* 5.

41. Ibid., 9.

42. Ibid., 23.

43. Ibid.

44. Ibid., 25.

45. Ibid., 26.

46. Florey, *Script and Scribble,* 46.

47. Ibid.

48. Ibid., 48–49.

49. Ibid., 50.

50. Ibid., 77.

51. Ibid., 78.

52. Ibid., 77.

53. Ibid., 80.

54. Ibid., 79.

55. Home page of Zaner-Bloser language arts and reading company, http://www.zaner-bloser.com/educator/products/handwriting/index.aspx?id=106 (accessed January 17, 2009).

56. Florey, *Script and Scribble,* 72.

57. Rhona Stainthorp, "Handwriting: A Skill for the 21st Century or Just a History Lesson?" *Literacy Today,* no. 26 (December 2006).

58. Thomas B. Connery, "Literary Aspects of Journalism: Journalistic Writing that Breaks Traditional Boundaries," in Blanchard, *History of the Mass Media in the United States,* 316–317.

59. Vincent Connelly, Julie E. Dockrell and Jo Barnett, "The Slow Handwriting of Undergraduate Students Constrains Overall Performance in Exam Essays," *Educational Psychology* 25, no. 1 (February 2005): 99.

CHAPTER 9

1. Walter J. Ong, *Orality and Literacy: The Technologizing of the Word* (New York: Routledge, 2003).

2. Marcus Tullius Cicero, *The Orations of Marcus Tullius Cicero* (Charleston, S.C: BiblioBazaar, 2008).

3. Neal Postman, "Informing Ourselves to Death" (paper presented at German Informatics Society, Stuttgart, Germany, October 11, 1990), http://w2.eff.org/Net_culture/Criticisms/informing_ourselves_to_death.paper (accessed December 8, 2008).

4. McLuhan, *Understanding Media.*

5. Harrington was not alone. Others also appeared to be sympathetic to the Confederacy during the Civil War but proclaimed sympathy for the Union following the war.

6. Records at the State Library of North Carolina do not confirm Harrington served as sheriff despite an election notice to that effect. According to the surviving records from the state, particularly the *Executive Legislative Documents Laid Before the General Assembly of North Carolina, Sessions* 1858–1859, 1860–1861, 1862–1863, 1863–1864, 1864–1865, 1868–1869, 1871–1872, 1873–1874, and 1887, Harrington was not listed as sheriff in Harnett County.

7. Ryfe, *News, Culture and Public Life.*

APPENDIX C

1. A beaver is a slang expression for a hat.
2. The answer: A stream.

SELECTED
WORKS CONSULTED

HARRINGTON'S NEWSPAPERS

Semi-Weekly News. July 20, 1860–August 13, 1860.
The Nation. April 17, 1858–September 8, 1858.
The Times. October 17, 1867–April 2, 1869.
Weekly News. June 7, 1860–March 2, 1864.
The Weekly News' Advertising Sheet. Monthly. February, March, April, 1861.
Weekly Eagle. April 20, 1860.
The Young American. January 1858–December 1858.

OTHER SOURCES

"Anthony Talks about Unusual NC Editor." *Newsline, A Publication of Campbell University Friends of the Library* 11, no. 3 (November 2003): 1.
Atwood, Roy Alden. "Captive Audiences: Handwritten Prisoner-of-War Newspapers of the Texan Santa Fe Expedition and the War Between the States." Paper, annual convention of the American Journalism Historians Association, Salt Lake City, UT, October 9, 1993.
———. "Handwritten Newspapers." In *History of the Mass Media in the United States: An Encyclopedia,* ed. Margaret A. Blanchard, 249–250. Chicago: Fitzroy Dearborn, 1998.
———. "Handwritten Newspapers of the Canadian-America West, 1842–1910." Paper, annual convention of the History Division, Association for Education in Journalism and Mass Communication, Kansas City, MO, August 11–14, 1993.
———. "Handwritten Newspapers on the Iowa Frontier, 1844–1854." *Journalism History* 7, no. 2 (Summer 1980): 56–59, 66–67.
———. "Shipboard News: Nineteenth Century Handwritten Periodicals at Sea." Paper, annual convention of the Association for Education in Journalism and Mass Communication, Chicago, IL, August 1, 1997.
Baldasty, Gerald J., and Jeffery Rutenbeck. "Money, Politics, and Newspapers: The Business Environment of Press Partisanship in the Late 19th Century." *Journalism History* 15, no. 2-3 (Summer/Autumn 1988): 60.
Barry, Stephen John. "Nathaniel Macon: The Prophet of Pure Democratic Republicanism, 1758–1837." PhD diss., State University of New York at Buffalo, 1967.
Birkerts, Sven. *The Gutenberg Elegies.* Boston: Faber & Faber, 1984.

Boeringer, Margaret J. "Joseph Gales: North Carolina Printer." Master's thesis, University of North Carolina Press at Chapel Hill, 1989.

Boyd, William K. *History of North Carolina*, vol. II, *The Federal Period, 1783–1860*. Chicago: Lewis Publishing, 1919.

Brier, Warren J. "The *Flumgudgeon Gazette and the Bumblebee Budget*." *Journalism Quarterly* 36 (Summer 1959): 317–320.

Brown, Dick. "To Roll the Presses He Took Pen in Hand." *Fayetteville Observer*, September 23, 1973, D1.

Buchholz, Michael. "The Penny Press, 1833–1861." In *The Media in America: A History*, 5th ed., ed. William David Sloan, 123–142. Northport, AL: Vision Press, 2002.

Callahan, Patricia. "Practically Everybody in Dunn, NC, Reads the Daily Newspaper." *Wall Street Journal*, August 10, 2001, A1, A4.

Cameron, Geneva H. "The James Stephens Harrington Family." In *The Heritage of Harnett County North Carolina*, vol. I, ed. Mary Alice Hasty, 209–210. Charlotte, NC: Delmar, 1993.

Carey, James W. *Communication as Culture: Essays on Media and Society*. Boston: Unwin Hyman, 1989.

Carter, Hodding. "Their Words Were Bullets: The Southern Press in War, Reconstruction and Peace," *Mercer University Lamar Memorial Lectures No. 12*. Athens, GA: University of Georgia Press, 1969.

Cheney, John L. Jr., ed. *North Carolina Government 1585–1979: A Narrative and Statistical History*. Raleigh, NC: North Carolina Department of Secretary of State, 1975.

Chiasson, Lloyd. *Three Centuries of American Media*. Englewood, CO: Morton Publishing, 1999.

Clarke, Mary Bayard. *Carolina Carols: A Collection of North Carolina Poetry*. Raleigh, NC: Pomeroy, 1854.

Claussen, Dane S. "Economics, Business, and Financial Motivations." In *American Journalism, History, Principles, Practices*, ed. William David Sloan, 106–115. Jefferson, NC: McFarland, 2002.

Cleveland, John F., and Horace Greeley. *A Political Text-Book for 1860: Comprising a Brief View of Presidential Nominations and Elections*. Whitefish, MT: Kessinger Publishing, 2007.

Connery, Thomas B. "Literary Aspects of Journalism: Journalistic Writing that Breaks Traditional Boundaries." In *History of the Mass Media in the United States: An Encyclopedia*, ed. Margaret A. Blanchard, 316–317. Chicago: Fitzroy Dearborn, 1998.

Conway, Kathleen. *North Carolina: Land of Contrasts*. Atlanta, GA: Clairmont Press, 2009.

Cox, Daisy Kelly. *Sion Harrington Family History Book*, unpublished history owned by John Burton Cameron III, Broadway, NC, 1960.

Cranford, Jane. "John McLean Harrington," Second in Radio Series for WCKB, Dunn, NC, 1955. Script available in the genealogy room of the Harnett County Library, Lillington, NC.

Croteau, David, and William Hoynes William. *Media/Society, Industries, Images and Audiences*. 3rd ed. Thousand Oaks, CA: Pine Forge Press, 2003.

Cummings, Carmen. *Devil's Game: The Civil War Intrigues of Charles A. Dunham*. Urbana: University of Illinois Press, 1994.

Cutler, Andrew, J. *The North Reports the Civil War*. Pittsburgh: University of Pittsburgh Press, 1955.

———. *The South Reports the Civil War*. Pittsburgh: University of Pittsburgh Press, 1970.

Czitrom, Daniel. *Media and the American Mind: From Morse to McLuhan*. Chapel Hill: University of North Carolina Press, 1982.

Dickens-Garcia, Hazel. "The Popular Press, 1833–1865." In *The Age of Mass Communication*, ed. William David Sloan, 147–170. Northport, AL: Vision Press, 1998.

Dyer, Carolyn Stewart. "Political Patronage of the Wisconsin Press, 1849/1860: New Perspectives on the Economics of Patronage." *Journalism Monographs* 109 (1989): 1–40.

Egnal, Marc. "Rethinking the Secession of the Lower South: The Clash of Two Groups." *Civil War History* 50, no. 3 (September 2004): 261–290.

Eisenstein, Elizabeth L. *The Printing Revolution in Early Modern Europe*. New York: Cambridge University Press, 1986.

———. "The Rise of the Reading Public." In *Communication in History: Technology, Culture, Society*, ed. David J. Crowley and Paul Heyer, 96–103. Boston: Pearson, 2007.

Ellen, John C., Jr. *Political Newspapers of the Piedmont Carolinas in the 1850s*. PhD diss., University of South Carolina, Columbia, 1959.

———. "Newspaper Finance in North Carolina's Piedmont and Mountain Section during the 1850s." *North Carolina Historical Review* 37 (1960): 488–505.

———. "Piedmont and Mountain Political Newspapers of North Carolina, 1850–1859: A Compendium." In *Essays in American History, East Carolina College Publications in History*, vol. 1, ed. Hubert A. Coleman et al., 165–182. Greenville, NC: East Carolina College, 1958.

Elliott, Robert Neal. *The Raleigh Register, 1799–1863*. Chapel Hill: University of North Carolina Press, 1955.

Endres, Kathleen, "The Press and the Civil War, 1861-1865." In *The Media in America: A History*, 5th ed., ed. William David Sloan, 159-174. Northport, AL: Vision Press, 2002.

Evans, William McKee. "Daniel Lindsay Russell." In *Dictionary of North Carolina Biography*, ed. William S. Powell, 5:271-273. Chapel Hill, NC: University of North Carolina Press, 1994.

Everett, George G. "The Age of New Journalism, 1883–1900." In *The Media in America: A History,* 5th ed., ed. William David Sloan, 223–248. Northport, AL: Vision Press, 2002.

Faulkner, Ronnie W. "Impending Crisis of the South." In *Encyclopedia of North Carolina,* ed. William S. Powell, 605–606. Chapel Hill: University of North Carolina Press, 2006.

Florey, Kitty Burns. *Script and Scribble: The Rise and Fall of Handwriting.* New York: Melville House Publishing, 2009.

Folk, Edgar E. "W. W. Holden and the North Carolina *Standard*, 1843–1848." *North Carolina Historical Review* 19 (January 1942): 22–47.

Fowler, Malcolm. "News of 'Boundless Continent' Mixed with Harnett Tid-bits." *Herald* (Sanford, NC), May 22, 1963, 6.

———. Fowler, Malcolm. *They Passed This Way: A Personal Narrative of Harnett County History.* Lillington, NC: Harnett County Centennial, 1955.

Hairr, John. *Harnett County: A History.* Charleston, SC: Arcadia Publishing, 2002.

"Handwritten Newspaper Was Published in Western Harnett." *Harnett County News,* February 2, 1944, 1, 6.

Harrington, Sion H., and John Hairr. *Eyewitnesses to Averasboro: The Confederates.* Erwin, NC: Averasboro Press, 2001.

Harrington, Zeb D., and Martha Harrington. *To Bear Arms: Civil War Information from Local "Folks," Chatham County and Adjacent Counties.* Moncure, NC: Private printing, 4780 Corinth Rd., 1984.

Harris, William C. *William Woods Holden: Firebrand of North Carolina Politics.* Baton Rouge: Louisiana State University Press, 1987.

Helper, Hinton Rowan. *Impending Crisis of the South: How to Meet It.* Ann Arbor, MI: Scholarly Publishing Office, 2004.

Hess, Miriam. "Newspapers." The University of Chicago, Theories of Media, Keywords Glossary, Winter 2003. http://csmt.uchicago.edu/glossary2004/newspaper.htm (accessed July 27, 2010).

"John McLean Harrington Papers." Chapel Hill: University of North Carolina, February 1958. In the Southern Historical Collection, University of North Carolina (accession number 3341, five items).

Karolevitz, Robert F. "Pen and Ink Newspapers of the Old West." *Frontier Times* 44, no. 2 (February–March 1970): 30–31, 62–64.

Kobre, Sidney. *The Development of the Colonial Newspaper.* Pittsburgh: Colonial Press, 1944.

Lapsansky-Werner, Emma J. *United States History.* Boston: Pearson/Prentice-Hall, 2009.

Mahone, E. T., Jr. "Earliest Printed County Newspaper Found." *The Harnett County News,* June 25, 1981, 2.

Maihafer, Harry J. *The General and the Journalists: Ulysses S. Grant, Horace Greeley, and Charles Dana.* Washington, DC: Brassey's, 1988.

Marszalek, John F. *Sherman's Other War: The General and the Civil War Press.* Kent, OH: Kent State University Press, 1999.

McFarland, Daniel Miles. "North Carolina Newspapers, Editors and Journalist Politics, 1815-1835." *North Carolina Historical Review* 30 (July 1953): 376-414.

McLuhan, Marshall. *Understanding Media: The Extensions of Man.* New York: New American Library, 1964.

Nerone, John C. "The Mythology of the Penny Press." *Critical Studies in Mass Communication* 4 (1987): 376-404.

Norton, Clarence Clifford. "Democratic Newspapers and Campaign Literature in North Carolina 1835-1861." *The North Carolina Historical Review* 5, no. 4 (October 1929): 345-363.

Ong, Walter. *Orality and Literacy: The Technologizing of the Word.* New York: Routledge, 2003.

Osthaus, Carl R. *Partisans of the Southern Press: Editorial Spokesmen of the Nineteenth Century.* Lexington: University Press of Kentucky, 1994.

Park, Robert. "The Natural History of the Newspaper." In *The City: Suggestions for Investigation of Human Behavior in the Urban Environment,* ed. Robert Park and Ernest W. Burgess, 80-98. Chicago: University of Chicago Press, 1925.

Perry, Stephen. *A Consolidated History of Media.* 4th ed. Bloomington, IL: Epistelogic, 2004.

———. "Pine Grove Lyceum Papers." *Nevada Historical Society Quarterly* 29, no. 3 (Fall 1985): 221-222.

Postman, Neal. *Amusing Ourselves to Death: Public Discourse in the Age of Show Business.* New York: Penguin, 1985.

Pratte, Paul A. "Origins of Mass Communication." In *The Media in America: A History,* 5th ed., William David Sloan, 1-16. Northport, AL: Vision Press, 2002.

Raper, Horace W. *The Papers of William Woods Holden,* vol. 1. Raleigh: Division of Archives and History, North Carolina Department of Cultural Resources, 2000.

Raper, Horace W. *William W. Holden: North Carolina's Political Enigma.* Chapel Hill: University of North Carolina Press, 1985.

Ratner, Lorman A., and Dwight L. Teeter, Jr., *Fanatics and Fire-Eaters: Newspapers and the Coming of the Civil War.* Urbana: University of Illinois Press, 2003.

Riley, Sam G., and Gary Selnow. "Southern Magazine Publishing, 1764-1984." *Journalism Quarterly,* 65, no. 4 (Winter 1988): 898-901.

Risley, Ford. *The Civil War: Primary Documents on Events from 1860 to 1865: Debating Historical Issues in the Media of the Time.* Westport, CT: Greenwood Press, 2004.

Rodman, George. *Mass Media in a Changing World*. New York: McGraw-Hill, 2006.

Ryfe, David M. "News, Culture and Public Life: A Study of 19th-Century American Journalism." *Journalism Studies* 7, no. 1 (2006): 60–77.

Schudson, Michael. *Discovering the News: A Social History of American Newspapers*. New York: Basic Books, 1978.

———. *The Good Citizen: A History of American Civic Life*. New York: Martin Kessler Books, 1998.

———. "The Politics of Narrative Form." In *The Power of News*, ed. Michael Schudson, 53–71. Cambridge, MA: Harvard University Press, 1995.

Scott, Rebecca. *Slave Emancipation in Cuba: The Transition to Free Labor, 1860–1899*. Pittsburgh: University of Pittsburgh Press, 2000.

Sloan, William David. *Perspectives on Mass Communication History*. Hillsdale, NJ: Lawrence Erlbaum Associates, 1991.

Sloan, William David, ed. *The Media in America: A History*, 5th ed. Northport, AL: Vision Press, 2002

Smythe, Ted Curtis, and Pauline D. Kilmer. "The Press and Industrial America 1865–1883." In *The Media in America: A History*, 5th ed., ed. William David Sloan, 199–222. Northport, AL: Vision Press, 2002.

Spencer, Henry Caleb. *Spencerian Key to Practical Penmanship*. New York: Ivison, Phinney, Blakeman, 1866.

Spencer, Platt Rogers. *Theory of Spencerian Penmanship for Schools and Private Learners*. Fenton, MI: Mott Media, 1985.

Startt, James D., and William David Sloan. *Historical Methods in Mass Communication*. Hillsdale, NJ: Lawrence Erlbaum Associates, 1989.

———. *The Significance of the Media in American History: Media in America*. Northport, AL: Vision Press, 1994.

Stephens, Mitchell. *A History of News: From the Drum to the Satellite*. New York: Penguin Books, 1988.

Thornton, Tamara Plakins. *Handwriting in America: A Cultural History*. New Haven, CT: Yale University Press, 1996.

Twyman, Michael. *Early Lithographed Books: A Study of the Design and Production of Improper Books in the Age of the Hand Press*. London: Farrand Press, 1990.

van Tuyll, Debra Reddin. "A Dozen Best, Top Books on the Civil War Press." *American Journalism* 24, no. 2 (Spring 2007): 151–160.

———. *The Southern Press in the Civil War*. Westport, CT: Greenwood Press, 2005.

Watson, Elgiva D. "Elisha Mitchell." In *Dictionary of North Carolina Biography*, ed. William S. Powell, 4:281-283. Chapel Hill: University of North Carolina Press, 1991.

Whisenhunt, Donald W. "The Frontier Newspapers: A Guide to Society and Culture. *Journalism Quarterly* 45, no. 4 (Winter 1968): 726–728.

Willey, Courtney E. "John McLean Harrington's 'Bridal Feast.'" 2005 Harnett County's Sesquicentennial Scholarly Presentation at Campbell University, Buies Creek, NC, October 18, 2005.

Williams, Walter E. "Rebellion in Oklahoma." *The Daily Record* (Dunn, NC), July 16, 2008, 4A.

Wimmer, Roger D., and Joseph R. Dominick. *Mass Media Research: An Introduction.* 8th ed. Independence, KY: Thomson-Wadsworth, 2006.

Winfield, Betty Houchin, and Janice Hume. "The Continuous Past: Historical Referents in Nineteenth-Century American Journalism." *Journalism Communication Monographs* 9, no. 3 (Autumn 2007): 120–174.

Working, D. W. "Some Forgotten Pioneer Newspapers." *The Colorado Magazine, State Historical Society of Colorado* 4, no. 3. (May 1927): 93–100.

INDEX

Abolition, abolitionists, 21, 24, 44, 74, 85, 86, 102
Acta Diruna, 31
Ad valorem, 6, 22
Advertising Sheet Monthly, The, 8, 75-78
Africa, 18
African Americans, 18, 49, 63, 85, 87, 103
Age of Literacy, 100
Aggregator (of news), xxi
Agricultural economy, 44
Alaska, 34
Alberta (Canada), 32
Alcohol, alcoholic, alcoholism, xviii, 13, 63, 101
Alden, Henry Mills, 42
American Colonization Society, 18
Americans Party, 25
American Whig Party, 25
Amish, 105
Amnesty, 102
Anderson, Maj. Robert, 75
Angier, 15
Anti-Federalists, 18
Archie Black's Academy, 11
Atlantic cable/telegraph, 50, 67
Atwood, Roy Alden, xiii-xv
Australia, 33
Austria, xiv
Autograph, 90
Avery, A. A., 51

Baghdad, 36
Balkans, 36
Baltimore Patriot, 63
Baptist associations, 18

Barbecue Presbyterian Church, 10
Barrel making, 7
Barometer (CA), 32
Battle of Fredericksburg, VA, 76
Battle of San Jacinto, TX, 32
Bennett, James Gordon, 94
Bentonville, NC, 2
Bible, Holy, 50, 52
Black Republicans, 24, 64, 65, 74
Blake, H.C., 35
Bledsoe, Moses A., 6
Blog, bloggers, blogging, xviii, xix, xxii, xxiii, 4, 22, 29, 36, 39, 105, 109
Bloser, Elmer Ward, 98
Boston, xiv, 31, 32, 66
Boston News-Letter, 31
Bridal, 57, 59, 100
British Columbia (Canada), 34
Brown, John, 5
Buchanan, James, 22
Budapest, xiv
Buffalo Springs, NC, 7, 8, 11, 39, 47, 59, 61, 66, 67
Burke, NC, 51
Burnside, Maj. Gen. Ambrose E., 77

Cape Fear Enterprise, 15
Cape Fear Pilot, 15
California, 5, 32, 34, 35
Calligraphy, 32, 93
Campbell, John, 31
Carolina Observer (Fayetteville), 17, 18
Catholic (Roman) schools, 97
Caucasians, 6
Cell phones, xiii
Central Times (Dunn, NC), 15

Charleston, SC, 75
Charleston Mercury, 76
Chatham County, 11
Charlotte Democrat, 58
Cherry Creek Pioneer (Rocky Mountains), 34
Chicago, xxii
China, Chinese, 33, 50
Chronicle (NC), 19
Christmas, 75, 85
Cincinnati, 55
Civil War, vii, viii, xviii, xix-xxi, 1, 2, 4, 6, 9, 11-26, 35, 41, 76, 78, 84, 90, 91, 94, 96, 101-103
Clark Street Sun (Montreal, Canada), 36,
Clarke, Mary Bayard, 51
Clay, U.S. Sen. Henry, 5
Coalfield Railroad, 7
Coca-Cola, 95
Coffee, 59, 66, 103
Colonial America, xiv, 31
Colorado, 34
Columbia Repository (Chapel Hill), 53
Columbus, Ohio, 97
Computer, xiii, 43
County Union (Harnett Co., NC), 15
Confederacy, 6, 13, 22, 33, 75, 77, 101, 102, 108
Confederate newspapers/press, 13, 26
Congress, U.S., 5, 6, 17, 22, 23, 26, 95, 123
Coolidge, Calvin, 97
Copperplate, 96, 97
Court heralds, xiii
Cuba, Cuban, 85, 86, 102
Cumberland County (NC), 10, 64, 65
Cumberland Gap, 78
Curtis, Cyrus, 91

Daily Intelligencer (Atlanta), 24
Daily Record, The (Dunn, NC), 15
Dana, Charles, 25

Dawk's News-Letter (London), 31
Day, Benjamin, 93, 94
Daybook, xxii
Declaration of Independence, 96
De La Floret, Countess de Villeneuve, 53
Democrats, Democratic Party, 2, 3, 6, 9, 12, 14, 15, 19-21, 23, 25, 40, 41, 46, 50, 51, 53, 58, 63, 64, 65, 68, 70, 74, 84, 95, 104, 106
Devil, 48
Diary, xxiv
Dixie, 73
Disunionists, 103
Domestic Quarterly Review (IA), 34
Douglas, Stephen, 2
Drawing, 45
Drug addiction, xviii
Drudge, Matt, xxi
Druggist, 45
Duhem, Pierre, 53
Duke University, 9, 10
Dunn Banner (NC), 15
Dunn Dispatch, The (NC), 15
Dunn Enterprise (NC), 15
Dunn Signboard (NC), 15

Easton Standard (NC), 65, 66
Elise (poet), 52, 59
Ellis, Gov. John W., 6, 21, 51, 59, 64, 65, 74
Emancipation Proclamation, 24
Emigrant, 32
Emigrant Soldier's Gazette and Cape Horn Chronicle, 34
England, Englishmen, 31, 34, 83, 106
Episcopal Church, 77
Ethernet, xviii
Europa (ship), 50
Europe, Europeans, 89, 103
Evening Star (UT), 35
Examiner (Richmond), 24
Execution, 31

Facebook, xx
Farmers, xviii, 42, 95, 104, 105
Fayetteville, N.C., 20, 39, 42, 45, 47, 61, 66, 67
Fayetteville Observer. Semi-Weekly., 46, 48, 49, 58, 61, 62, 68
Federalist, 17
Female Tract Society, Raleigh, 18
Fire-eaters, 24
Flesch-Kincaid readability scale, 102
Flumgudgeon Gazette and Bumblebee Budget (OR), 33
Foolscap, 33
Fort Bragg, NC, 10
Fort Moultrie, SC, 75
Forster, Anthony, 18
Foster, Capt. John L., 75
Fowler, Malcolm, 2
France, 106
Franklin, Benjamin, 56, 97
Fredericksburg, VA, 77, 78
French Revolution, 53, 55, 100
Fruit crop, 50, 67

Gales, Joseph, 18, 61
Garfield, James, 95
Garrison, William Lloyd, 40
Gazette (Fayetteville, NC), 19
Gazette (London), 31
Gazette (Oxford), 31.
Georgia, Augusta, 63
Gettysburg, 33
Gold rush, 34
Gogol, Nikolai, 1
Good Samaritan, xviii, xix, xxiv
Governor of North Carolina, xviii, 21, 26
Grantham, G. K., 15
Great Eastern (ship), 50
Grizzly bear, 67

Hamburg, 50
Hancock, John, 96

Handwriting, handwritten newspapers, xv, xviii, xx, xxii-xiv, 1-6, 8-10, 15, 18, 21, 27, 29-36, 39-40, 42-44, 46, 53, 61-62, 70, 73, 76-77, 86, 89-108
Hardee, Gen. William, 2
Harnett County, vii, viii, xx, xxiii, 1, 2, 4, 6-8, 10, 12-13, 15, 23, 39, 42, 51, 55, 60, 64-65, 73-74, 85-87, 91, 92, 102, 104, 105
Harnett Courier, 15
Harnett County News, 11
Harnett Leader, 15
Harper's (magazine), 42, 58
Harrington's publications (table), 8
Harrington Post Office, 60
Harrington
   David, 7
   James, 7
   James Stephen, 10, 12
   John McLean, xiv, xv, xviii, 1, 6, 10, 11, 13, 18, 61, 73, 89, 90, 91, 95, 99, 108
   Louis, 7
   Margaret, 7, 10
   Sarah, 7
   Sion, 7, 14, 15, 70
Harris, Benjamin, 31
Hay, John, 25
Haywood, NC, 11
Henderson, Phil, 55
Henry, Sgt. M., 76
Herald (New York), 94
Herzon (soldier), 73
Hillsboro, NC, 19
Holden, William Woods, 12, 19-24
Holly Springs, NC, 15
Holograph, holography, xxii, 90, 91, 95
House of Commons (NC), 10
Humor, 103
Hungarian Natural Archives, xiv

Illiteracy, 19
India, Chennai, 31
Industrial Press (era), 94
Information culture, xiii
Ink, ink stamp, xx, xxii, 26, 29, 33, 45
Internet, xiii-xv, 34, 46, 98
Interpretative writing, 39
Iowa, 32, 34

Jackson, Andrew, 6, 18, 103
Jesus Christ, xvii
Jiangsu Province, Nanjing, 33
Job, Book of, 52
Joke, 64, 103
Johnson, Andrew, 12-14, 22, 95
Johnson, Finley, 54
Jones, Elkins, 60
Journalism history, 37-38
Journalist, literary, 106-107
Journal (ship's), xxii

Kansas-Nebraska Act, 5, 22
Kiplinger Newsletter, 2
Knowledge Seekers (UT), 35
Know Nothings, 21
Kossuth, Lajos, xiv

Leasure Hour, 9, 70
Lecompton Constitution, 22, 65
Lee, Robert E., 77
Letters (as type of communication),
  99, 100
Leviathan (ship), 49, 50, 103
Liberator (Boston), 40
Lincoln, Abraham, 2, 24, 25, 64, 74,
  86
Lightning lines (telegraph), xiii
Liquor, 50
Literature, xviii
Literary journal, xxi
Little River Record (NC), 15
London, 31, 36
London Gazette, 31

Longhand, 30, 33
Loring, Thomas, 19
Los Angeles County (CA), 64

Macon, U.S. Sen. Nathaniel, 44
Mail, 104
Maine, 104
Manti Herald (UT), 35
Massachusetts, 19
Matrimony, 37
McKay, William, 66
McLean, John Tyler, 15
McLuhan, Marshall, 43, 100
McRae, Duncan K., 21, 64
McRae, John, 18
Mecklenburg Jeffersonian (NC), 20
Melbourne Advertiser (Australia), 33
Mexico, 5
Military posts, 34
Mining, 34, 35
Missouri Compromise, 5
Mitchell, Elisha, 56
Moncure, NC, 11
Monks, 30
Moon, Capt., 76
Moore County, NC, 85
Moravians, 18
Mormon, Mormons, 34, 35
Mt. Pisgah Presbyterian Church, 10

Napoleon, 50
Nation, The, xv, xxi, 1, 2, 4, 8-10, 39,
  40, 46, 48, 54, 55, 60-73, 87, 100-
  104, 108
Native Americans, 33
Naval stores, 60
Nevada, 32
New American, The, 68
New Bern, NC, 65
New Orleans, 32
Newsgathering, 23
Newspaper (definition), 30
Newsprint, 26

New York, 36, 106
New York Times, xx, xxiii, 43, 96,
News, xx, 23, 24, 25, 35, 40
News artist/artisan, 29, 30
News sheets, xiv
Neya Powagans, 32
North (U.S.), xix, 23, 25, 26, 58, 67,
    84, 103
North Carolina, 5, 6, 9, 11, 17-24, 32,
    52, 53, 61, 74, 76, 78, 91, 101, 103,
    106
North Carolina militia, 12
North Carolina State House, 46
Northern (U.S.) press, 26

Objectivity (press), 40
Obituaries, 101
Old Testament, 52
Opium, 33
Opposition Party, 25
Oregon, 22, 33
Orrell, Maj. R. M., 84
Overcoat, The, 1
Outer Banks, NC, 25

Pacific Coast, 34
Pacific Northwest, 33
Palmer, Austen N., 97
Paris, 21
Park, Robert E., 38
Partisanship, 41, 94
Party press, 94
Patent medicine, 21
Pen, penmanship, xxiii, xix, 33, 40,
    43, 104, 108
Penny Press, 94
Pennsylvania, 68
Personal journalist, 3, 4
Pescud, P. F., 21
Petrel, The (CA), 32
Philadelphia, 60
Pickett, Charles Edward, 33
Piedmont (area of NC), 7, 24, 25

Pine Forest, NC, 11
Poet, poetry, xviii, 55, 92, 107
Polk, James K., 33
Poor Richard's Almanac, 56
*Port Phillip Patriot and Melbourne
    Advertiser*, 33
Postman, Neal, 99
Print media, mainstream, 40
Printers, xx
Printing (commercial), 17, 18
Printing press, xiii, xiv, 31
Prisoner-of-war newspapers, 31
Prisons, 34
Prison Bee, The (NY), 36
Propaganda (political), 25
Proslavery, 23, 24
Pro-Constitutional Union, 23
Pro-Southern rights, 23
Provisional government, 26
*Publick Occurrences Both Forreign and
    Domestick*, 31
Pudget's [sic] Sound, 73

Quarterly Visitor (IA), 34
Quill pen, 97

Radio, xiii
Railroads, 7, 23, 44, 65
Raleigh, NC, 1, 12, 39, 42, 61
Raymond, Henry, 94
Rebel colonies, 67
Reconstruction, 22
Redwing Carrier Pigeon, The (KS), 35
Register (Raleigh), 18, 20, 21, 61
Reporter (Harnett County), 15
Reporter-publishers, 4
Republicans, Republican Party, 3, 5,
    12, 14, 22, 64, 95, 106
Revival (religious), 104
Richmond, VA, 76
Richmond Whig, 77
Rip Van Winkle, 47, 52
Rocky Mountains, 33, 34

Rocky Mountain Gold Register and Rocky Mountain City Herald, 34
Rome (ancient), 31
Romans (ancient), xiv
Roman Catholic Church, xiv, 97
Rowan County, NC, 64
Rowan Whig and Western Advocate (Salisbury, NC), 20
Russell, Daniel L., 14

Santa Claus, 77
Scarlet fever, 51
Saturday Evening Post, xxi, 48, 91
Schultze, Quentin J., xvii-xxiii
Scorpion, The (NV), 34
Scriptorium, xiv
Scott, Walter, 78, 84
Scotland, Scotsmen, 78, 84
Scott, Dred, 5
Secession (from the Union), 22-24, 63, 74, 101-103
Semantic code, 32
Semantic reality, 30
*Semi-Weekly News, 8, 46, 73, 78, 84, 85, 92, 102, 108
Senter, David Henry, 15
Sermons, 18
Shakespeare, 107
Shark, The (CA), 32
Sherman, William Tecumseh, 25
Shipboard newspapers, 31, 34
Signature, 90
Skype, 43,
Slavery, xviii, 5, 6, 18, 22, 24, 39, 44, 58, 66, 85, 86, 95, 100, 102, 105, 107
Society news, 18
South, Southerners, xix, 4-6, 12, 22, 24, 26, 34, 44, 60, 63, 65, 74, 75, 95, 99, 103
Spain, 50
Spencer, Henry Cable, 96
Spencer, Platt Rogers, 95

Spencerian handwriting, 95, 96, 97, 101
Sponheim, Abbot of, 89
Standard (Raleigh), 19-24, 64, 65, 103
Stage drivers, 17
State Journal (Raleigh), 23
Stavitsky, Sid, 36
Stedman's (magazine), 66, 73, 90, 93, 101
Stewart, Charles T., 15
Stone, Joseph T., 15
Stowe, Harriet Beecher, 5
Storytellers, storytelling, 24, 90, 93, 101
Sun, New York, 93, 94

Thames, 2
*Times., The, xviii, 2, 8, 9, 46, 78, 84, 85, 92, 102
Tobacco and Manufacturers' Guide, 15
Twitter, xviii, xix

Uncle Tom's Cabin, 5
Union, 4, 22-24, 26, 75, 77, 84, 101, 103
University of North Carolina at Chapel Hill, 91
University of Pennsylvania, 97
University Magazine (Literary Society of University of North Carolina at Chapel Hill), 53
Upper Little River District, 12, 14
Urdu, 32
Utah, 34, 35

Vancouver Island, BC (Canada), 34
Van Buren, Martin, 18
Venice, 31
Victorians, 2, 96, 100
Virginia, 5
Von Radetz, Austrian Field Marshal Joseph Radetzky, 50

Walker, F. A., 14

Wall Street Journal, 43
Washington Shark (IA), 34
Weddings, 101
Weekly Eagle, 8, 9, 73, 108
Weekly Guide (NC), 15
Weekly News, 8, 46, 73-78, 92, 103
*Weekly News' Advertising Sheet.
    Monthly.*, 8, 9, 75
Weekly North Carolina Standard, 13
West Africa, 18
Western Railroad, 7
West, 33, 34
Whig, 6, 19, 20, 21, 25
White, Elijah, 33
Wickens, Elizabeth, 85
Wilkesboro, NC, 34
Wilmington, NC, 11, 76, 85
Wilmington Herald, 50, 68
Wilmington Journal, 67
Wilson, Frank I., 22
Wood-notes, 52
WordPress, xx
World (New York), 93
Worth, David and Julia A., 51
Worth, J., 68
Worth, J and D.G., 11, 60
Wurzburg, St. James at, 89

Young, E.F., 15
Young American, The, xv, xxiii, 1, 2,
    4, 7-9, 39, 45-60, 62, 68-71, 73, 87,
    93, 100-104, 108
Young Ladies' Thoughts, 35

Zaner-Bloser, 97
Zaner, Charles Paxton, 98

* denotes one of Harrington's planned
    or published papers

LaVergne, TN USA
16 March 2011
220373LV00001B/6/P